CCNP Self-Study
# CCNP CIT
# Exam Certification Guide

## Second Edition

**Amir S. Ranjbar**
MSc., CCIE No. 8669

# Cisco Press

Cisco Press
800 East 96th Street, 3rd Floor
Indianapolis, Indiana 46240 USA

# CCNP CIT Exam Certification Guide
## Second Edition

Amir S. Ranjbar, MSc., CCIE No. 8669

Copyright© 2004 Cisco Systems, Inc.

Published by:
Cisco Press
800 East 96th Street, 3rd Floor
Indianapolis, IN 46240 USA

Printed in the United States of America 1 2 3 4 5 6 7 8 9 0

First Printing November 2003

Library of Congress Cataloging-in-Publication Number: 2002115790

ISBN: 1-58720-081-3

## Warning and Disclaimer

This book is designed to provide information about Cisco internetwork troubleshooting. Every effort has been made to make this book as complete and as accurate as possible, but no warranty or fitness is implied.

The information is provided on an "as is" basis. The authors, Cisco Press, and Cisco Systems, Inc., shall have neither liability nor responsibility to any person or entity with respect to any loss or damages arising from the information contained in this book or from the use of the discs or programs that may accompany it.

The opinions expressed in this book belong to the author and are not necessarily those of Cisco Systems, Inc.

## Feedback Information

At Cisco Press, our goal is to create in-depth technical books of the highest quality and value. Each book is crafted with care and precision, undergoing rigorous development that involves the unique expertise of members from the professional technical community.

Readers' feedback is a natural continuation of this process. If you have any comments regarding how we could improve the quality of this book or otherwise alter it to better suit your needs, you can contact us through e-mail at feedback@ciscopress.com. Please make sure to include the book title and ISBN in your message.

We greatly appreciate your assistance.

## Corporate and Government Sales

Cisco Press offers excellent discounts on this book when ordered in quantity for bulk purchases or special sales. For more information, please contact **U.S. Corporate and Government Sales** 1-800-382-3419 corpsales@pearsontechgroup.com.

For sales outside of the U.S. please contact **International Sales** 1-317-581-3793 international@pearsontechgroup.com.

# Trademark Acknowledgments

All terms mentioned in this book that are known to be trademarks or service marks have been appropriately capitalized. Cisco Press or Cisco Systems, Inc. cannot attest to the accuracy of this information. Use of a term in this book should not be regarded as affecting the validity of any trademark or service mark.

**Publisher:** John Wait

**Editor-in-Chief:** John Kane

**Executive Editor:** Brett Bartow

**Production Manager:** Patrick Kanouse

**Development Editor:** Andrew Cupp

**Project/Copy Editor:** Karen A. Gill

**Team Coordinator:** Tammi Barnett

**Cover/Interior Designer:** Louisa Adair

**Composition:** Interactive Composition Corporation

**Indexer:** Tim Wright

**Cisco Representative:** Anthony Wolfenden

**Cisco Press Program Manager:** Sonia Torres Chavez

**Manager, Marketing Communications, Cisco Systems:** Scott Miller

**Cisco Marketing Program Manager:** Edie Quiroz

**Technical Editors:** Craig Dorry, Don Johnston, Jay Swan

CISCO SYSTEMS

**Corporate Headquarters**
Cisco Systems, Inc.
170 West Tasman Drive
San Jose, CA 95134-1706
USA
http://www.cisco.com
Tel:   408 526-4000
        800 553-NETS (6387)
Fax:  408 526-4100

**European Headquarters**
Cisco Systems Europe
11 Rue Camille Desmoulins
92782 Issy-les-Moulineaux
Cedex 9
France
http://www-europe.cisco.com
Tel:   33 1 58 04 60 00
Fax:  33 1 58 04 61 00

**Americas Headquarters**
Cisco Systems, Inc.
170 West Tasman Drive
San Jose, CA 95134-1706
USA
http://www.cisco.com
Tel:   408 526-7660
Fax:  408 527-0883

**Asia Pacific Headquarters**
Cisco Systems Australia, Pty., Ltd
Level 17, 99 Walker Street
North Sydney
NSW 2059 Australia
http://www.cisco.com
Tel: +61 2 8448 7100
Fax: +61 2 9957 4350

**Cisco Systems has more than 200 offices in the following countries. Addresses, phone numbers, and fax numbers are listed on the Cisco Web site at www.cisco.com/go/offices**

Argentina • Australia • Austria • Belgium • Brazil • Bulgaria • Canada • Chile • China • Colombia • Costa Rica • Croatia • Czech Republic • Denmark • Dubai, UAE • Finland • France • Germany • Greece • Hong Kong Hungary • India • Indonesia • Ireland • Israel • Italy • Japan • Korea • Luxembourg • Malaysia • Mexico The Netherlands • New Zealand • Norway • Peru • Philippines • Poland • Portugal • Puerto Rico • Romania Russia • Saudi Arabia • Scotland • Singapore • Slovakia • Slovenia • South Africa • Spain • Sweden Switzerland • Taiwan • Thailand • Turkey • Ukraine • United Kingdom • United States • Venezuela • Vietnam Zimbabwe

# About the Author

**Amir S. Ranjbar**, MSc., CCIE No. 8669, is an instructor and senior network architect for Global Knowledge, the largest Cisco training partner. He is a certified Cisco Systems instructor who teaches the Cisco Internetwork Troubleshooting course on a regular basis. Born in Tehran, Iran, Amir moved to Canada in 1983 and obtained his bachelor's degree in computing and information science (1988) and master of science degree in knowledge-based systems (1991) from the University of Guelph (Guelph, Ontario).

After graduation, Amir developed software applications in the areas of statistical analysis and systems simulation for a number of institutes, such as Statistics Canada, University of Waterloo, and University of Ottawa. Amir started his training career by joining Digital Equipment Corporation's Learning Services in 1995. After a few years of working exclusively as a Microsoft Certified Trainer (MCSE, MCT), he decided to shift his focus to Cisco Systems internetworking products. In 1998, Amir joined Geotrain Corporation, which was acquired by Global Knowledge in 1999.

Amir obtained his Cisco Certified Internetwork Expert status in January 2002. Among the courses Amir teaches are Interconnecting Cisco Network Devices (ICND), Building Cisco Remote Access Networks (BCRAN), Building Cisco Multilayer Switched Networks (BCMSN), Building Scalable Cisco Internetworks (BSCI), Cisco Internetwork Troubleshooting (CIT), Cisco Multiprotocol Label Switching (MPLS), OSPF, ISIS, and Advanced BGP. You can contact Amir by e-mail at aranjbar@rogers.com.

# About the Technical Reviewers

**Craig Dorry**, CCIE No. 9072, is a network architect and Tier 3 network support engineer for AT&T Solutions, where he is the escalation contact for high-profile and business-impacting network issues. Craig has more than eight years of experience in network implementation and support at the LAN and WAN level. He has strong knowledge of routing protocol performance issues as well as network diagnostic and management equipment.

**Don Johnston** is a certified Cisco Systems instructor and consultant with 20 years of experience teaching computing and networking. He is currently teaching CCNP courses with Global Knowledge as a contract instructor. Don consults with clients on routing and switching design, implementation, and diagnosis of existing problems.

**Jay Swan** teaches Cisco courses with Global Knowledge. He holds CCSI, CCNP, and CCSP certifications, as well bachelor's and master's degrees from Stanford University. Prior to joining Global Knowledge, Jay worked in the ISP and higher education fields. He lives in southwest Colorado.

# Dedication

I would like to dedicate this book to those whose lives have a positive impact on the lives of others. I wish that people would live and take actions based on their beliefs, rather than merely have beliefs and take no actions. I thank my parents and sisters; my wife, Elke; my children; and the rest of my invaluable family and friends for making my life better. I am confident that my children, Thalia, Ariana, and Armando, will have a life full of health, prosperity, and happiness; however, my hope is that they will fulfill their duty to participate in elevating the quality of our society and our environment. I will then feel very proud and successful.

—Amir

# Acknowledgments

I did not have the pleasure of getting to know or communicating with all the individuals who have put their valuable time and effort into this book, but I would like to take this opportunity to sincerely thank each and every one of them. Among those with whom I worked directly were Brett Bartow (executive editor) and Andrew Cupp (development editor). These gentlemen are always a pleasure to work with, and I thank them for their patience, professionalism, and understanding. I would also like to thank Karen Gill (project/copy editor) for her hard work and patience, and, of course, the technical editors, Craig Dorry, Don Johnston, and Jay Swan, for their valuable suggestions and corrections. Finally, I acknowledge once again that this is a work done by a team, and I shake the hands of every member of this team for their dedication and hard work.

Thank you all!

# Contents at a Glance

# Contents

# Icons Used in This Book

Router

Bridge

Hub

DSU/CSU

Catalyst
Switch

Multilayer
Switch

ATM
Switch

ISDN/Frame Relay
Switch

Communication
Server

Gateway

Access
Server

PC

PC with
Software

Sun
Workstation

Macintosh

Terminal

File
Server

Web
Server

Cisco Works
Workstation

Modem

Printer

Laptop

IBM
Mainframe

Front End
Processor

Cluster
Controller

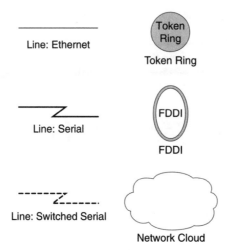

## Command Syntax Conventions

The conventions used to present command syntax in this book are the same conventions used in the IOS Command Reference. The Command Reference describes these conventions as follows:

- Vertical bars (|) separate alternative, mutually exclusive elements.

- Square brackets [ ] indicate optional elements.

- Braces { } indicate a required choice.

- Braces within brackets [{ }] indicate a required choice within an optional element.

- **Boldface** indicates commands and keywords that are entered literally as shown. In actual configuration examples and output (not general command syntax), boldface indicates commands that are manually input by the user (such as a **show** command).

- *Italic* indicates arguments for which you supply actual values.

# Foreword

*CCNP CIT Exam Certification Guide, Second Edition* is a complete study tool for the CCNP CIT exam, allowing you to assess your knowledge, identify areas to concentrate your study, and master key concepts to help you succeed on the exam and in your daily job. The book is filled with features that help you master the skills necessary to troubleshoot suboptimal performance in a converged network environment. This book was developed in cooperation with the Cisco Internet Learning Solutions Group. Cisco Press books are the only self-study books authorized by Cisco for CCNP exam preparation.

Cisco and Cisco Press present this material in text-based format to provide another learning vehicle for our customers and the broader user community in general. Although a publication does not duplicate the instructor-led or e-learning environment, we acknowledge that not everyone responds in the same way to the same delivery mechanism. It is our intent that presenting this material via a Cisco Press publication will enhance the transfer of knowledge to a broad audience of networking professionals.

Cisco Press will present study guides on existing and future exams through these *Exam Certification Guides* to help achieve Cisco Internet Learning Solutions Group's principal objectives: to educate the Cisco community of networking professionals and to enable that community to build and maintain reliable, scalable networks. The Cisco Career Certifications and classes that support these certifications are directed at meeting these objectives through a disciplined approach to progressive learning.

To succeed on the Cisco Career Certifications exams, as well as in your daily job as a Cisco certified professional, we recommend a blended learning solution that combines instructor-led, e-learning, and self-study training with hands-on experience. Cisco Systems has created an authorized Cisco Learning Partner program to provide you with the most highly qualified instruction and invaluable hands-on experience in lab and simulation environments. To learn more about Cisco Learning Partner programs that are available in your area, please go to www.cisco.com/go/authorizedtraining.

The books that Cisco Press creates in partnership with Cisco Systems will meet the same standards for content quality demanded of our courses and certifications. It is our intent that you will find this and subsequent Cisco Press certification and training publications of value as you build your networking knowledge base.

Thomas M. Kelly
Vice-President, Internet Learning Solutions Group
Cisco Systems, Inc.
October 2003

# Introduction

This book is one of the members of the Cisco Press family of publications that has been developed to help you prepare for the Cisco Certification examinations. This book's specific target is the new 642-831 CIT exam. I am a certified Cisco Systems instructor, and CIT is one of the courses that I teach. I started teaching this course in the first quarter of 1999. I have passed the old CIT exam, the later Support exams, and most recently the beta exam for the new CIT exam.

CCNP candidates often ask me how I think the new CIT exam is different from the previous Support exam and the old CIT 4.0 exam. The new CIT course (v5.0) is more focused on troubleshooting methodology rather than the actual internetworking technologies. The lecture component of the CIT instructor-led course and its student kit is focused on documentation, troubleshooting resources, and troubleshooting methodologies. The lab component of the CIT instructor-led course leads students into exercising those techniques learned during the lecture about those internetworking technologies covered in the BCRAN, BCMSN, and BSCI courses. Therefore, I respond to those who ask by saying that the new course and its corresponding exam are both troubleshooting methodology oriented. Technology-specific material is assumed to have been covered by the other CCNP courses and exams.

The CIT exam is one of the four exams you will need to pass to achieve Cisco Certified Network Professional (CCNP) certification in the Routing and Switching career track. The other three exams are the 642-801 BSCI (routing), 642-811 BCMSN (switching), and 642-821 BCRAN (remote access) exams. Note that Cisco Certified Network Associate (CCNA) status is a prerequisite to becoming CCNP certified.

## Objective of This Book

During the time that I was preparing this book, I kept my focus on only one goal: preparing the readers for the 642-831 CIT exam. Throughout the book, I present what I think is absolutely essential for you to know before you attempt the new CCNP CIT exam. The content is similar to that of the CIT course, but the large volume of exam-oriented tools such as the summary tables, figures, questions and answers, and, of course, the accompanying CD make this book ideal for exam preparation. My presentation is short, to the point, and oriented toward exam preparation. The "Scenarios" section of this book mimics lab exercises by presenting real-life style cases showing you how to apply the troubleshooting methods and techniques covered throughout.

## Who Should Read This Book?

This book's target audience is primarily those who want a condensed, exam-oriented book to prepare them for the 642-831 CIT CCNP exam. I would like to share the following thought with the readers of this book: This book is not a magic tool that somebody without the proper background can pick up, read, and use to pass the exam. My assumption of the target audience's background is a more-than-basic familiarity with internetworking, routing, switching, and wide-area networking.

This means the reader should have at least a CCNA level of Cisco networking knowledge and experience. With reference to the Cisco training curriculum, this book's prerequisite is similar to the CIT course's prerequisite. In other words, I assume that the reader has a good grasp of the material presented in the ICND (or CRLS/ICRC), BSCI (or BSCN/ACRC), and BCMSN (or CLSC) Cisco official training curriculum courses.

# The Organization and Features of This Book

Because the new CIT examination closely reflects the material presented in the Cisco official CIT training material, I made a point of making sure the flow of this book matches that of the CIT's official training curriculum.

This book is also accompanied by a CD-ROM that offers multiple-choice questions out of the entire book's content. The simulated exam and study tools are specifically designed to complement the material in this book, provide a thorough study medium, and prepare you for the CIT exam.

## Book Organization

This book's 13 chapters are broken into 7 parts. This section summarizes the contents of this book.

### Part I: Establishing a Baseline

One of the goals of network support professionals and engineers is to eliminate or at least minimize the down time of a network. Having a complete and up-to-date network baseline helps accomplish that goal. The network baseline can be defined as a snapshot of the configuration of a network while it is operating under normal conditions. During troubleshooting or disaster recovery, the baseline is used as a guide to return the network to its normal condition efficiently. Without guesswork and with peace of mind backed by documentation, the network can be restored to its working condition without wasting time.

The elements of a network can be classified into two groups:

- Networking devices, such as routers and switches
- End systems, such as servers and workstations

The baseline must include information on both of these groups. Chapter 1 describes creating network configuration table and topology diagrams. These documents should store information about networking devices when they are in good working condition (networking devices' baseline information). Chapter 2 covers creating end system configuration tables and end-to-end topology diagrams. These documents, in contrast, should store information about end system devices when they are in good working condition (end system devices' baseline information).

## Part II: Determining an Effective Troubleshooting Strategy

An organization needs an effective troubleshooting strategy. An effective troubleshooting strategy facilitates discovery of the source of the problem, isolating the problem area, and solving the problem. This process needs to be time and cost sensitive; otherwise, business opportunities are lost and user confidence in the organization's competence is reduced.

Chapters 3–6 cover different aspects and topics related to effective troubleshooting strategy. Chapter 3 emphasizes understanding of the layered model and the encapsulation/decapsulation process. Chapter 4 presents a simple three-stage troubleshooting model and flowchart. Chapter 5 is dedicated to gathering network and user symptoms. Chapter 6 compares and contrasts top-down versus bottom-up versus divide-and-conquer approaches to troubleshooting.

## Part III: Resolving Problems at the Physical and Data Link Layers

After you have gathered the symptoms of a problem and selected a troubleshooting approach, the next step is to use those symptoms to isolate the problem(s) and take the necessary actions to correct them. Chapters 7 and 8 discuss the isolation and correction phases of the general troubleshooting process to resolve network performance, optimization, and failure issues at the physical and data link layers of the OSI model.

## Part IV: Resolving Problems at the Network Layer

Because the processes and methods of gathering symptoms, isolating problems, and correcting problems at the physical and data link layers have been dealt with, Part IV moves on to accomplishing the same tasks at the network layer. The goal of Chapters 9 and 10 is to show you how to perform the isolation and correction phases of the general troubleshooting process to resolve failure and optimization problems at the network layer of the OSI model. As you will notice, the symptoms of the problem, as well as the commands and applications used to successfully resolve problems, are different at the network layer.

Chapter 9 focuses on isolating the problem, and Chapter 10 delves into correcting the problem at the network layer. Problem isolation is presented in Chapter 9 through identifying the symptoms of problems occurring at the network layer and analyzing the Cisco and end system commands and application output. Correcting the problem is Chapter 10's task, accomplished by presenting common Cisco and end system commands and examples and listing network layer support resources.

## Part V: Resolving Problems at the Transport and Application Layers

The process for isolating and correcting problems at the transport and application layers is the same as the process of isolating and correcting problems at the lower layers. However, at the transport and application layers, the symptoms that the problems present, as well as the commands, applications, and steps used to successfully resolve them, are different. Part V discusses the isolation and correction phases of the general troubleshooting process to resolve failure and optimization problems at the transport and application layers of the OSI model.

Chapters 11 and 12 focus on isolating and correcting problems that are rooted at the transport and application layers of the TCP/IP layered model. Chapter 11 presents the common symptoms of transport and application layers and lists some important commands that can help you with problem isolation. Chapter 12 focuses on problem correction. It provides some of the most useful commands as well as a list of support resources.

## Part VI: Scenarios

Chapter 13 is composed of several scenarios. These scenarios review some of the material, but more importantly, they show how the troubleshooting techniques presented in the course and this book can be applied to real-life cases.

## Part VII: Appendix

Appendix A contains the answers and explanations to the chapter quizzes.

# Features of This Book

This book features the following:

- **"Do I Know This Already?" Quizzes**—Each chapter begins with a quiz that helps you determine the amount of time you need to spend studying that chapter. If you follow the directions at the beginning of the chapter, the "Do I Know This Already?" quiz directs you to study all or particular parts of the chapter.

- **Foundation Topics**—These are the core sections of each chapter. They explain the protocols, concepts, and configuration for the topics in that chapter. If you need to learn about the topics in a chapter, read the "Foundation Topics" section.

- **Foundation Summaries**—Near the end of each chapter, a summary collects the most important information from the chapter and pulls it into lists, tables, and figures. The "Foundation Summary" section is designed to help you review the key concepts in the chapter if you scored well on the "Do I Know This Already?" quiz. This section is an excellent tool for last-minute review.

- **Q&A**—Each chapter ends with a "Q&A" section that forces you to exercise your recall of the facts and processes described inside that chapter. The questions are generally harder than the actual exam, partly because the questions are in "short answer" format instead of multiple choice. These questions are a great way to increase the accuracy of your recollection of the facts.

- **Scenarios**—Chapter 13 contains scenarios that you should read and work on after you feel you have mastered all the topics presented in the book.

- **Test Questions**—Using the test engine on the CD-ROM, you can take simulated exams. You can also choose to be presented with several questions on a topic that you need more work on. This testing tool provides you with practice that will make you more comfortable when you actually take the CIT exam.

# CIT Exam Topics

Cisco lists the topics for the CIT exam on its Web site at http://www.cisco.com/warp/public/10/wwtraining/certprog/testing/current_exams/642-831.html. The list provides key information about what the test covers. Table I-1 lists the CIT exam topics and the corresponding parts in this book that cover those topics. Each part begins with a list of the topics covered in that part. Use these references as a road map to find the exact materials you need to study to master the CIT exam topics. Note, however, that because all exam information is managed by Cisco Systems and is therefore subject to change, candidates should monitor the Cisco Systems site for course and exam updates at www.cisco.com/go/training.

**Table I-1**  *CIT Topics*

| Topic | Description | Part |
|---|---|---|
| **Technology** | | |
| 1 | Identify troubleshooting methods. | II |
| 2 | Explain documentation standards and the requirements for document control. | I |
| **Implementation and Operation** | | |
| 3 | Establish an optimal system baseline. | I |
| 4 | Diagram and document system topology. | I |
| 5 | Document end system configuration. | I |
| 6 | Verify connectivity at all layers. | III, IV, V |
| 7 | Select an optimal troubleshooting approach. | II |
| **Planning and Design** | | |
| 8 | Plan a network documentation system. | I |
| 9 | Plan a baseline monitoring scheme. | I |
| 10 | Plan an approach to troubleshooting that minimizes system down time. | II |

**Table I-1** *CIT Topics (Continued)*

| Topic | Description | Part |
|---|---|---|
| **Troubleshooting** | | |
| 11 | Use Cisco IOS commands and applications to identify system problems at all layers. | III, IV, V |
| 12 | Isolate system problems to one or more specific layers. | III, IV, V |
| 13 | Resolve suboptimal system performance problems at Layers 2 through 7. | III, IV, V |
| 14 | Resolve local connectivity problems at Layer 1. | III |
| 15 | Restore optimal baseline service. | III, IV, V |
| 16 | Work with external providers to resolve service provision problems. | III, IV, V |
| 17 | Work with system users to resolve network-related end-use problems. | III, IV, V |

Table I-2 shows which topics are covered in each part.

**Table I-2** *Part-by-Part Listing of CIT Topics*

| Book Part | CIT Topic |
|---|---|
| I | 2–5, 8–9 |
| II | 1, 7, 10 |
| III | 6, 11–17 |
| IV | 6, 11–13, 15–17 |
| V | 6, 11–13, 15–17 |

If you feel that your knowledge of a particular chapter's subject matter is strong, you might want to proceed directly to that chapter's exercises to assess your true level of preparedness. If you are having difficulty with those exercises, make sure to read over that chapter's "Foundation Topics." Also, be sure to test yourself by using the CD-ROM's test engine. Finally, if you are lacking in certain internetworking-technologies knowledge, be sure to review the reference materials provided in the appendix and glossary. Regardless of your background, you should begin with Chapter 1.

## About the CIT Exam

The CCNP is a hands-on certification that requires a candidate to pass the Cisco Internetwork Troubleshooting exam. The emphasis in the exam is on troubleshooting the router if the configuration for it has failed. CCNP is currently one of the most sought-after certifications, short of the Cisco Certified Internetworking Expert (CCIE).

The exam is a computer-based exam that has multiple choice, fill-in-the-blank, and list-in-order style questions. The fill-in-the-blank questions are filled in using the complete syntax for the command, including dashes and the like. For the fill-in-the-blank questions, a tile button is given to list commands in alphabetical order. This is a real lifesaver if you can't remember whether there is a dash or an s at the end of a command. Knowing the syntax is key, however, because the list contains some bogus commands in addition to the real ones.

The exam can be taken at any Pearson VUE testing center (http://www.vue.com/cisco/) or Thomson Prometric testing center (1-800-829-NETS or http://www.2test.com). As with most Cisco exams, you cannot mark a question and return to it. In other words, you must answer a question before moving on, even if this means guessing. Remember that a blank answer is scored as incorrect.

## Test Preparation, Test-Taking Tips, and Using This Book

This section contains recommendations that will increase your probability of passing the CIT exam.

The following are some additional suggestions for using this book and preparing for the exam:

- Familiarize yourself with the exam topics in Table I-1 and thoroughly read the chapters on topics that you are not familiar with. Use the assessment tools provided in this book to identify areas where you need additional study. The assessment tools include the "Do I Know This Already?" quizzes, the "Q&A" questions, and the sample exam questions on the CD-ROM.

- Take all quizzes in this book and review the answers and the answer explanations. It is not enough to know the correct answer. You must also understand why one answer is correct and the others are incorrect. Retake the chapter quizzes until you pass with 100 percent.

- Take the CD-ROM test in this book and review the answers. Use your results to identify areas where you need additional preparation.

- Review other documents, RFCs, and the Cisco Web site for additional information. If this book references an outside source, it is a good idea to spend some time looking at it.

- Review the chapter questions and CD-ROM questions the day before your scheduled test. Review each chapter's "Foundation Summary" when you are making your final preparations.

- If you are not sure about the correct answer to a question, attempt to eliminate incorrect answers.

My personal opinion about preparing for any of the examinations is an orthodox one. I believe that after someone meets the prerequisites of a course, he should take the official training curriculum course. Next, he should practice the material learned in the course through hands-on experimentation or using other reference material, such as this book. This method is solid and effective and has been proven effective repeatedly. Indeed, that is how I prepare myself for the exams that I attempt.

However, we are not all the same, and we do not all have the same budget, time, or learning behaviors. I can't and won't, in good conscience, tell you that this book is *all* you need to have to pass the new CIT exam, even though it is tempting to say so. What I can tell you with all honesty is that this book familiarizes you with all the topics you need to master to pass the CIT exam. This book also includes many of the details of these topics, but you will have to rely on your overall troubleshooting and networking knowledge as specified by the CIT prerequisites to pass the CIT exam. If you come across a topic in this book that you do not feel comfortable with even after working through the book, you should do further research. At the very minimum, make sure you meet the course prerequisite, familiarize yourself with the CIT course materials, and then use all the tools presented in this book.

The following CIT exam topics are covered in this part. (To view the CIT exam outline, visit www.cisco.com/go/training.)

- Explain documentation standards and the requirements for document control.

- Establish an optimal system baseline.

- Diagram and document system topology.

- Document end system configuration.

- Plan a network documentation system.

- Plan a baseline monitoring scheme.

# Part I: Establishing a Baseline

## This chapter covers the following subjects:

- Components of a network configuration table

- Components of a topology diagram

- Discovering network configuration information

- The process of creating network documentation

- Guidelines for creating network documentation

# Creating Network Configuration Documentation

The elements of a network can be classified into two groups:

- Networking devices, such as routers and switches

- End systems, such as servers and workstations

The *network baseline* must include information on both of these groups. The network baseline and network configuration documentation can serve as a troubleshooting tool to diagnose a problem and, more importantly, to correct it. The network baseline information (about network devices) is recorded in network configuration tables and topology diagrams. These documents help to restore the network devices and components to their normal configuration, operation, and performance. This chapter identifies the components of a network configuration table and topology diagram, explains how to discover and record (document) network configuration information, and provides guidelines on best practices while creating network documentation.

> **NOTE** Remember that baseline information about network devices is recorded in network configuration tables and topology diagrams. Each of the sections to follow has a specific focus that also needs attention.

## "Do I Know This Already?" Quiz

The purpose of the "Do I Know This Already?" quiz is to help you decide if you really need to read this entire chapter. If you already intend to read the entire chapter, you do not need to answer these questions now.

The 15-question quiz, derived from the major sections in the "Foundation Topics" portion of the chapter, helps you determine how to spend your limited study time.

Table 1-1 outlines the major topics discussed in this chapter and the "Do I Know This Already?" quiz questions that correspond to those topics.

**Table 1-1** *"Do I Know This Already?" Foundation Topics Section-to-Question Mapping*

| Foundation Topics Section | Questions Covered in This Section |
|---|---|
| "Components of a Network Configuration Table" | 3 |
| "Components of a Topology Diagram" | 2 |
| "Discovering Network Configuration Information" | 5 |
| "The Process of Creating Network Documentation" | 1 |
| "Guidelines for Creating Network Documentation" | 4 |

**CAUTION** The goal of self-assessment is to gauge your mastery of the topics in this chapter. If you do not know the answer to a question or are only partially sure of the answer, you should mark this question wrong for purposes of the self-assessment. Giving yourself credit for an answer you correctly guess skews your self-assessment results and might provide you with a false sense of security.

1. Which of the following is the most accurate list of information recorded in a network configuration table?

   a. IP address, controller event, multipoint DLCI, map statement, Kshell

   b. Bridge zone, OSPF area, LightStream PZ, Router ID, subnet mask

   c. Device name, interface name, MAC address, Duplex, access lists

   d. IP address, subnet mask, checksum, bytes, data flow status

2. Which two of the following would be the minimum required and most important components of a network topology diagram?

   a. Devices

   b. Contact information

   c. Loaded firmware

   d. Connections between devices

   e. Interface Spanning Tree configuration

3.  Which IOS command would you use to view a list of devices that are directly connected to the device that you are requesting from?

    a.  **show ip interfaces**

    b.  **show spanning-tree**

    c.  **show cdp neighbors**

    d.  **show connected devices**

4.  Which stage of the process of creating network configuration documentation involves the use of the IOS **show cdp neighbors** command?

    a.  Login

    b.  Document

    c.  Transfer

    d.  Discover Devices

5.  Which of the following is not one of the guidelines for creating useful network configuration documentation?

    a.  Use consistent symbols, terminology, and styles.

    b.  Know the scope of the documentation.

    c.  Update the documentation at least once a year.

    d.  Store the documents in a logical location.

6.  Which one of the following is *not* an essential piece of information that a network configuration table must document about each networking device?

    a.  Device name

    b.  Data link layer addresses and implemented features

    c.  Network layer addresses and implemented features

    d.  Size (number of entries) of its routing table

    e.  Important information about the physical aspects of the device

**7.**  Which one of the following is *not* usually recorded in a network configuration table for routers?

    **a.**  Interface name

    **b.**  Interface speed

    **c.**  MAC address

    **d.**  IP address (and subnet mask)

    **e.**  IP routing protocol(s)

**8.**  To illustrate the important components of a network at the Internet layer (TCP/IP model), which of the following might be included in the network topology diagram? (Choose three.)

    **a.**  IP addresses

    **b.**  Subnet masks

    **c.**  MAC addresses

    **d.**  Routing protocols

    **e.**  Spanning tree states

**9.**  Which of the following is *not* one of the steps taken in discovering network configuration information on routers?

    **a.**  Determine the model of the device and its operating system version using the **show version** command.

    **b.**  Get into the ROM Monitor by modifying the configuration register using the **config-register** command.

    **c.**  Display a summary of the interfaces along with their IP address/mask, interface name, media type, and physical and data link operational status using the **show ip interfaces brief** command.

    **d.**  Discover the IP address and MAC address of each interface using the **show ip interfaces** and **show interfaces** commands.

**10.**  Which of the following is *not* one of the steps taken in discovering network configuration information on routers?

    **a.**  List the active IP routing protocols using the **show ip protocols** command.

    **b.**  Reveal the details about the spanning tree using the **show spanning-tree** (or **show spantree**) command.

    **c.**  Display the detail of content-addressable memory using the **show memory** command.

    **d.**  Display the list of Cisco devices that are connected to a device using the **show cdp** command and see details about each of those listed using the **show cdp entry** *device-id* command.

**11.** Which of the following is *not* one of the steps taken in discovering network configuration information on standard switches?

   **a.** View a summary of the ports, including port names, port status, duplex, and speed, using the **show interfaces status** command.

   **b.** Display a summary of the EtherChannel configuration using the **show etherchannel summary** command.

   **c.** Display a summary of the Trunk status using the **show interfaces trunk** command.

   **d.** Reveal the content of the ARP cache using the **show arp** command.

**12.** Which of the following is the correct order of the 5-stage process of creating network documentation?

   **a.** Login, Interface Discovery, Document, Diagram, Device Discovery

   **b.** Login, Document, Diagram, Interface Discovery, Device Discovery

   **c.** Login, Interface Discovery, Diagram, Document, Device Discovery

   **d.** Login, Device Discovery, Interface Discovery, Document, Diagram

   **e.** Diagram, Device Discovery, Login, Interface Discovery, Document

**13.** Which of the following elements of the network documentation guidelines asks the troubleshooter to collect only relevant data?

   **a.** Determine the scope.

   **b.** Know your objective.

   **c.** Be consistent.

   **d.** Keep the documents accessible.

   **e.** Maintain the documentation.

**14.** Which of the following elements of network documentation guidelines asks the troubleshooter to know which devices are part of your domain of responsibility?

   **a.** Determine the scope.

   **b.** Know your objective.

   **c.** Be consistent.

   **d.** Keep the documents accessible.

   **e.** Maintain the documentation.

**15.** Which of the following elements of network documentation guidelines asks the troubleshooter to avoid conflicting abbreviations, terminology, and style?

  **a.** Determine the scope.

  **b.** Know your objective.

  **c.** Be consistent.

  **d.** Keep the documents accessible.

You can find the answers to the "Do I Know This Already?" quiz in Appendix A, "Answers to the 'Do I Know This Already?' Quizzes and 'Q&A' Sections." The suggested choices for your next step are as follows:

- **12 or less overall score**—Read the entire chapter. This includes the "Foundation Topics" and "Foundation Summary" sections, as well as the "Q&A" section.

- **13–15 overall score**—If you want more review on these topics, skip to the "Foundation Summary" section and then go to the "Q&A" section. Otherwise, move to the next chapter.

# Foundation Topics

## Components of a Network Configuration Table

*Network configuration tables* store accurate information about the hardware and software components of a network. Recording data into these tables, referring to these tables to look up information, and maintaining the accuracy of these tables are easier and more pleasant than using documentation that is composed of massive amounts of text and configuration printouts. Network configuration tables should hold essential information about the network devices and not be cluttered with unimportant data. The following is a list of important information that a network configuration table should include about each networking device:

■ Device name and model, as well as IOS name and version

■ Data link layer addresses and implemented features

■ Network layer addresses and implemented features

■ Important information about the physical aspects of the device

■ Other information that someone who is familiar with the network or has experience troubleshooting it considers important to the document

> **NOTE**    Remember the list of information that a network configuration table must include about each networking device.
>
> The content of a network configuration table might vary based on its planned usage. For example, a table that will serve budgetary/inventory purposes will have some information that is different from a table to be used for troubleshooting/maintenance purposes. The focus of this book is on internetwork troubleshooting.

You can simplify the network configuration table by organizing it with respect to the layers of the TCP/IP protocol stack (that is, physical/data link, Internet (network), transport, and application layers). You can surely appreciate that certain pieces of information are device specific. For example, you can often find variable speed ports in switches, not routers. Even though you can record information about routers, switches, and multilayer switches in the same table, you generally want to keep the information about these devices in separate tables. Table 1-2 shows different types of information tabulated in accordance to the OSI (or TCP/IP) layer they correspond to.

**Table 1-2** *Elements/Components of Network Configuration Table (Classified)*

| Layer | Information |
|---|---|
| Physical | CPU type |
| | Flash memory |
| | DRAM |
| | MAC address |
| | Media type |
| | Speed |
| | Duplex |
| | Trunk status |
| Data link | Device name |
| | Device model (+ IOS version) |
| | MAC address |
| | Duplex |
| | Port identifier |
| | STP status |
| | PortFast |
| | EtherChannel |
| | Username/password |
| Network | IP address |
| | Secondary IP address |
| | Subnet mask |
| | IP routing protocol(s) |
| | Access lists |
| | VLANs (if any) |
| | IP address of neighboring device(s) |
| | Interface name(s) |

Table 1-3 shows an example of a network configuration table for routers. In Table 1-3, the following information is recorded for each of the shown routers:

■   Device name and model

■   Interface name

■   MAC address (or other Layer 2 address)

■   IP address (and subnet mask)

■   IP routing protocol(s)

**Table 1-3**   *Example of a Network Configuration Table for a Router*

| Device Name, Model | Interface | MAC Address | IP Address/ Subnet Mask | IP Routing Protocol(s) |
|---|---|---|---|---|
| Long Island, Cisco1760-V | fa0/0 | 0007.8500.a159 | 10.2.3.1/16 | EIGRP 100 |
| | fa0/1 | 0007.8500.a160 | 10.0.1.1/16 | EIGRP 100 |
| | s0/1 | HDLC | 192.168.34.1/24 | OSPF 100 |
| | s1/1 | PPP | 172.18.1.1/16 | EIGRP 100 |
| New York, Cisco2611XM | s0/1 | FR DLCI 200 | 192.168.34.2/24 | OSPF |
| | s1/0 | HDLC | 172.18.2.1/16 | EIGRP 100 |

Table 1-4 shows an example of a network configuration table for switches. In Table 1-4, the following information is recorded for each of the shown switches:

■   Device name and model

■   Management VLAN and IP address

■   Port name

■   Speed

■   Duplex

■   STP state

■   PortFast

■   Trunk status

- EtherChannel

- VLANs

**Table 1-4**   *Example of a Network Configuration Table for a Switch*

| Catalyst Switch Name Model, Management IP Management VLAN | Port | Speed | Duplex | STP State (Fwd/ Block) | Port-Fast (Yes/ No) | Trunk Status | Ether-Channel L2 or L3 | VLAN(s) |
|---|---|---|---|---|---|---|---|---|
| Lexington WS-C3550-24-SMI 10.3.2.33/27 VLAN 1 | Fa0/1 | 10 | Full | Fwd | No | On | — | All |
| | Fa0/2 | 100 | Full | Block | No | Off | — | 2 |
| | Fa0/3 | 100 | Half | Fwd | Yes | Off | — | 3 |
| | Fa0/4 | 100 | Auto | Fwd | No | On | L2 | All |
| | Fa0/5 | 100 | Auto | Fwd | No | On | L2 | All |
| | Fa0/6 | 100 | Auto | Fwd | No | On | L2 | All |
| | Fa0/7 | 100 | Auto | Fwd | No | On | L2 | All |

# Components of a Topology Diagram

The *network topology diagram* is the second piece of documentation (after the network configuration table), and it is considered an essential part of any network baseline. This diagram is a graphical representation of the network that must illustrate all the devices and how they are connected. Physical and logical detail about the network are revealed using consistent notations and symbols. Figure 1-1 is an example of a network topology diagram. In Figure 1-1, you can see a network cloud symbol with the title *Internet*. A network cloud symbol is often used to represent a network that is under control of another group (or company, or autonomous system, and so on). At times, the network cloud symbol is used within a network topology diagram to show an area whose detail is outside the scope of the diagram.

The information displayed in the network topology diagram might correspond to different layers of the TCP/IP model. For example, to illustrate the important components of a network at the Internet layer (TCP/IP model), you might include IP addresses, subnet masks, and routing protocols (see Table 1-5).

**NOTE**   Remember that a network topology diagram shows all the devices and how they are physically and logically connected. The device name, interface or port name, IP address, and routing protocol(s) are a few of its important components.

**Figure 1-1**  *Network Topology Diagram*

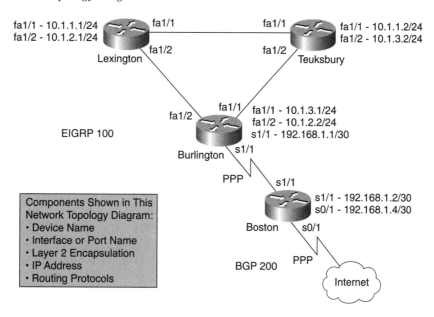

**Table 1-5**  *Components of a Topology Diagram Classified Based on the TCP/IP Model*

| Layer | Information |
|---|---|
| Physical | Device name |
| | Media type |
| Data link | MAC address |
| | Encapsulation |
| | DLCI, VPI/VCI |
| | Trunk or access/VLAN number |
| Network | IP address |
| | Subnet mask |
| | Interface name |
| | Routing protocol(s) |

## Discovering Network Configuration Information

You must collect from each device the information that you need to record in network configuration tables and network topology diagrams by entering appropriate commands. In this section, two sets of commands for discovering network configuration information are presented. The first set is the commands to be used on routers and multilayer switches, and the second set is the commands to be used on standard switches. You should start the process of collecting the network configuration information from one device and continue it until you have visited all devices and collected their information.

On a router or multilayer switch, you are interested in discovering the following information:

- The device's name, its model, and the IOS version it is running. You can discover these required pieces of information by using the following command:

  ```
  show version
  ```

- The number and types of the device's interfaces, along with their data link layer information and IP addresses. Following is the command that will generate that output:

  ```
  show interfaces
  ```

  If a particular interface is of interest, you must enter the interface type and number as follows:

  ```
  show interfaces interface-type number
  ```

  For example:

  ```
  show interfaces Ethernet 0
  ```

- Network/IP layer information about all the interfaces. Several significant pieces of information are available—in addition to IP address and mask—such as access lists applied to each interface and each interface's proxy ARP setting. The following command produces such output:

  ```
  show ip interfaces
  ```

- If you want a brief list of interfaces along with their IP address, media type, data link and physical status, use the **brief** keyword with the **show ip interfaces** command to yield the desired output:

  ```
  show ip interfaces brief
  ```

- The IP routing protocol (or protocols) running on the device along with the networks it is active on, the neighbors that it has received routes from, and any inbound or outbound routing filters that have been applied to that protocol. You can retrieve all of this from the following output:

  ```
  show ip protocols
  ```

■  Spanning tree information is desirable on bridging and switching devices. You can use the following commands to assist in disseminating spanning tree detail on those devices:

```
show spanning-tree summary
show spanning-tree vlan vlan-number
```

■  The names of adjacent devices, along with each device's model, capabilities, and at least one IP address. If Cisco Discovery Protocol (CDP) is active on the local device and its neighbor, these pieces of information are readily available through usage of the following:

```
show cdp neighbors [detail]
show cdp entry device-id
```

■  Commands related to the routing protocol that is active between a device and its neighbors also can reveal useful information about the neighbors. Following are examples of such commands:

```
show ip ospf neighbors
show ip eigrp neighbors
```

**NOTE**    The **show tech-support** command is a useful command that produces the previous information. Beware of the fact that this command generates much output.

You can extract some of the information that you want to discover from the routers from standard access switches of the network. However, you must obtain other kinds of more switch-oriented information by using appropriate commands. The following is a list of the sought information from a standard switch along with the commands that you must use to obtain them:

■  The device's name, its model, and the operating system version it is running obtained by using the following command:

```
show version
```

■  The number and types of the device's ports along with their name, status, duplex, and speed. The following commands reveal all those to you:

```
show interfaces description
show interfaces status
```

■  Information about the status of port channeling and EtherChannel configuration gathered by using the following command:

```
show etherchannel summary
```

■  The list of ports configured for trunking along with their status retrieved from the following output:

```
show interfaces trunk
```

■  Spanning tree information, which is desirable on bridging and switching devices. The following commands assist in disseminating spanning tree detail on those devices (based on IOS version):

```
show spanning-tree
show spantree
```

■ The names of adjacent devices, along with each device's model, capabilities, and at least one IP address. If CDP is active on the local device and its neighbor, these pieces of information are readily available through usage of the following:

```
show cdp neighbors [detail]
show cdp entry device-id
```

# The Process of Creating Network Documentation

To create *network documentation*, you must log into each device, one at a time, and discover and document its network configurations. You can hop from one device to its undocumented neighbor(s) and repeat this process until you are finished. Figure 1-2 depicts the stage-by-stage process of creating network documentation by using a flow chart. Table 1-6 provides an explanation for each of the stages shown in Figure 1-2.

**Figure 1-2**  *Creating Network Documentation*

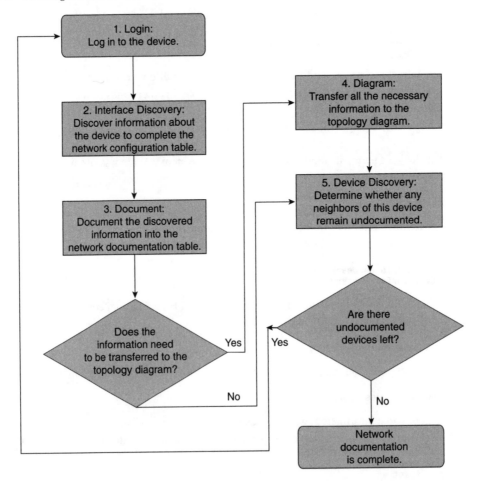

**Table 1-6**  *Explanation for Each Stage of the Network Documentation Process*

| Stage | Description |
|---|---|
| 1. Login | You must log in to the device and switch to the privileged mode; then you can type the commands necessary for network discovery. |
| 2. Interface Discovery | Discover the necessary information about the device so that you can complete the network configuration table. |
| 3. Document | Document/record the discovered information in the network configuration table and determine whether you need to record any of it in the network topology diagram. If you must record any information in the network topology diagram, proceed to Stage 4; otherwise, move to Stage 5. |
| 4. Diagram | Transfer the necessary information about the device from the network configuration table to the network topology diagram. If you need to document more information about the device, return to Stage 2; otherwise, move to Stage 5. |
| 5. Device Discovery | Determine whether any neighboring device is undocumented; if there is one, go to Stage 1. Otherwise, if there are no undocumented network devices, it means that network documentation is completed. |

# Guidelines for Creating Network Documentation

To produce effective, efficient, and easy-to-use network documentation, you should determine the documentation's scope, know its objective, be consistent, make it available yet secure, and keep it up to date by properly maintaining it. These points are listed and briefly explained in Table 1-7.

**Table 1-7**  *Guidelines for Creating Network Documentation*

| Guideline | Explanation |
|---|---|
| Determine the scope. | Know which devices are part of your domain of responsibility. |
| Know your objective. | Collect data that is relevant to your objective and provide sufficient detail information. Avoid extraneous data because it renders the documentation difficult to use. |
| Be consistent. | Use consistent terminology, abbreviations, and style. Use templates when possible, and keep a library of symbols and graphics icons that you can reuse. |

*continues*

**Table 1-7** *Guidelines for Creating Network Documentation (Continued)*

| Guideline | Explanation |
|---|---|
| Keep the documents accessible. | Store the network documentation in a location where it is readily available on the job; keep another copy of it in a secure location off-site. |
| Maintain the documentation. | As the network undergoes changes, modify the network documentation accordingly to keep it accurate and up to date.<br><br>Note: Many organizations have deployed a formal process called *change control* . This process enforces reporting of network changes, maintaining version control, and assigning responsibility for modifying and distributing updated documents. |

# Foundation Summary

The "Foundation Summary" section of each chapter lists the most important facts from that chapter. Although this section does not list every fact from the chapter that will be on your CCNP exam, a well-prepared CCNP candidate should at a minimum know all the details in each "Foundation Summary" before taking the exam.

A network baseline documentation has two components:

■ Network configuration documentation

■ End system (network) configuration documentation

A network configuration table must document the following about each networking device:

■ Device name

■ Data link layer addresses and implemented features

■ Network layer addresses and implemented features

■ Important information about the physical aspects of the device

■ Other information that someone who is familiar with the network or who has experience troubleshooting it considers important to document

A network topology diagram is a graphical representation of the network that must illustrate all the devices and how they are connected. It should reveal the following physical, data link, and network layer information:

■ Physical layer:

— Device name

— Media type

■ Data link layer:

— MAC address

■ Network layer:

— IP address

— Subnet mask

— Interface name

— Routing protocol(s)

You need to gather and record some significant network configuration information about routers and switches. This information, along with the commands used to gather them, is outlined in Tables 1-8 and 1-9.

**Table 1-8** *Discovering Network Configurations on Routers and Multilayer Switches*

| Information Sought | Command Used to Gather That Information |
|---|---|
| Name of the device<br><br>Model of the device<br><br>Operating system version | **show version** |
| MAC address of the interface(s) | **show interfaces**<br><br>**show interfaces** *interface-type number* |
| Active interfaces and their address | **show ip interfaces** |
| Summary of the interfaces along with their IP address, interface name, media type, and physical and data link operational status | **show ip interfaces brief** |
| Summary of the active IP routing protocols | **show ip protocols** |
| Details about the spanning tree | **show spanning-tree summary**<br><br>**show spanning-tree vlan** *vlan-number* |
| List of the Cisco devices that are directly connected to this device | **show cdp neighbors [detail]**<br><br>**show cdp entry** *device-id* |
| Details about any device that is connected to this device | **show ip ospf neighbors**<br><br>**show ip eigrp neighbors** |

**Table 1-9**  *Discovering Network Configurations on Standard Switches*

| Information Sought | Command Used to Gather That Information |
|---|---|
| Name and model of the device<br><br>Operating system version | **show version** |
| Active ports and their addresses | **show interfaces description** |
| Summary of the ports, including port names, port status, duplex, and speed | **show interfaces status** |
| Summary of the EtherChannel configuration | **show etherchannel summary** |
| Summary of the trunk status | **show interfaces trunk** |
| Details about the spanning tree | **show spanning-tree**<br><br>**show spantree** |
| List of the Cisco devices that are directly connected to this device | **show cdp neighbors** |
| Details about any device that is connected to this device | **show cdp entry** *device-id* |

The following enlists the 5-step process of creating network documentation:

- **Stage 1: Login**—Log in to the device.

- **Stage 2: Interface Discovery**—Discover all the necessary information for the network documentation table.

- **Stage 3: Document**—Record the discovered information into the network documentation table and determine whether you need to record any of it in the network topology diagram as well.

- **Stage 4: Diagram**—Update the network topology diagram with the information that you determined must be transferred to the network topology diagram.

- **Stage 5: Device Discovery**—Determine whether the device has a neighbor that has not yet been discovered and documented. If no devices remain to be documented, the documentation concludes; otherwise, proceed to Step 1.

The guidelines for creating network documentation are as follows:

- Determine the scope.

- Know your objective.

- Be consistent.

- Keep the documents accessible.

- Maintain the documentation.

# Q&A

As mentioned in the introduction, you have two choices for review questions. The questions that follow give you a bigger challenge than the exam because they use an open-ended question format. By reviewing now with this more difficult question format, you can exercise your memory better and prove your conceptual and factual knowledge of this chapter. You can find the answers to these questions in Appendix A.

For more practice with exam-like question formats, including questions that use a router simulator and multiple choice format, use the exam engine on the CD.

1.  What are the two components of network baseline documentation?

2.  Name at least three pieces of information that a network configuration table must document.

3.  The network topology diagram is a graphical representation of the network that must illustrate all the devices and how they are connected. Name at least three pieces of information that reveal physical, data link, or network layer information about a device.

4.  List at least three commands that are useful for discovering network configurations on routers and multilayer switches.

5.  List at least three commands that are useful for discovering network configurations on standard switches.

6.  List the five stages of the process of creating network documentation.

7.  What are the rules/guidelines for creating network documentation?

## This chapter covers the following subjects:

- Components of an end system network configuration table

- Components of an end system network topology diagram

- Commands and applications used to gather information about end system network configurations

- Discovering end system network configuration information

- Creating end system network configuration documentation

# CHAPTER 2

# Creating End System Network Configuration Documentation

Similar to their intermediate system counterparts (routers and switches), *end systems* are important components of a network, and restoring their configuration is a vital part of troubleshooting efforts. Personal computers, laptops, and various types of servers—such as e-mail servers, Web servers, and e-commerce (database) servers—are all examples of end systems. This chapter discusses configuration documentation for end systems: what that documentation should include and how it should be created effectively. End system network configuration documentation should include network configuration tables and network topology diagrams. Including end system network configuration information in the baseline renders troubleshooting timely and efficient.

## "Do I Know This Already?" Quiz

The purpose of the "Do I Know This Already?" quiz is to help you decide if you really need to read the entire chapter. If you already intend to read the entire chapter, you do not need to answer these questions now.

The 10-question quiz, derived from the major sections in the "Foundation Topics" portion of the chapter, helps you determine how to spend your limited study time.

Table 2-1 outlines the major topics discussed in this chapter and the "Do I Know This Already?" quiz questions that correspond to those topics.

**Table 2-1**  *"Do I Know This Already?" Foundation Topics Section-to-Question Mapping*

| Foundation Topics Section | Questions Covered in This Section |
|---|---|
| "Components of an End System Network Configuration Table" | 2 |
| "Components of an End System Network Topology Diagram" | 1 |
| "Commands and Applications Used to Gather Information About End System Network Configurations" | 3 |
| "Creating End System Network Configuration Documentation" | 4 |

> **CAUTION**   The goal of self-assessment is to gauge your mastery of the topics in this chapter. If you do not know the answer to a question or are only partially sure of the answer, you should mark this question wrong for purposes of the self-assessment. Giving yourself credit for an answer you correctly guess skews your self-assessment results and might provide you with a false sense of security.

1.   Which list includes only components of an end system network configuration table?

   a.   PortFast, IP address, network applications, trunk status

   b.   IOS type/version, subnet mask, default gateway address, STP state

   c.   IP address, subnet mask, routing protocol, duplex

   d.   DNS server address, IP address, OS type/version, high-bandwidth applications

2.   Which of the following items is not a usual network application running on an end system?

   a.   FTP

   b.   HTTP

   c.   SMTP

   d.   VTP

3.   Which of the following lists only components of a topology diagram that relate to end systems?

   a.   Trunk status, PortFast, subnet mask

   b.   Device name, network applications, IP address

   c.   Duplex, interface name, routing protocol

   d.   IP address, subnet mask, STP state

4.   Which end system command (MS-Windows) is used to view the address that a host dynamically obtains from DHCP?

   a.   **ping**

   b.   **route print**

   c.   **show ip resolve**

   d.   **ipconfig /all**

5. While performing discovery of end system network configurations, which command (MS-Windows) is used to list the active routes for a host?

   a. **ipconfig /all**

   b. **tracert**

   c. **route print**

   d. **show route**

6. Which of the following commands displays the content of the local end system's ARP cache table (IP address to MAC address mappings)?

   a. **arp print**

   b. **arp –a**

   c. **arp –p**

   d. **show arp print**

7. To reduce the amount of paperwork generated by documenting end systems, which guideline should you follow?

   a. Document all possible aspects of the hardware and network configuration of an end system.

   b. Create separate end system topology diagrams instead of adding end systems to existing network diagrams.

   c. Determine an objective for the documentation and collect data that meets that objective.

   d. Document desktops and laptops along with infrastructure devices.

8. Which one of the following is not one of the guideline elements for creating end system network configuration documentation?

   a. Know the objective.

   b. Know the scope.

   c. Keep the documents locked up.

   d. Maintain the documentation.

9. Many organizations have deployed a formal process that enforces reporting of network changes, maintaining version control, and assigning responsibility for modifying and distributing updated documents. What is this process called?

   a. Priority policy

   b. Strict priority

   c. Change control

   d. Firewall policy

**10.** Using templates and keeping a library of symbols and graphics icons that can be reused helps you follow which of the following guidelines for creating end system network configuration documentation?

    **a.** Determine the scope.

    **b.** Know your objective.

    **c.** Be consistent.

    **d.** Keep the documents accessible.

    **e.** Maintain the documentation.

You can find the answers to the "Do I Know This Already?" quiz in Appendix A, "Answers to the 'Do I Know This Already?' Quizzes and 'Q&A' Sections." The suggested choices for your next step are as follows:

- **8 or less overall score**—Read the entire chapter. This includes the "Foundation Topics" and "Foundation Summary" sections, as well as the "Q&A" section.

- **9 or 10 overall score**—If you want more review on these topics, skip to the "Foundation Summary" section and then go to the "Q&A" section. Otherwise, move to the next chapter.

# Foundation Topics

## Components of an End System Network Configuration Table

The purpose of this section is to identify the information that you should record in an *end system network configuration table* used to troubleshoot end systems. The network configuration table, as baseline documentation, should hold accurate and up-to-date information about the software and hardware used in end systems. The following is a list of items to record in an end system network configuration table:

- Device name and its role or function (purpose), if any

- Operating system/version

- IP address/subnet mask

- Default gateway, DNS server, and WINS server addresses

- Any high-bandwidth, latency-sensitive, or business-critical network applications that the end system runs

The content of an end system network configuration table is essentially dictated by its function. For example, if the table is used for inventory management, it might store information such as asset number or date of purchase. You might store location or backup-related information in the end system network configuration table. Finally, the table might be intended to serve as a troubleshooting resource—that is, to hold up-to-date baseline information. Even in this case, the content of the table varies based on the type of device that is documented. Table 2-2 shows the type of information you need to record about an end system, based on the TCP/IP protocol stack the device maps to.

Some end systems serve a special purpose. For example, they might run a special server application, harbor a high-bandwidth network application, or store a large data bank. Identifying those types of end systems and storing specific information about them can be beneficial for troubleshooting purposes. Streaming video—such as QuickTime—and multicast applications—such as IPTV—are examples of high-bandwidth applications. Table 2-3 displays a sample end system network configuration table providing useful information for end system recovery and troubleshooting.

**Table 2-2**   *End System Configuration Table Components Classified Based on the TCP/IP Protocol Stack Layers*

| Layer | Information |
|---|---|
| Physical/data link | Physical location<br>Manufacturer/model<br>CPU type/speed<br>RAM<br>Storage<br>Device name<br>Device function or purpose<br>Access VLAN<br>MAC address |
| Network | IP address<br>Subnet mask<br>Default gateway<br>DNS address<br>WINS address |
| Application | Operating system/version<br>Network applications<br>High-bandwidth applications<br>Latency-sensitive applications<br>Business-critical applications |

**Table 2-3**   *End System Network Configuration Table Example*

| Device Name Function/ Purpose | Operating System Version | IP Address Subnet Mask Default Gateway | WINS Address DNS Address | Network Application | Delay-Sensitive or High-Bandwidth Application |
|---|---|---|---|---|---|
| DHCPserv (DHCP Server) | Windows NT 4.0 | 10.1.1.3<br>255.255.255.0<br>10.1.1.1 | —<br>— | — | — |
| PrimWINS (Primary WINS Server) | Windows 2000 | 10.1.1.5<br>255.255.255.0<br>10.1.1.1 | —<br>10.1.1.7 | MS-Exchange<br>SMTP | — |
| PrimeDNS (Domain Name Server) | Linux | 10.1.1.7<br>255.255.255.0<br>10.1.1.1 | 10.1.1.5<br>— | Telnet | — |

**Table 2-3**   *End System Network Configuration Table Example (Continued)*

| Device Name Function/ Purpose | Operating System Version | IP Address Subnet Mask Default Gateway | WINS Address DNS Address | Network Application | Delay-Sensitive or High-Bandwidth Application |
|---|---|---|---|---|---|
| Ecommsvr (E-Commerce DB Server) | UNIX | 10.32.1.5 255.255.255.0 10.32.1.1 | 10.1.1.5 10.1.1.7 | Oracle Database | E-Commerce |
| WebnFTP (Web Server/ FTP Server) | UNIX | 10.32.1.6 255.255.255.0 10.32.1.1 | 10.1.1.5 10.1.1.7 | HTTP FTP | — |

# Components of an End System Network Topology Diagram

The *end system network topology diagram* has its focus on the end systems it graphically depicts. It illustrates how end systems are both physically and logically connected to the network. An end system network topology diagram is a graphical presentation of its counterpart end system network configuration table. Nonetheless, it is not practical for a network topology diagram to include every component of the end system network configuration table. Therefore, vital and essential information—such as each end device's name, an illustration of the device, and how it is connected to the network—are depicted without cluttering the diagram (see Figure 2-1). The network information in Figure 2-1 comes from Table 2-3.

**Figure 2-1**   *End System Network Topology Diagram Example*

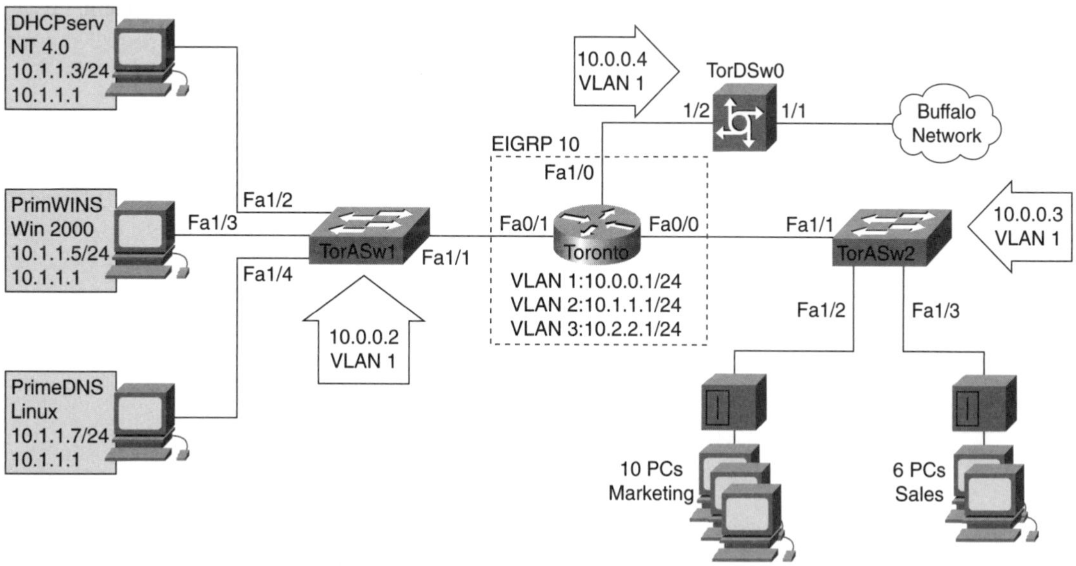

The information recorded about each end system in a topology diagram depends on the TCP/IP layer that the device maps to or functions at. Table 2-4 shows for each TCP/IP layer the type of data that you would record about each end system.

**Table 2-4**   *End System Topology Diagram Components Classified Based on the TCP/IP Protocol Stack Layers*

| Layer | Information |
|---|---|
| Physical | Physical location |
| Network/data link | IP address |
| | Subnet mask |
| | Default gateway |
| | Device name |
| | Device purpose |
| | Access VLAN |
| | MAC address |
| Application | Operating system/version |
| | Network applications |

The level of detail that an end system topology diagram depicts about network devices varies. An end system-focused topology diagram might represent the network components as a network cloud symbol with the details of the end systems connected to it. On the other hand, all the details of the network device configuration might be included on the same diagram as the end systems. Figure 2-2 shows a topology diagram that includes both network devices and end systems. It includes the following information about end systems:

- Device name and purpose

- Operating system

- IP address

**Figure 2-2**   *End System Network Topology Diagram Depicting Information About End Systems and Network Devices*

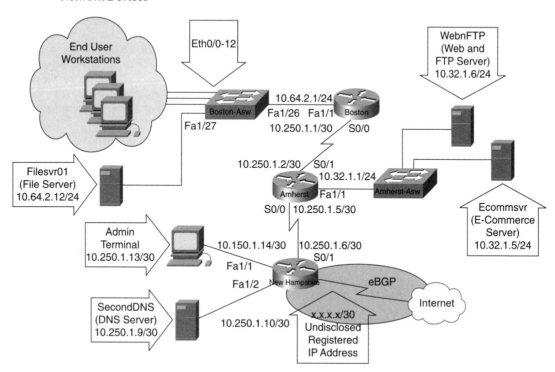

# Commands and Applications Used to Gather Information About End System Network Configurations

You use many commands and applications to gather information or to perform diagnosis on end systems (IP hosts). An operating system might support some commands similar to other operating systems and might support some unique commands or applications. Table 2-5 lists some general commands offered on most operating systems.

**Table 2-5**   *General End System Network Configuration Information Gathering Commands*

| Command | Description |
|---------|-------------|
| **ping** {*host* | *ip-address*} | Sends an ICMP echo request to the host name or IP address specified and waits for an ICMP echo reply from that host. |
| **arp –a** | Displays the content of the local device's ARP cache table (IP address to MAC address mappings). |

*continues*

**Table 2-5**   *General End System Network Configuration Information Gathering Commands (Continued)*

| Command | Description |
|---|---|
| **telnet** *{host | ip-address}* | Builds a Telnet session with the host name or IP address specified. Telnet is a TCP/IP application layer tool to gain terminal access to an IP device on the network. A successful Telnet session is an indication that the end system's IP address is valid, it is reachable from the local host, and it is running a Telnet server application. |

Microsoft Windows operating systems offer several TCP/IP commands, utilities, and applications. Some commands are universal, but some are not supported on all Microsoft operating systems. Table 2-6 lists Microsoft Windows commands that you can use to gather information about the network configuration of an end system.

**Table 2-6**   *Microsoft Windows Commands to Gather Information About End Systems*

| Command | Description |
|---|---|
| **ipconfig /all** | Displays IP information for hosts that are running Windows NT/Windows 2000/Windows XP operating systems |
| **tracert** *{host | ip-address}* | Verifies connectivity to the host name or IP address specified and shows the address of intermediate IP device(s) on that path |
| **winipcfg** | Displays IP information for hosts that are running Windows 9x and Windows Me |
| **route print** | Displays the content of local devices' IP routing tables |

Finally, Table 2-7 shows similar commands used on UNIX and Mac OS X operating systems.

**Table 2-7**   *UNIX/Mac OS X Commands to Gather Information About End Systems*

| Command | Description |
|---|---|
| **ifconfig –a** | Displays IP information for UNIX and MAC OS X hosts |
| **traceroute** *{host | ip-address}* | Verifies connectivity to the host name or IP address specified and shows the address of intermediate IP device(s) on that path |
| **route -n** | Displays the content of local devices' IP routing tables |

# Discovering End System Network Configuration Information

This section presents an 8-step method for discovering network configuration information of end systems. Each step is about discovering a specific piece of information and requires executing a special action or command. These steps along with their descriptions and their corresponding actions and commands are organized and presented in Table 2-8.

**Table 2-8**  *Discovering End System Network Configurations*

| Step | Description | OS-Dependent Action or Command |
|------|-------------|-------------------------------|
| 1 | Discover and view information about the operating system and hardware of the device. | On a Windows end system, you can access information about the operating system and hardware by choosing **Start > Settings > Control Panel** and then double-clicking the **Systems** icon. <br><br> On a Mac running Mac OS X, click the **Apple** icon and choose **About This Mac**. |
| 2 | Access a command line. | To access a command line on a Windows end system, choose **MS-DOS** or **Command Prompt** from the **Start** menu. <br><br> You can find the command-line Terminal utility on Mac OS X in the Utilities folder located in the Applications directory. |
| 3 | View detailed information about the TCP/IP settings of the device. | You can do this by entering the **ipconfig /all** or **winipcfg** commands in a Windows command prompt or entering **ifconfig -a** in a UNIX or Mac OS X command line. The important information to record includes the IP address/subnet mask, default gateway address, and any DNS or WINS server addresses. It is also useful to note if the IP address of a device is static or if it has been temporarily assigned through Dynamic Host Configuration Protocol (DHCP). |

*continues*

**Table 2-8**  *Discovering End System Network Configurations (Continued)*

| Step | Description | OS-Dependent Action or Command |
|---|---|---|
| 4 | Display any active routes. | You accomplish this by entering the **route print** command in a Windows command prompt or entering **route –n** in a UNIX or Mac OS X command line. |
| 5 | View Address Resolution Protocol (ARP) information (table). | Enter the **arp –a** command in the command line. |
| 6 | Check connectivity to remote devices. | Use the **ping** {*ip-address* | *host* } utility to test connectivity to other/remote devices. |
| 7 | View the route that is used to connect to a remote address, such as the default gateway. | View the route that is used to connect to a remote address, such as the default gateway. To accomplish this, enter **tracert** {*ip-address* | *hostname* } in a Windows command prompt or enter **traceroute** {*ip-address* | *hostname* } in a UNIX or Mac OS X command line. |
| 8 | Check that TCP is available and functioning on the end system. | Check that TCP is available and functioning on the end system by entering the **telnet** {*ip-address* | *hostname* } command.

Note that successful Telnet requires that the end device run a Telnet server application. |

# Creating End System Network Configuration Documentation

The purpose of this section is to provide guidelines on creating good end system network configuration documentation. Good documentation provides up-to-date, sufficient, and accurate information about the end systems' network configuration. The guidelines are listed and explained in Table 2-9.

**Table 2-9**  *Guidelines for Creating End System Network Configuration Documentation*

| Guideline | Explanation |
|---|---|
| Determine the scope. | Find out exactly which end systems you are responsible for and focus your effort on those. |
| Know the objective. | Collect relevant data only. Make sure you provide sufficient detail but avoid extraneous information because that can make the documentation difficult to use. |
| Be consistent. | Use consistent terminology, abbreviations, and style. Make sure the documents are well organized and easy to understand. Use templates and keep a library of symbols and graphics icons that you can reuse. |
| Keep the documents accessible. | Store the network documentation in a location where it is readily available and accessible to the appropriate personnel on the job. Keep a copy of the documentation in a secure location off-site. |
| Maintain the documentation. | Modify your network documentation as conditions and devices in the network change. Keeping network documentation up to date is especially important.<br><br>Note: Many organizations have deployed a formal process called *change control*. This process enforces reporting of network changes, maintaining version control, and assigning responsibility for modifying and distributing updated documents. |

# Foundation Summary

The "Foundation Summary" section of each chapter lists the most important facts from that chapter. Although this section does not list every fact from the chapter that will be on your CCNP exam, a well-prepared CCNP candidate should at a minimum know all the details in each "Foundation Summary" before taking the exam.

End system documentation is composed of the following:

- End system network configuration table

- End system network topology diagram

An end system network configuration table is baseline documentation that stores the following types of information about hardware, software, and configuration of end systems:

- Physical layer:

  — Device name and purpose

  — Physical location

  — Manufacturer/model

  — CPU type/speed

  — RAM

  — Storage

- Data link and network layer:

  — MAC address

  — Access VLAN number

  — IP address/subnet mask

  — Default gateway

  — WINS address

  — DNS address

- Application layer:

  — Operating system/version

  — Network application

  — High-bandwidth requirements/specifications

An end system network topology diagram graphically represents how the end device(s) logically and physically fit into the network. The diagram should depict (illustrate) every device along with its name and how it connects to the network.

Following are the commands and applications used to gather information about end system network configurations:

■ General commands:

— **ping**

— **arp –a**

— **telnet**

■ Windows commands:

— **ipconfig /all**

— **tracert**

— **winipcfg**

— **route print**

■ UNIX/Mac OS X commands:

— **ifconfig -a**

— **traceroute**

— **route -n**

The following steps outline the procedure for discovering the network configuration of an end system:

**Step 1**    View information about the operating system and hardware of the device:

• Windows: **System** icon in the Control Panel

• Mac OS: **About This Mac** from **Apple** icon

**Step 2**    Access a command line:

• Windows: **MS-DOS** or **Command Prompt**

• Mac OS: Utilities folder in Applications directory

**Step 3**    View detailed information about the TCP/IP settings of the device:

• Windows: **ipconfig /all** or **winipcfg**

• UNIX or Mac OS: **ifconfig -a**

**Step 4**        Display any active routes:

- Windows: **route print**

- UNIX or Mac OS: **route -n**

**Step 5**        View ARP information:

- **arp -a**

**Step 6**        Check connectivity to remote devices:

- **ping**

**Step 7**        View the route that connects to a remote address, such as the default gateway:

- Windows: **tracert**

- UNIX or Mac OS: **traceroute**

**Step 8**        Check that the TCP/Telnet server is available and functioning on the end system:

- **telnet**

Following are some guidelines for creating effective end system network documentation:

- Determine the scope.

- Know your objective.

- Be consistent.

- Keep the documents accessible.

- Maintain the documentation.

# Q&A

As mentioned in the introduction, you have two choices for review questions. The questions that follow give you a bigger challenge than the exam because they use an open-ended question format. By reviewing now with this more difficult question format, you can exercise your memory better and prove your conceptual and factual knowledge of this chapter. You can find the answers to these questions in Appendix A.

For more practice with exam-like question formats, including questions that use a router simulator and multiple choice format, use the exam engine on the CD.

1. Name the two main components of end system network documentation.

2. Identify at least three pieces of information recorded in the end system network configuration table that relate to the TCP/IP physical layer.

3. List at least three types of information recorded in the end system network configuration table that relate to the TCP/IP Internet/network layer.

4. Name at least two types of information recorded in the end system network configuration table that relate to the TCP/IP application layer.

5. What is the end system network topology diagram, and what should it depict?

6. Identify the end system network configuration information-gathering command(s) that list the set of active routes on an end system running Windows and on an end system running a UNIX/MAC operating system.

7. Name the general end system network configuration information-gathering command that displays the content of the local end system's ARP cache table.

8. Provide the command that displays IP information for hosts that are running Windows NT/Windows 2000/Windows XP and its counterpart command for Windows 9x/Windows Me.

9. Identify the command that displays IP information for UNIX and MAC OS X hosts.

10. Name at least three guidelines for creating end system network configuration documentation.

The following CIT exam topics are covered in this part. (To view the CIT exam outline, visit www.cisco.com/go/training.)

- Identify troubleshooting methods.

- Select an optimal troubleshooting approach.

- Plan an approach to troubleshooting that minimizes system downtime.

# Part II: Determining an Effective Troubleshooting Strategy

# This chapter covers the following subjects:

- The encapsulated data flow process

- Comparing layered networking models

- The layers of a logical model

CHAPTER **3**

# Applying a Logical Layered Model to a Physical Network

The popular networking models of today separate network functionality into modular layers. Applying a logical layered model to a physical network divides the complexity of the problem into more manageable and understandable parts. This simplifies the task of isolating network problems, expedites problem solving, and creates divisions of labor.

## "Do I Know This Already?" Quiz

The purpose of the "Do I Know This Already?" quiz is to help you decide if you really need to read this entire chapter. If you already intend to read the entire chapter, you do not need to answer these questions now.

The 10-question quiz, derived from the major sections in the "Foundation Topics" portion of the chapter, helps you determine how to spend your limited study time.

Table 3-1 outlines the major topics discussed in this chapter and the "Do I Know This Already?" quiz questions that correspond to those topics.

**Table 3-1** *"Do I Know This Already?" Foundation Topics Section-to-Question Mapping*

| Foundation Topics Section | Questions Covered in This Section |
| --- | --- |
| "The Encapsulated Data Flow Process" | 5 |
| "Comparing Layered Networking Models" | 1 |
| "The Layers of a Logical Model" | 4 |

**CAUTION** The goal of self-assessment is to gauge your mastery of the topics in this chapter. If you do not know the answer to a question or are only partially sure of the answer, you should mark this question wrong for purposes of the self-assessment. Giving yourself credit for an answer you correctly guess skews your self-assessment results and might provide you with a false sense of security.

1. How many stages make up the encapsulated data flow process?

   a. 2.

   b. 3.

   c. 4.

   d. 5.

   e. It is a direct process.

2. During which stage of the encapsulated data flow process does an end system receive data from a network and begin the process of removing data control information to make it usable with an application?

   a. Stage 1: Encapsulation

   b. Stage 2: Transmission

   c. Stage 3: Forwarding/Filtering

   d. Stage 4: Decapsulation

   e. Stage 5: Decompression

3. Which stages of the encapsulated data flow process alternate until the data flows through all devices that are necessary to reach the interface of the target end system?

   a. Stages 1 and 2: Encapsulation and Transmission

   b. Stages 2 and 3: Transmission and Forwarding

   c. Stages 3 and 4: Forwarding and Decapsulation

   d. Stages 4 and 5: Decapsulation and Decompression

   e. Stages 5 and 1: Fragmentation and Reassembly

4. During which stage of the encapsulated data flow process is data passed over the physical medium as bits?

   a. Stage 1: Encapsulation

   b. Stage 2: Transmission

   c. Stage 3: Forwarding/Filtering

   d. Stage 4: Decapsulation

   e. Stage 5: Reassembly

**5.** During which stage of the encapsulated data flow process are segmentation and encapsulation performed?

    **a.** Stage 1

    **b.** Stage 2

    **c.** Stage 3

    **d.** Stage 4

    **e.** Stage 5

**6.** Which of the following is the correct mapping of the TCP/IP model layers with the OSI model layers?

    **a.** The network interface and data link layers of the TCP/IP model map to the physical layer, the Internet layer maps to the network layer, the transport layer maps to the transport and session layers, and the application layer maps to the presentation and application layers.

    **b.** The network interface layer of the TCP/IP model maps to the physical layer, the Internet layer maps to the data link and network layers, the transport layer maps to the transport and session layers, and the application layer maps to the presentation and application layers.

    **c.** The physical layer of the TCP/IP model maps to the transport and application layers, the network interface layer maps to the physical layer, the transport layer maps to the data link layer, and the network layer maps to the Internet, session, and presentation layers.

    **d.** The network interface layer of the TCP/IP model maps to the physical and data link layers, the Internet layer maps to the network layer, the transport layer maps to the transport layer, and the application layer maps to the session, presentation, and application layers.

    **e.** Mapping between the two models does not exist.

**7.** A multilayer switch is considered a _____ device.

    **a.** TCP/IP network interface layer 1

    **b.** TCP/IP Internet layer 1

    **c.** TCP/IP transport layer 3

    **d.** TCP/IP application layer 3

    **e.** TCP/IP political layer 5

**8.** Identify the logical layers that pertain to a hub.

   **a.** TCP/IP network interface layer 1 and OSI physical layer 1

   **b.** TCP/IP network interface layer 1 and OSI data link layer 2

   **c.** TCP/IP network interface layer 1 and TCP/IP network layer 2

   **d.** TCP/IP network interface layer 1, TCP/IP network layer 2, and TCP/IP transport layer 3

   **e.** All the TCP/IP layers

**9.** Identify the logical layers that pertain to an end system.

   **a.** TCP/IP network interface layer 1 and OSI physical layer 1

   **b.** TCP/IP network interface layer 1 and OSI data link layer 2

   **c.** TCP/IP network interface layer 1 and TCP/IP network layer 2

   **d.** TCP/IP network interface layer 1, TCP/IP network layer 2, and TCP/IP transport layer 3

   **e.** All the TCP/IP layers

**10.** A standard LAN switch is considered a _____ device.

   **a.** TCP/IP network interface layer 1 and OSI physical layer 1

   **b.** TCP/IP network interface layer 1 and OSI data link layer 2

   **c.** TCP/IP network interface layer 1 and TCP/IP network layer 2

   **d.** TCP/IP network interface layer 1, TCP/IP network layer 2, and TCP/IP transport layer 3

   **e.** All the TCP/IP layers

You can find the answers to the "Do I Know This Already?" quiz in Appendix A, "Answers to the 'Do I Know This Already?' Quizzes and 'Q&A' Sections." The suggested choices for your next step are as follows:

■ **8 or less overall score**—Read the entire chapter. This includes the "Foundation Topics" and "Foundation Summary" sections, as well as the "Q&A" section.

■ **9 or 10 overall score**—If you want more review on these topics, skip to the "Foundation Summary" section and then go to the "Q&A" section. Otherwise, move to the next chapter.

# Foundation Topics

## The Encapsulated Data Flow Process

This section discusses the stages of data flow through a network that interconnects remote end systems and segments using Cisco routers and switches. This discussion includes the topic of encapsulation and decapsulation (or de-encapsulation), along with the different forwarding/filtering performed by routers and switches. Figure 3-1 shows end system Host A and end system Host B communicating on a network. The encapsulated data flow process has four stages. In Figure 3-1, Stages 1 through 4 point to different components of the network. The stages are as follows:

- Stage 1—Encapsulation

- Stage 2—Transmission

- Stage 3—Forwarding/Filtering

- Stage 4—Decapsulation

**Figure 3-1**  *The Process of Encapsulated Data Flow on a Simple Connection*

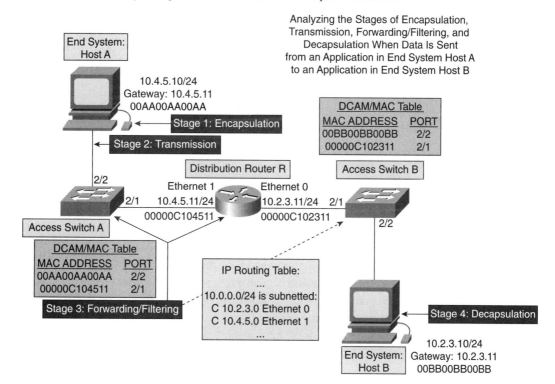

A description for each stage is provided next.

Stage 1 is encapsulation. First, you must convert the data into segments. At times, data is too large to be sent as one piece. For example, a file transfer might require the file to be broken into several pieces and sent as such. Each segment encapsulates some data, but it also has a header that identifies the sending application on one device (source) and the receiving application on its counterpart device (destination). The sending and receiving applications are usually identified using source and destination port numbers. Next, you add a header that includes network address information to each segment, effectively converting each segment into a packet (packet encapsulates segment). From there, you encapsulate each packet into a frame. The frame header includes physical addressing information (frame encapsulates packet). Finally, you are ready to transmit the frame as bits.

In Figure 3-1, end system Host A (using the TCP/IP protocol suite) takes data from an application and encapsulates the data as several pieces, as needed, in several segments. The segments are then encapsulated in packets with Host A's IP address as the source and Host B's IP address as the destination. Because Host A, comparing its IP address and subnet mask to the destination IP address, realizes that the destination IP address is a remote host, Host A must encapsulate the IP packet in a frame with the MAC address of Host A's default gateway (MAC address of 10.4.5.11) as the destination MAC address. If Host A does not have the MAC address associated to 10.4.5.11 in its ARP table, it must send an ARP request (which is a broadcast) to request and receive it. As a result, the packets sent will have 10.4.5.10 (Host A's IP address) as their source IP address and 10.2.3.10 (Host B's IP address) as their destination IP address. Those packets will be encapsulated in frames whose source MAC address will be 00AA00AA00AA (Host A's fictional MAC address), and their destination address will be 00000C104511 (Router R's Ethernet 1 MAC address). The frames that encapsulate IP packets—which encapsulate TCP or UDP (or other payload types such as RTP) segments, which in turn encapsulate application data—are ready for transmission into the media (transmission over a physical network).

NOTE    Even though most people use the term *packet* as the Layer 3 protocol data unit (PDU), the true Layer 3 PDU is a *datagram*. A packet is a fragment of a datagram that was fragmented due to insufficient MTU at a particular network segment. However, unless a datagram is segmented, a packet and a datagram are identical.

Stage 2 of the encapsulated data flow process is about passing the data over the physical medium as bits. Stage 3 is about how the intermediate network devices (routers, switches, hubs, and so on) change or alter and forward or filter (not forward) the data. When data reaches a network device, the device removes data control information as needed. Standard Layer 2 switches read physical addressing information (destination MAC address) and forward frames to a port or an interface based on the content of the dynamic content-addressable memory (DCAM) table. Routers, firewalls, and multilayer switches, generally speaking, read network addressing information (destination IP addresses) and forward packets to an interface based on the content of the IP routing table. Stages 2 and 3 alternate until the data flows through all devices that are necessary to reach the interface of the target end system.

In Figure 3-1, the frames that are leaving Host A (encapsulating packets that are destined to Host B) have 00AA00AA00AA as their source MAC address and 00000C104511 as their destination MAC address because Host A transmits them into the media. As frames enter Switch A via port 2/2, Switch A looks up their destination MAC address in its DCAM. Previously in its DCAM, Switch A learned and stored 00000C104511 and mapped it to port 2/1. Therefore, those frames are only forwarded to port 2/1. (If the MAC address were not present in Switch A's DCAM, the switch would flood them to all other ports that belong to the same VLAN as port 2/2.)

The frames now leave Switch A's port 2/1 (Transmission stage) and enter Router R's Ethernet 1 interface. Because the destination MAC address of the frames matches Router R's Ethernet 1 MAC address, Router R will decapsulate packets from inside the frames (reducing their TTL and recomputing their CRC). Because the destination IP address of those packets is not one of Router R's IP addresses, Router R will attempt to forward the packets based on its IP routing table. Router R's IP process (after doing lookups on its routing table) finds out that it is directly connected to the network to which the IP packets are destined; therefore, it forwards the packets out of its Ethernet 0 interface.

The packets need to be encapsulated in Ethernet frames. The source MAC address of those frames will be 00000C102311 (Ethernet 0's MAC address), and the destination MAC address of the frames can be discovered using ARP (by sending an ARP request and receiving an ARP reply) on Ethernet 0 (unless they are already present in Router R's ARP table). The frames will have 00000C102311 as their source MAC address and 00BB00BB00BB as their destination MAC address, and they will be transmitted to the media connected to the Ethernet 0 interface of Router R (Transmission stage, once again). Those frames subsequently enter Switch B's 2/1 port. After a lookup in its DCAM, Switch B decides that it must forward the frame out of its port 2/2 only. The frames are transmitted to the media connecting to Switch B's 2/2 port. The frames have 00000C102311 as their source MAC address (Router R's Ethernet 1 MAC address) and 00BB00BB00BB as their destination MAC address (Host B's Ethernet network interface card's MAC address). These frames encapsulate packets that were sent from Host A (which means their source IP address is 10.4.5.10) and are destined to Host B (which means their destination IP address is 10.2.3.10).

Stage 4 is called the Decapsulation stage. In Figure 3-1, Stage 4 points to end system Host B, meaning that end system Host B receives the data from the physical medium, removes the data control information, and converts the data as needed for use with the target application. In Figure 3-1, after frames enter Host B's network interface card, the network interface card discovers that the frames' destination MAC address matches the MAC address. The network interface card generates an interrupt to the CPU and the frame is copied from the network interface card's buffer to the main memory of Host A. Each frame's packet is decapsulated (the frame header and check sequence are removed), each packet's segment is decapsulated (the packet header and cyclic redundancy check are removed), and the data encapsulated in each segment is decapsulated and passed to the destination application based on the destination port number of the segments.

## Comparing Layered Networking Models

This section explains the 4-layer TCP/IP model by comparing it to the OSI model and by describing the function of each of its layers. Figure 3-2 displays the 7-layer OSI model and the 4-layer TCP/IP model side by side. As displayed, similar to the OSI networking model, the TCP/IP networking model divides networking architecture into modular layers. Figure 3-2 shows how the TCP/IP networking model maps to the layers of the OSI networking model.

**Figure 3-2**   *Comparing the OSI Model with the TCP/IP Model*

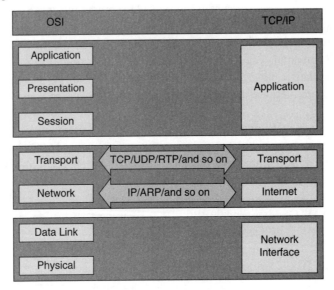

The network interface layer of the TCP/IP model maps to the physical and data link layers of the 7-layer OSI model. The network interface layer communicates directly with the network and provides an interface between the architecture of the network and the Internet layer.

The Internet layer of the TCP/IP model maps to the network layer of the 7-layer OSI model. The Internet layer of the TCP/IP protocol model is responsible for addressing and routing. Segments are received from the transport layer protocol (TCP or UDP), and Layer 3 (header and CRC) information—such as source and destination IP address—is added to the segment. The formed PDU is a datagram (or packet); the routing process and routing information determine the method of forwarding.

The transport layer of the TCP/IP model maps to the transport layer of the 7-layer OSI model. The transport layer is responsible for exchanging segments among devices on a TCP/IP network. Depending on whether the transport layer is connection oriented (like TCP) or connectionless (like UDP), and whether it is reliable (like RTP) or best effort (like UDP), the transport layout protocol could perform synchronization, sequence numbering, acknowledging, windowing, and so on.

The application layer of the TCP/IP model maps to the session, presentation, and application layers of the 7-layer OSI model. The TCP/IP model illustrates the close relationship between the session, presentation, and application OSI layers by combining them into a single layer. The application layer provides communication among applications (such as FTP, HTTP, and SMTP) on separate hosts.

> **NOTE**   Most internetworking professionals, especially those who are close to or at the CCNP level, are familiar with the OSI model, the TCP/IP model, and the correspondence between those layers. However, you should review the topic and recognize that when you support networks and troubleshoot their problems that are for the most part TCP/IP based, your frame of mind must be mostly in line with the TCP/IP 4-layer model. For instance, when protocol-analyzer software displays and deciphers a frame encapsulating an IP packet, you should observe frame information, packet information, segment information, and application data/information. When you are troubleshooting TCP/IP networks, it is easier to think in 4-layer terms than in 7-layer terms. Problem isolation becomes much more effective and quick, division of labor and responsibilities turns out to be more simple, and corrective actions are much more crisp and discrete.

## The Layers of a Logical Model

This section identifies the logical layers that you should focus on when troubleshooting specific networking devices. The ability to identify which layers of the logical networking model pertain to a networking device allows a troubleshooter to minimize the complexity of a problem by dividing the problem into manageable parts. Table 3-2 shows what logical layers the different internetworking devices map to.

The ability to map networking devices to logical network layers can focus troubleshooting efforts on the relevant elements and prevent wasted time and effort. For example, knowing that Layer 3 issues are of no importance to a switch (standard Layer 2 switch, not a multilayer switch) defines the boundaries of the task at hand to Layers 1 and 2. Because there is still plenty to consider at only these two layers, this simple knowledge can prevent you from troubleshooting irrelevant possibilities and will significantly reduce the amount of time spent attempting to correct a problem. However, it is important to note that some network applications can still be active on these devices that map to Layers 5–7. For example, a Layer 2 switch that receives SNMP configuration commands or generates SNMP traps is performing actions that are beyond its basic Layer 2 functions. Therefore, if someone tries to find out why an SNMP trap from a switch was not delivered to the SNMP manager, even though he might isolate the problem to be on the Layer 2 switch, the actual problem might have its roots at higher layers.

**Table 3-2**  *Network Devices Mapped to a Logical Layered Model*

| Device | Physical (TCP/IP Network Interface Layer 1) | Data Link (TCP/IP Network Interface Layer 1) | Network (TCP/IP Internet Layer 2) | Transport (TCP/IP Transport Layer 3) | Application 1 (TCP/IP Application Layer 4) |
|---|---|---|---|---|---|
| Router | X | X | X | * | |
| Firewall | X | X | X | * | |
| Multilayer Switch | X | X | X | * | |
| Standard Switch | X | X | | | |
| Hub | X | | | | |
| End System | X | X | X | X | X |

[1]In the *Cisco Internetwork Troubleshooting 5.0 Student Guide*, the session, presentation, and application layers are often grouped together as the application layer, similar to the TCP/IP model.

The asterisks (*) in Table 3-2 indicate that even though the device performs certain actions at the transport layer, those actions are not the primary functions of the device.

# Foundation Summary

The "Foundation Summary" section of each chapter lists the most important facts from that chapter. Although this section does not list every fact from the chapter that will be on your CCNP exam, a well-prepared CCNP candidate should at a minimum know all the details in each "Foundation Summary" before taking the exam.

Table 3-3 summarizes a simple process of encapsulated data flow between two end systems.

**Table 3-3** *Sending Encapsulated Data Between Two End Systems*

| Stage | Description |
|---|---|
| Stage 1: Encapsulation | The sending end system takes data from an application and converts it as needed for transmission over a physical network. This involves the following: <br><br> • Converting data into segments <br><br> • Encapsulating segments with a header that includes network addressing information and converting segments into packets <br><br> • Encapsulating packets with a header that includes physical addressing information and converting packets into frames <br><br> • Converting frames into bits |
| Stage 2: Physical Transmission | Data passes over the physical medium as bits. |
| Stage 3: Forwarding/ Filtering | When data reaches a network device, the device removes data control information as needed. Standard switches read physical addressing information and forward frames to a port (or an interface). Routers, firewalls, and multilayer switches read network addressing information and forward packets out of an interface. Stages 2 and 3 alternate until the data flows through all devices that are necessary to reach the interface of the target end system. |
| Stage 4: Decapsulation | The interface of the receiving end system receives the data from the physical medium, removes the data control information, and converts the data as needed for use with the target application. |

Table 3-4 displays the 7-layer OSI model and the 4-layer TCP/IP model side by side; it shows how the TCP/IP networking model maps to the layers of the OSI networking model.

**Table 3-4**  *Comparing the OSI Model to the TCP/IP Model*

| OSI | TCP/IP |
|---|---|
| Application (Layer 7)<br>Presentation (Layer 6)<br>Session (Layer 5) | Application |
| Transport (Layer 4) | Transport |
| Network (Layer 3) | Internet |
| Data link (Layer 2)<br>Physical (Layer 1) | Network interface |

Table 3-5 shows what logical layer(s) the different internetworking devices map to.

**Table 3-5**  *Network Devices Mapped to a Logical Layered Model*

| Device | Physical (TCP/IP Network Interface Layer 1) | Data Link (TCP/IP Network Interface Layer 1) | Network (TCP/IP Internet Layer 2) | Transport (TCP/IP Transport Layer 3) | Application [1] (TCP/IP Application Layer 4) |
|---|---|---|---|---|---|
| Router | X | X | X | * | |
| Firewall | X | X | X | * | |
| Multilayer Switch | X | X | X | * | |
| Standard Switch | X | X | | | |
| Hub | X | | | | |
| End System | X | X | X | X | X |

[1] In the *Cisco Internetwork Troubleshooting 5.0 Student Guide*, the session, presentation, and application layers are often grouped together as the application layer, similar to the TCP/IP model.

The asterisks (*) in Table 3-5 indicate that even though the device performs certain actions at the transport layer, those actions are not the primary functions of the device.

# Q&A

As mentioned in the introduction, you have two choices for review questions. The questions that follow give you a bigger challenge than the exam because they use an open-ended question format. By reviewing now with this more difficult question format, you can exercise your memory better and prove your conceptual and factual knowledge of this chapter. You can find the answers to these questions in Appendix A.

For more practice with exam-like question formats, including questions that use a router simulator and multiple choice format, use the exam engine on the CD.

1. At which stage of the encapsulated data flow process is a header that includes network address information added to each segment?

2. Explain Stage 2 of the encapsulated data flow process.

3. Explain Stage 3 of the encapsulated data flow process.

4. Explain Stage 4 of the encapsulated data flow process.

5. List the layers of the OSI model that TCP/IP's network interface layer maps to.

6. Name the layer or layers of the OSI model that TCP/IP's Internet layer maps to.

7. Identify the layer or layers of the OSI model that TCP/IP's application layer maps to.

8. List the layer or layers of the OSI model that TCP/IP's transport layer maps to.

9. Which logical layers does a router map to?

10. Name the logical layers that a firewall maps to.

11. List the logical layers that a multilayer switch maps to.

12. What are the logical layers that a standard Layer 2 switch maps to?

13. Identify the logical layer that a hub maps to.

14. Name the logical layers that an end system maps to.

## This chapter covers the following subjects:

- The general troubleshooting process

- The Gather Symptoms stage

- The Isolate the Problem stage

- The Correct the Problem stage

# The General Troubleshooting Process

Solving network problems effectively and in a timely manner requires following a systematic troubleshooting methodology. The goal of this chapter is to present a general process and methodology that you can use in any network troubleshooting situation. The benefit of applying this general process is that it helps you systematically resolve problems quicker and more cost effectively, with less confusion and wasted time.

To appreciate the importance of using a systematic troubleshooting method, you must first understand the steps and scope of systematic troubleshooting. Everyone has a definition of systematic troubleshooting in mind. When asked, many people describe systematic troubleshooting as step-by-step, ordered, organized, thoughtful, and methodological. That's all true. In addition to those, a troubleshooting method is systematic if it guarantees progress. A method that gets into circles and causes you to become more confused than when you started is *not* a systematic method.

You can't afford *not* to use a systematic troubleshooting method. In today's internetworks, downtime can mean large amounts of money or opportunities lost. In some cases, downtime might even lead to a company's bankruptcy. In any case, network support people are usually under tremendous pressure to discover and fix problems quickly. If you know the cause of a failure and can fix it, you should do it without hesitation. However, for most occasions, that will not be the case. Therefore, you must deploy a technique that can eliminate different possibilities and move you step by step toward the real causes of your problem. This way, you are always making progress and will not get into loops and confusion. Ultimately, you will either recognize what has broken, failed, or been misconfigured (problem isolation), or you can make a report of everything you have done and discovered and hand the case over to somebody else who can then use that information in further troubleshooting efforts. The important thing is that you will not be wasting your own and other people's time, and your effort will produce results regardless of whether you have fixed the problem.

Readers who have previous knowledge of recommended troubleshooting methods and strategies or those who have attended the previous version of the Cisco Internetwork Troubleshooting (CIT) course will notice that the current version of this course presents the systematic troubleshooting method differently. The models presented elsewhere and in the previous version of this book are valid; however, the new model, presented here, is more general and has less discrete steps. For instance, the new model does not specify the problem definition as a separate and initial step. Neither does it call documentation a separate and final step.

Nevertheless, defining the problem and documenting the actions taken are part of the troubleshooting process. Therefore, the current version of the CIT course, which presents a 3-stage troubleshooting method, considers problem definition as part of Stage 1 and documenting the results and actions taken as part of Stage 3. Because this book's goal is not to teach internetwork troubleshooting from the author's point of view, but to prepare you for the new CIT certification exam, the focus of this short chapter is to introduce the CIT 3-stage troubleshooting method, describing the actions taken and the processes involved at each stage.

# "Do I Know This Already?" Quiz

The purpose of the "Do I Know This Already?" quiz is to help you decide if you really need to read this entire chapter. If you already intend to read the entire chapter, you do not need to answer these questions now.

The 10-question quiz, derived from the major sections in the "Foundation Topics" portion of the chapter, helps you determine how to spend your limited study time.

Table 4-1 outlines the major topics discussed in this chapter and the "Do I Know This Already?" quiz questions that correspond to those topics.

**Table 4-1**   *"Do I Know This Already?" Foundation Topics Section-to-Question Mapping*

| Foundation Topics Section | Questions Covered in This Section |
| --- | --- |
| "The General Troubleshooting Process" | 3 |
| "The Gather Symptoms Stage" | 3 |
| "The Isolate the Problem Stage" | 2 |
| "The Correct the Problem Stage" | 2 |

**CAUTION**   The goal of self-assessment is to gauge your mastery of the topics in this chapter. If you do not know the answer to a question or are only partially sure of the answer, you should mark this question wrong for purposes of the self-assessment. Giving yourself credit for an answer you correctly guess skews your self-assessment results and might provide you with a false sense of security.

1.   How many stages make up the general troubleshooting process?

  a.  2

  b.  3

  c.  4

  d.  5

2.  What are the stages of the general troubleshooting process?

    a.  Gather Symptoms

    b.  Translate the Symptoms

    c.  Isolate the Problem

    d.  Correct the Problem

3.  Which of the following describes the Gather Symptoms stage of the general troubleshooting process?

    a.  Determining what network components have been affected

    b.  Implementing, testing, and documenting a solution

    c.  Selecting the most likely cause

    d.  Making configuration changes to the routing table

4.  Which of the following describes the Isolate the Problem stage of the general troubleshooting process?

    a.  Implementing, testing, and documenting a solution

    b.  Backing up the current configuration

    c.  Determining which network components have been affected

    d.  Selecting the most likely cause

5.  Which of the following describes the Correct the Problem stage of the general troubleshooting process?

    a.  Determining what network components have been affected

    b.  Implementing, testing, and documenting a solution

    c.  Interviewing an end user

    d.  Selecting the most likely cause

6.  In which stage of the general troubleshooting process are you if you are testing the network to ensure that you have not introduced an additional problem?

    a.  Gather Symptoms stage

    b.  Isolate the Problem stage

    c.  Correct the Problem stage

    d.  Create More Problems stage

**7.** Which stage in the general troubleshooting process involves interviewing a user?

   **a.** Gather Symptoms stage

   **b.** Isolate the Problem stage

   **c.** Correct the Problem stage

   **d.** Ignore the Problem stage

**8.** Given three possible causes of a network problem, you enter commands that help you decide which one is most likely the cause of the problem. Which stage in the general troubleshooting process are you performing?

   **a.** Gather Symptoms stage

   **b.** Isolate the Problem stage

   **c.** Correct the Problem stage

   **d.** Interview Users stage

**9.** Which of the following lists the correct order of the stages in the general troubleshooting process?

   **a.** Gather Symptoms, Correct the Problem, Isolate the Problem

   **b.** Isolate the Problem, Correct the Problem, Gather Symptoms

   **c.** Gather Symptoms, Isolate the Problem, Correct the Problem

   **d.** Isolate the Problem, Gather Symptoms, Correct the Problem

**10.** You read from a system log that the link of an interface has been flapping up and down repeatedly. This situation is an example of which stage of the general troubleshooting process?

   **a.** Gather Symptoms stage

   **b.** Isolate the Problem stage

   **c.** Correct the Problem stage

   **d.** Deny the Problem stage

You can find the answers to the "Do I Know This Already?" quiz in Appendix A, "Answers to the 'Do I Know This Already?' Quizzes and 'Q&A' Sections." The suggested choices for your next step are as follows:

- **8 or less overall score**—Read the entire chapter. This includes the "Foundation Topics" and "Foundation Summary" sections, as well as the "Q&A" section.

- **9 or 10 overall score**—If you want more review on these topics, skip to the "Foundation Summary" section and then go to the "Q&A" section. Otherwise, move to the next chapter.

# Foundation Topics

## The General Troubleshooting Process

The general troubleshooting process is composed of three major stages:

1. Gather Symptoms

2. Isolate the Problem

3. Correct the Problem

The spirit of this model is that gathering symptoms and any relevant data should help eliminate what is *not* the problem and lead you toward what might *be* the problem. After you have isolated the problem, you can correct it. These stages are not independent, and each of them involves several tasks. Not all problems are solved in a 1-2-3 fashion; in fact, few are. At times, you might have to hop back and forth between two stages before you succeed. For example, while you are trying to correct a problem, your action might cause another unidentified problem. As a result, you need to gather more symptoms, isolate the new problem, and correct it. Figure 4-1 depicts the stages of this general troubleshooting process, the order of their execution, and how they can result in a solution in one or more iterations.

**Figure 4-1**  *The General Troubleshooting Process*

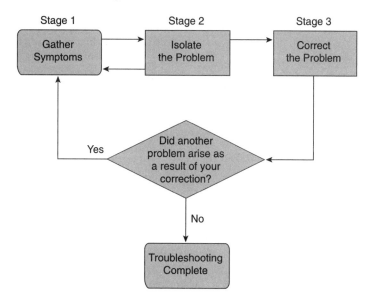

Each stage of the troubleshooting process and all the tasks associated with each stage need to be formally defined and carefully described. Many organizations have policies regarding how each stage should be executed so that it is guaranteed to succeed. The way changes are made (usually one at the time), authorized, and subsequently documented are also usually enforced rigorously.

## The Gather Symptoms Stage

During the Gather Symptoms stage of the general troubleshooting process, you gather and document symptoms from the network, end systems, or users. The process is usually initiated when someone reports a problem verbally, via e-mail or voice mail, or through another form of problem reporting. Subsequently, you must try to define the problem. Defining the problem usually involves interviewing users, seeing the problem first hand, and talking to peers, support staff, and engineers. The symptoms that the users and the troubleshooters observe vary. Whereas the users mostly report that applications don't work or resources are not reachable, the support staff/engineers notice symptoms such as alerts from the network management system or console log messages. Ideally, you must notice any and all deviations from the baseline. Find out what is broken, what doesn't work, or what is not normal. Following are some good questions to ask:

- Did it ever work before?

- When was the last time it worked?

- Do you know what has changed?

Even though Gather Symptoms is only the first of the three stages of troubleshooting, during this stage, you must start thinking of possibilities. The plan is to identify a problem area, and from the problem area, identify a problem device. From the problem device, identify a problem component. In networks that have redundancy (such as component, device, link), it is best to bypass the problem area. This way, data can travel across the network while a particular area is investigated and repaired. Transition from the Gather Symptoms stage to the Isolate the Problem stage happens when the problem has been defined, the gathering of symptoms is complete, and from the initial set of possibilities, some are ruled out and the other remain as probable culprits.

## The Isolate the Problem Stage

Isolating the problem starts when, based on the gathered symptoms, initial interviews, and so on, some of the initial possibilities are ruled out, and the others remain as probable culprits. However, the remaining possibilities must be ranked based on their likelihood, and their validity should be evaluated individually. The way that the possibilities are tested, reinstated, or overthrown is based on the tests conducted and the fact-gathering methods that were employed.

Gathering symptoms is discussed in the next chapter in three sections: "Gathering Network Symptoms," "Gathering User Symptoms," and "Gathering End System Symptoms." The number of tests that you can perform and the facts that you can gather are numerous and virtually endless. Therefore, you must select an approach that can swiftly eliminate some possibilities so that you can rank and test a manageable number of remaining possibilities. Three major approaches are often taken: top-down, bottom-up, and divide-and-conquer. These approaches are discussed in Chapter 6, "Selecting a Troubleshooting Approach." Remember your aim to identify an isolated problem area, isolate a problem segment or device, and then isolate a problem component. It is only then that you can proceed to the next stage, which is to correct the problem and observe the results.

## The Correct the Problem Stage

After you have an isolated problem at hand, you must propose the corresponding corrective action(s). If the actions are multiple and independent (atomic), implement them one at a time. Making few or one change at a time allows for more granular and discrete observation and evaluation of their results; moreover, one or a few actions are easier to roll back if necessary. Therefore, note that not all changes stick; you might have to withdraw some.

Furthermore, keep in mind that one or few changes might not correct the problem; some or all of the symptoms might remain. Even though those actions that created more problems or were proven unnecessary have been rolled back, some actions might have to remain, even though they might not fix the problem(s). Further actions to be followed might then, finally, resolve all the issues. Therefore, you must decide on each action: roll back or remain. You must communicate with others those actions that remain and document them thoroughly.

Eventually, after one, a few, or more changes or actions, the symptoms disappear, and the problem is fixed. All the corrective actions are documented and communicated. In many organizations, these actions must be authorized before they can be implemented. In contrast, you might end up in a situation in which you can imagine (propose) no more possibilities. At that point, you feel as if a dead end has been reached. In those cases, chances are good that you do not have enough facts. Another possibility is that the faulty device runs an IOS that has an operational bug. Therefore, when you exhaust all possibilities, you must seek other people's (such as Cisco's Technical Assistance Center) assistance, gather more facts, or use Cisco's Bug Toolkit to find out if the problem is due to an existing bug. Some problems have specific solution(s) that completely fix/correct them. Other problems have a workaround, and still other problems might not have a clear and present solution due to limitations in technology or the operating system. Resolving the problems at different layers of the OSI model is discussed in Chapters 7 through 12.

# Foundation Summary

The "Foundation Summary" section of each chapter lists the most important facts from the chapter. Although this section does not list every fact from the chapter that will be on your CCNP exam, a well-prepared CCNP candidate should at a minimum know all the details in each "Foundation Summary" before taking the exam.

The general troubleshooting process is composed of three major stages:

1.  **Gather Symptoms**—Gather and document symptoms from the network and end systems to determine how the state of the network has changed compared to the baseline.

2.  **Isolate the Problem**—Identify the characteristics of problems at the logical layers of the network so that you can select the most likely cause.

3.  **Correct the Problem**—Correct an identified problem by implementing, testing, and documenting a solution.

# Q&A

As mentioned in the introduction, you have two choices for review questions. The questions that follow give you a bigger challenge than the exam because they use an open-ended question format. By reviewing now with this more difficult question format, you can exercise your memory better and prove your conceptual and factual knowledge of this chapter. You can find the answers to these questions in Appendix A.

For more practice with exam-like question formats, including questions that use a router simulator and multiple choice format, use the exam engine on the CD.

1. What are the stages of the general troubleshooting process?

2. What do you do in the first stage of the troubleshooting process?

3. What do you do in the second stage of the troubleshooting process?

4. What do you do in the third stage of the troubleshooting process?

5. True or false: You should establish a policy for each stage of the troubleshooting process.

6. True or false: You have not truly isolated the problem until you have identified a single problem or a set of related problems.

## This chapter covers the following subjects:

- Gathering network symptoms

- Gathering user symptoms

- Gathering end system symptoms

# CHAPTER 5

# Gathering Symptoms

The previous chapter presented the general troubleshooting process. In the first stage of the process, you gather symptoms of the problem. By gathering symptoms, you build a knowledge base about potential reasons for the problem(s). This chapter presents how to gather symptoms from network devices, end users, and end systems.

## "Do I Know This Already?" Quiz

The purpose of the "Do I Know This Already?" quiz is to help you decide if you really need to read this entire chapter. If you already intend to read the entire chapter, you do not need to answer these questions now.

The 10-question quiz, derived from the major sections in the "Foundation Topics" portion of the chapter, helps you determine how to spend your limited study time.

Table 5-1 outlines the major topics discussed in this chapter and the "Do I Know This Already?" quiz questions that correspond to those topics.

**Table 5-1** *"Do I Know This Already?" Foundation Topics Section-to-Question Mapping*

| Foundation Topics Section | Questions Covered in This Section |
|---|---|
| "Gathering Network Symptoms" | 5 |
| "Gathering User Symptoms" | 3 |
| "Gathering End System Symptoms" | 2 |

**CAUTION**   The goal of self-assessment is to gauge your mastery of the topics in this chapter. If you do not know the answer to a question or are only partially sure of the answer, you should mark this question wrong for purposes of the self-assessment. Giving yourself credit for an answer you correctly guess skews your self-assessment results and might provide you with a false sense of security.

1. Which of the following is the correct description for the Analyze Existing Symptoms stage in the process of gathering network symptoms?

   a. Identifying whether a problem is inside or outside the boundary of control for you as a troubleshooter.

   b. You either solve the problem at this stage, or you move on to the Isolating phase.

   c. Determining whether the problem is with the hardware or the software configuration.

   d. Getting a description of the problem.

   e. Identifying whether the problem is at the core, distribution, or access layer of the network.

2. Which of the following is the correct description for the Determine Ownership stage in the process of gathering network symptoms?

   a. Identifying whether a problem is inside or outside the boundary of control for you as a troubleshooter.

   b. You either solve the problem at this stage, or you move on to the Isolating phase.

   c. Determining whether the problem is with the hardware or the software configuration.

   d. Getting a description of the problem.

   e. Identifying whether the problem is at the core, distribution, or access layer of the network.

3. Which of the following is the correct description for the Narrow Scope stage in the process of gathering network symptoms?

   a. Identifying whether a problem is inside or outside the boundary of control for you as a troubleshooter.

   b. You either solve the problem at this stage, or you move on to the Isolating phase.

   c. Determining whether the problem is with the hardware or the software configuration.

   d. Getting a description of the problem.

   e. Identifying whether the problem is at the core, distribution, or access layer of the network.

**4.** Which of the following is the correct description for the Determine Symptoms stage in the process of gathering network symptoms?

    **a.** Identifying whether a problem is inside or outside the boundary of control for you as a troubleshooter.

    **b.** You either solve the problem at this stage, or you move on to the Isolating phase.

    **c.** Determining whether the problem is with the hardware or the software configuration.

    **d.** Getting a description of the problem.

    **e.** Identifying whether the problem is at the core, distribution, or access layer of the network.

**5.** Which of the following is the correct description for the Document Symptoms stage in the process of gathering network symptoms?

    **a.** Identifying whether a problem is inside or outside the boundary of control for you as a troubleshooter.

    **b.** You either solve the problem at this stage, or you move on to the Isolating phase.

    **c.** Determining whether the problem is with the hardware or the software configuration.

    **d.** Getting a description of the problem.

    **e.** Identifying whether the problem is at the core, distribution, or access layer of the network.

**6.** If a user in your company network tells you that he cannot send e-mail, what would be the most pertinent question to ask?

    **a.** Are you using a laptop or a desktop computer?

    **b.** Is the SMTP server correctly configured?

    **c.** When did you first notice the problem?

    **d.** Can you open a word processing application?

**7.** Select the items that fit in the guidelines for gathering user symptoms.

    **a.** Ask questions that are pertinent to the problem.

    **b.** Do not speak to the user so that he doesn't feel responsible for the problem.

    **c.** Use each question as a means to either eliminate or discover possible problems.

    **d.** Speak at a technical level that the user can understand.

    **e.** Use the terminology that is accurate and that *you* are comfortable with.

8.  Select the items that fit in the guidelines for gathering user symptoms.

    a.  If possible, ask the user to re-create the problem.

    b.  Ask the user to try to fix the problem so that he can fix it the next time, without calling you.

    c.  Determine the sequence of events that took place before the problem occurred.

    d.  Try to collect statistics on the number of trouble calls each user makes so that they become more conscious of the process and more careful.

    e.  Match the symptoms that the user describes with common problem causes.

9.  After you have gathered all the symptoms at an end system and realized you cannot solve the problem, what should you do next?

    a.  Get a new IP address for the end system.

    b.  Replace the end system.

    c.  Reboot the end system.

    d.  Copy all network configuration information (such as IP address, subnet mask, and so on) from another device that is in good working order.

    e.  Begin isolating the symptoms to identify a single problem.

10. Which of the following lists in correct order the stages of gathering symptoms from end systems?

    a.  Document, determine, and analyze the symptoms.

    b.  Interview the user(s), analyze the symptoms, determine the symptoms, and document them.

    c.  Document the symptoms, analyze them, and then interview the user.

    d.  Interview the user, document the symptoms, and then fix the problem if possible.

    e.  Interview the user, determine the symptoms, analyze the symptoms, and then document them.

You can find the answers to the "Do I Know This Already?" quiz in Appendix A, "Answers to the 'Do I Know This Already?' Quizzes and 'Q&A' Sections." The suggested choices for your next step are as follows:

- **8 or less overall score**—Read the entire chapter. This includes the "Foundation Topics" and "Foundation Summary" sections, as well as the "Q&A" section.

- **9 or 10 overall score**—If you want more review on these topics, skip to the "Foundation Summary" section and then go to the "Q&A" section. Otherwise, move to the next chapter.

# Foundation Topics

Gathering a comprehensive collection of symptoms allows you to understand and recognize the problem and be able to describe and document it. Misunderstanding or having an incomplete perception of the problem can waste valuable time and resources on factors that might not be relevant to the problem. The time it takes you to collect a comprehensive set of symptoms is well worth it because it helps focus your efforts on the problem at hand. Therefore, it is essential that if you are planning to diagnose and fix problems in a network, you must invest time and effort in gathering enough symptoms and facts. This enables you to understand and define the problem before starting to form opinions about the causes and taking corrective actions. In this chapter, gathering symptoms is described in three sections:

■ "Gathering Network Symptoms"

■ "Gathering User Symptoms"

■ "Gathering End System Symptoms"

## Gathering Network Symptoms

Figure 5-1 displays the process of gathering symptoms from a network using a flowchart. Figure 5-1 sends the message that you must first ascertain that the problem is within your area of responsibility. Next, you must determine whether the symptoms and facts gathered are enough to identify the cause and take corrective actions. Sometimes gathering more facts is necessary; when you have gathered enough information and determined the cause, you can take corrective actions.

The stages of gathering network symptoms are as follows:

■ **Stage 1: Analyze Existing Symptoms**—In Stage 1, you must define the problem. This entails analyzing any gathered symptoms from the trouble ticket, the users, or from the end systems that are affected by the problem. The problem description must be short yet accurate.

■ **Stage 2: Determine Ownership**—In Stage 2, you must determine whether solving the problem at hand is your responsibility or must be handled by someone else. If the problem is in the system that you are responsible for, move on to Stage 3. If the problem is outside the boundary of control for you, contact an administrator for the external system.

■ **Stage 3: Narrow Scope**—In Stage 3, you determine whether the problem is at the core, distribution, or access layer of the network. At the identified layer, analysis of existing symptoms and knowledge of the network topology helps determine which segment, device, or component is the most likely culprit.

**Figure 5-1**    *The Process of Gathering Symptoms from a Network*

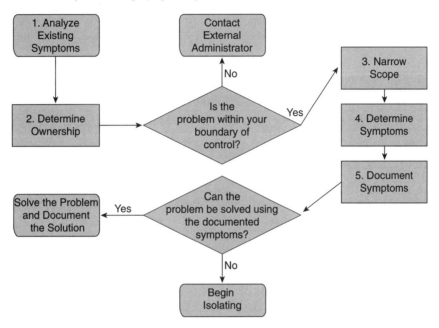

- **Stage 4: Determine Symptoms**—During Stage 4, you gather hardware and software symptoms from the suspect devices using a layered troubleshooting approach. You must start with the most likely culprit and use your knowledge and experience to determine whether the problem is more likely a hardware or software configuration problem. Gathering symptoms and facts about hardware that is perceived to be malfunctioning is effective if you physically inspect the suspected devices. In contrast, when you are gathering symptoms for possible software configuration problems, you should use Cisco IOS commands to check the status of various aspects of the suspected devices.

- **Stage 5: Document Symptoms**—In Stage 5, you document any hardware or software symptoms. If you can solve the problem by using the documented symptoms, you should solve the problem and document the solution. If you cannot solve the problem, you must begin the Isolating phase of the general troubleshooting process. Table 5-2 describes the common Cisco IOS commands that you can use to gather symptoms about a network.

**Table 5-2**    *Cisco IOS Commands for Gathering Network Symptoms*

| Command | Description |
|---|---|
| **ping** {*host* | *ip-address* } | Sends an echo request packet to an address and then waits for a reply. The {*host* | *ip-address*} variable is the IP alias or IP address of the target system. |
| **traceroute** {*host* | *ip-address*} | Identifies the path that a packet takes through the network. The {*host* | *ip-address*} variable is the IP alias or IP address of the target system. |

*continues*

**Table 5-2** *Cisco IOS Commands for Gathering Network Symptoms (Continued)*

| Command | Description |
|---|---|
| **telnet** {*host* | *ip-address*} | Connects to an IP device using the Telnet application. The {*host* | *ip-address*} variable is the IP alias or IP address of the target system. |
| **show ip interface** [**brief**] | Displays a summary of the status of all interfaces on a device. |
| **show ip route** | Displays the current state of the IP routing table. |
| **show running-config** | Displays the contents of the currently running configuration file. |
| [**no**] **debug ?** | Displays a list of options for enabling or disabling debugging events on a device. |

**NOTE** Be prudent with your use of the **debug** command on a network. It generates enough output to noticeably affect the performance of a network device. Be sure to disable debugging as soon as you have achieved your objectives.

# Gathering User Symptoms

This section provides a set of guidelines for gathering symptoms from users, a set of general questions to ask the users during the Gathering Symptoms process, and an example of how to follow the guidelines and put the general questions to use.

The following list presents the guidelines for gathering symptoms for a user's hardware or software:

■ Ask questions that are pertinent to the problem.

■ Use each question as a means to either eliminate or discover possible problems.

■ Speak at a technical level that a user can understand.

■ Ask the user when he first noticed the problem.

■ If possible, ask the user to re-create the problem.

■ Determine the sequence of events that took place before the problem occurred.

■ Match the symptoms that the user describes with common problem causes.

The following list is a good set of general questions to ask a user during the process of gathering symptoms:

■ What does not work?

■ What does work?

- Are the things that do and do not work related?

- Has the thing that does not work ever worked before?

- When did you first notice the problem?

- What has changed since the last time it worked?

- When exactly does the problem occur?

- Can you reproduce the problem? If yes, how do you reproduce it?

- Are you the only affected user or are others in your office experiencing similar problems?

Now look at an example of how you can use the provided guidelines and the general set of questions. Assume that a user calls you and claims that she cannot get on the Internet. You ask a few questions and find out that the user first noticed the problem within the past few minutes. You then ask the user to try to re-create the problem by opening a browser and attempting to reach an Internet site. She cannot make the connection, and she gets a "Cannot Reach Server or DNS Error" message. She states that she already tried this, and that the only site she can reach successfully is the site run by the department in which she works. This allows you to eliminate several possible culprits. Knowing that the user can reach local servers but not anything outside the company network, you suspect that a routing issue might be the problem.

Feeling confident that the gateway router is operating correctly, you try to determine the sequence of events that took place before the problem arose by asking if the user has recently accessed the Network settings in the Control Panel. This is something the user says she does not know, but a little while ago, she was checking out the Preferences for the browser and "clicked on some stuff." She does not think she changed anything important, though. Hearing this, you visit the user's computer and discover that she inadvertently removed the address for the default gateway.

Your use of an effective interviewing technique allowed you to come up with a clear description of the problem. Your next step will be either to use the gathered symptoms to correct the problem or begin isolating.

# Gathering End System Symptoms

This section presents a process you can use to gather symptoms from end systems. Figure 5-2 displays this process with a flowchart. The process starts with interviewing the user and then calls for analyzing, determining, and documenting the symptoms. Finally, you correct the problem if it is possible.

**NOTE**    This book focuses on troubleshooting network connectivity. You might need to seek help from external vendors or workstation and server administrators to effectively troubleshoot problems at end systems.

**Figure 5-2**   *The Process of Gathering Symptoms from an End System*

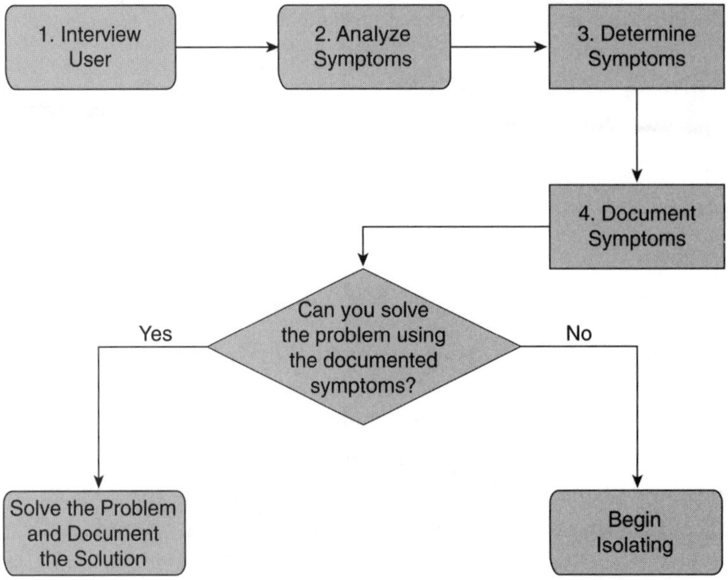

The stages of gathering end system symptoms are as follows:

- **Stage 1: Interview User**—At Stage 1, if possible, you gather initial symptoms from the user and use these symptoms as a platform to gather symptoms at the end system later.

- **Stage 2: Analyze Symptoms**—In Stage 2, you form a description of the problem by analyzing any gathered symptoms from the user.

- **Stage 3: Determine Symptoms**—During Stage 3, you gather hardware and software symptoms from the end system using a layered troubleshooting approach, starting with the most likely culprit. You must rely on experience to decide whether the problem is more likely a hardware or a software problem. Starting with the most obvious symptom—gathering symptoms and facts about hardware that is perceived to be malfunctioning—is effective if you physically inspect the suspected devices. Information you gather from the user helps determine the most obvious places to begin. When you are gathering symptoms for perceived software problems, you should test the network applications on the end system. Information you gather from the user helps determine the most obvious applications to test.

- **Stage 4: Document Symptoms**—In Stage 4, you document all the hardware and software symptoms. If you can solve the problem using the documented symptoms, you must do so and document the solution. If you cannot solve the problem at this point, you must then begin the Isolating phase of the general troubleshooting process. Table 5-3 lists and describes the commands used to gather symptoms on end systems.

**Table 5-3**    *Commands for Gathering Symptoms on End Systems*

| Command | Description |
|---|---|
| **ping** {*host* \| *ip-address*} | Sends an echo request packet to the target system and then waits for a reply. The {*host* \| *ip-address*} variable is the IP alias or IP address of the target system. |
| **telnet** {*host* \| *ip-address*} | Connect to an IP address or host name using the Telnet application. |
| Windows: **tracert** [*destination* ]<br><br>Mac/UNIX: **traceroute** [*destination* ] | Identifies the path that a packet takes through the network. The [*destination* ] variable is the host name or IP address of the target system. |
| Windows: **ipconfig /all**<br><br>Mac/UNIX: **ifconfig –a** | Displays information relating to the IP configuration of an end system. |
| **arp –a** | Displays the contents of the entire ARP table (local mappings of MAC addresses to their corresponding IP addresses). |
| **route print** | Displays the contents of the entire IP routing table (on the end device). |
| **netstat [-a] [-e]**<br><br>    **[-n] [-p** *proto*]<br><br>    **[-r] [-s]** | Displays protocol statistics and current TCP/IP network connections:<br><br>**-a** Displays all connections and listening ports.<br><br>**-e** Displays Ethernet statistics.<br><br>**-n** Displays addresses and port numbers in numerical form.<br><br>**-p** *proto* Shows connections for the protocol specified by *proto*; *proto* can be **TCP** or **UDP**.<br><br>**-r** Displays the routing table.<br><br>**-s** Displays per-protocol statistics. By default, statistics are shown for TCP, UDP, and IP; you can use the **-p** option to specify a subset of the default. |

# Foundation Summary

The "Foundation Summary" section of each chapter lists the most important facts from that chapter. Although this section does not list every fact from the chapter that will be on your CCNP exam, a well-prepared CCNP candidate should at a minimum know all the details in each "Foundation Summary" before taking the exam.

Table 5-4 categorizes the process of gathering symptoms.

**Table 5-4** *Categories of Gathering Symptoms*

| Category | Description |
| --- | --- |
| Gathering Network Symptoms | Gathering symptoms from network devices (five stages) |
| Gathering User Symptoms | Gathering hardware and software symptoms from user feedback to complete a list of symptoms at the end system |
| Gathering End System Symptoms | Gathering data at the end system to complete a list of hardware and software symptoms displayed at the end system (four stages) |

## Gathering Network Symptoms

You can gather network symptoms in five stages:

1. Analyze Existing Symptoms
2. Determine Ownership
3. Narrow Scope
4. Determine Symptoms
5. Document Symptoms

The following Cisco IOS commands are useful for gathering network symptoms:

- **ping** {*host* | *ip-address*}
- **traceroute** {*host* | *ip-address*}
- **telnet** {*host* | *ip-address*}
- **show ip interface brief**

- **show ip route**

- **show running-config**

- **[no] debug** ?

## Gathering User Symptoms

The following list presents the guidelines for gathering symptoms for a user's hardware or software:

- Ask questions that are pertinent to the problem.

- Use each question as a means to either eliminate or discover possible problems.

- Speak at a technical level that a user can understand.

- Ask the user when he first noticed the problem.

- If possible, ask the user to re-create the problem.

- Determine the sequence of events that took place before the problem occurred.

- Match the symptoms that the user describes with common problem causes.

The following list is a good set of general questions to ask a user during the process of gathering user symptoms:

- What does not work?

- What does work?

- Are the things that do and do not work related?

- Has the thing that does not work ever worked before?

- When did you first notice/experience the problem?

- What has changed since the last time it worked?

- When exactly does the problem occur?

- Can you reproduce the problem? If yes, how do you reproduce it?

## Gathering End System Symptoms

You can perform the process of gathering symptoms from an end system in four stages:

1. Interview User

2. Analyze Symptoms

3. Determine Symptoms

4. Document Symptoms

The following commands are useful for gathering symptoms on end systems:

- **ping** {*host* | *ip-address*}

- **telnet** {*host* | *ip-address*}

- Windows: **tracert** {*host* | *ip-address*}

- Mac/UNIX: **traceroute** {*host* | *ip-address*}

- Windows: **ipconfig /all**

- Mac/UNIX: **ifconfig –a**

- **arp -a**

- **route print**

- **netstat -n**

# Q&A

As mentioned in the introduction, you have two choices for review questions. The questions that follow give you a bigger challenge than the exam because they use an open-ended question format. By reviewing now with this more difficult question format, you can exercise your memory better and prove your conceptual and factual knowledge of this chapter. You can find the answers to these questions in Appendix A.

For more practice with exam-like question formats, including questions that use a router simulator and multiple choice format, use the exam engine on the CD.

1.  What is the first stage in the general troubleshooting process, and why is it important and useful?

2.  What three categories can the Gathering Symptoms process be broken into?

3.  What are the five stages of the Gathering Network Symptoms process?

4.  Provide three Cisco IOS **show** commands for gathering network symptoms.

5.  Provide three Cisco IOS diagnostic and troubleshooting commands for gathering network symptoms (No **show** or **debug** commands).

6.  Provide at least four guidelines for gathering symptoms for a user's hardware or software.

7.  List at least four general questions you can ask a user during the process of gathering user symptoms.

8.  What are the four stages in the process of gathering symptoms from an end system?

9.  What Windows command identifies the path a packet takes through the network? What is the Mac/UNIX counterpart for this command?

10.  What Windows command displays information relating to the IP configuration of the end system?

## This chapter covers the following subjects:

■ The bottom-up troubleshooting approach

■ The top-down troubleshooting approach

■ The divide-and-conquer troubleshooting approach

■ Selecting a troubleshooting approach

# CHAPTER 6

# Selecting a Troubleshooting Approach

You cannot perform troubleshooting on an ad hoc basis in serious production environments; to effectively solve a problem, you must follow a specific methodology. This chapter presents three main approaches to troubleshooting and describes how to select a suitable troubleshooting approach for the problem at hand. As a troubleshooter, you must take your knowledge and aptitude into account and take the approach you feel is most suitable. With a method to follow, you can solve the problem more quickly and cost effectively than if you approached the problem haphazardly. After you have chosen an approach, do not switch to another one in the midst of the troubleshooting effort. Switching methods often causes confusion, wastes time and effort, and impedes the resolution efforts.

## "Do I Know This Already?" Quiz

The purpose of the "Do I Know This Already?" quiz is to help you decide if you really need to read this entire chapter. If you already intend to read the entire chapter, you do not need to answer these questions now.

The 10-question quiz, derived from the major sections in the "Foundation Topics" portion of the chapter, helps you determine how to spend your limited study time.

Table 6-1 outlines the major topics discussed in this chapter and the "Do I Know This Already?" quiz questions that correspond to those topics.

**Table 6-1** *"Do I Know This Already?" Foundation Topics Section-to-Question Mapping*

| Foundation Topics Section | Questions Covered in This Section |
|---|---|
| "The Bottom-Up Troubleshooting Approach" | 2 |
| "The Top-Down Troubleshooting Approach" | 3 |
| "The Divide-and-Conquer Troubleshooting Approach" | 3 |
| "Selecting a Troubleshooting Approach" | 2 |

> **CAUTION** The goal of self-assessment is to gauge your mastery of the topics in this chapter. If you do not know the answer to a question or are only partially sure of the answer, you should mark this question wrong for purposes of the self-assessment. Giving yourself credit for an answer you correctly guess skews your self-assessment results and might provide you with a false sense of security.

1. Which of the following is an example of a problem that would take place at the network level of the bottom-up approach to troubleshooting?

   a. An interface malfunctions.

   b. A routing loop occurs.

   c. A router heat sink needs to be replaced.

   d. The duplex setting of a port is incorrectly set.

2. If you have exhausted the possibility of the problem occurring in all but the final level of the top-down troubleshooting approach, which layer are you concerned with?

   a. Physical

   b. Data link

   c. Transport

   d. Application

3. Using a divide-and-conquer approach, which layer would you begin with if you isolated the problem to an access list on a router?

   a. Physical

   b. Data link

   c. Network

   d. Transport

4. The power of the Cisco IOS command set encourages which troubleshooting approach?

   a. Bottom-up

   b. Top-down

   c. Divide-and-conquer

   d. Weighted fair

**5.** During the course of a troubleshooting case, you started checking the physical devices first. Which approach have you taken?

   **a.** Bottom-up

   **b.** Top-down

   **c.** Divide-and-conquer

   **d.** LLQ (Low Latency)

**6.** A user has initiated a trouble call, and it seems like a trivial case. Which approach should you most likely take?

   **a.** Bottom-up

   **b.** Top-down

   **c.** Divide-and-conquer

   **d.** Priority approach

**7.** Which one of the following is a problem that would occur at the first level of the top-down troubleshooting approach?

   **a.** The PortFast setting on a port is incorrectly set to off.

   **b.** The STP state on an interface is incorrectly set to forward.

   **c.** A jabbering port is identified.

   **d.** An FTP client application is found to be corrupt.

**8.** Which of the following provides the guidelines for selecting the best troubleshooting approach?

   **a.** Apply experience, analyze the symptoms, and solve the problem.

   **b.** Select a troubleshooting approach and determine the scope of the problem.

   **c.** Determine the scope of the problem, analyze it using your experience, and solve it.

   **d.** Determine the scope of the problem, apply experience, and analyze the symptoms.

**9.** Using the divide-and-conquer troubleshooting approach, you decide to begin troubleshooting a TCP/IP problem at the network layer. You determine that the network layer is working properly. Based on this knowledge, which of the following layers is/are *not* assumed to be working properly?

   **a.** Physical layer

   **b.** Data link layer

   **c.** Transport layer

   **d.** Application layer

10. Which troubleshooting approach is most appropriate to implement if the problem is located at the network interface?

    **a.** Bottom-up

    **b.** Top-down

    **c.** Divide-and-conquer

    **d.** Class-based weighted

You can find the answers to the "Do I Know This Already?" quiz in Appendix A, "Answers to the 'Do I Know This Already?' Quizzes and 'Q&A' Sections." The suggested choices for your next step are as follows:

- **8 or less overall score**—Read the entire chapter. This includes the "Foundation Topics" and "Foundation Summary" sections, as well as the "Q&A" section.

- **9 or 10 overall score**—If you want more review on these topics, skip to the "Foundation Summary" section and then go to the "Q&A" section. Otherwise, move to the next chapter.

# Foundation Topics

The first three sections describe the top-down, bottom-up, and divide-and-conquer approach to troubleshooting based on the OSI layered network model. The final section provides the guidelines on how to select the most effective troubleshooting approach.

## The Bottom-Up Troubleshooting Approach

The *bottom-up* approach to troubleshooting a networking problem starts with the physical components of the network and works its way up the layers of the OSI model. If you conclude that all the elements associated to a particular layer are in good working condition, you inspect the elements associated with the next layer up until the cause(s) of the problem is/are identified. Figure 6-1 shows the bottom-up troubleshooting approach.

**Figure 6-1**   *A Bottom-Up Troubleshooting Approach*

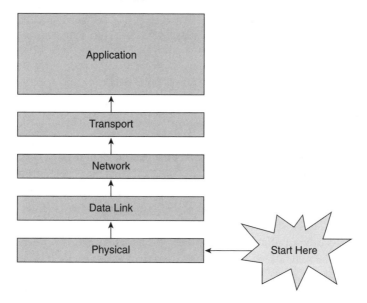

Bottom-up troubleshooting is an effective and efficient approach for situations when the problem is suspected to be physical. Most networking problems reside at the lower levels, so implementing the bottom-up approach often results in effective and perhaps fast results. When faced with a complex troubleshooting case, the bottom-up approach is usually favored. That is because after you ascertain that the elements associated with a particular OSI layer are in good working condition, you can shift your focus on the next layer above, and so on, until you identify the faulty layer.

The downside to the bottom-up approach is that it requires you to check every device, interface, and so on. In other words, regardless of the nature of the problem, the bottom-up approach starts with an exhaustive check of all the elements of each layer, starting with the physical layer, and works its way up. At each layer, selecting the element to start with is somewhat arbitrary because it is up to you as the troubleshooter. One way to avoid having to start troubleshooting from the bottom layer (physical layer) is to test the health of the bottom layers by using the ping or traceroute/tracert tool. A fully successful ping across a link eliminates the possibility of broken hardware (physical layer) or data link layer issues such as mismatch encapsulations or inactive frame relay DLCIs. Ping or traceroute/tracert failure would tell you that problems might exist at the lower layers, requiring investigation.

> **NOTE**   When you are testing tools such as ping and traceroute (or tracert on Windows operating systems), you must first ascertain that those applications or the protocols they utilize are supported in the network. In other words, in certain environments, in accordance with management policies, internetworking devices drop or filter packets associated with utilities such as ping or traceroute. In such circumstances, failure of those applications can be misleading or confusing. You can verify whether those applications (or the protocols and the associated application port numbers they utilize) are supported by talking to the administrators or the network engineers. Otherwise, you must inspect the access lists on routers or firewalls.

# The Top-Down Troubleshooting Approach

As its name implies, when you apply a *top-down* approach to troubleshooting a networking problem, you start with the user application and work your way down the layers of the OSI model. Figure 6-2 shows the top-down troubleshooting approach. If a layer is *not* in good working condition, you inspect the layer below it. When you know that the current layer is not in working condition and you discover that a lower layer works, you can conclude that the problem is within the layer above the lower working layer. After you have discovered which layer is the lowest layer with problems, you can begin identifying the cause of the problem from within that layer.

You usually choose the top-down approach when you have reason to believe that the problem is most likely at the application or other upper OSI layers. Past experiences, new software installations, changes in user interface, or added security features are common reasons for believing that the reported problems are most likely user, application, or at least upper OSI layer-related. The top-down troubleshooting approach is usually most suitable for problems experienced by one person or only a few people; that is because lower layer (that is, network infrastructure) problems usually affect more than one person.

You usually take the top-down approach for simpler cases. The disadvantage to selecting this approach is that if the problem turns out to be more complex or happens to spring from lower-layer culprits (physical, data link, or network), you will have wasted time and effort on examining the user applications or upper OSI layer components. Furthermore, if you have internetwork expertise, you might not necessarily have the expertise to diagnose or correct application layer issues. Network engineers often examine the components that fall within their area of responsibility, and if those happen to be in good working condition, the problem is then referred to the workstation, server, or application expert.

**Figure 6-2**   *A Top-Down Troubleshooting Approach*

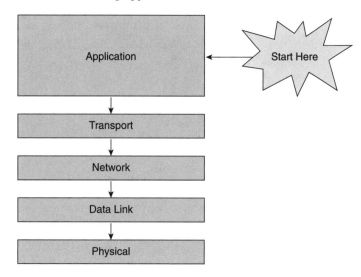

## The Divide-and-Conquer Troubleshooting Approach

The *divide-and-conquer* approach to network troubleshooting, unlike its top-down and bottom-up counterparts, does not always commence its investigation at a particular OSI layer. When you apply the divide-and-conquer approach, you select a layer and test its health; based on the observed results, you might go in either direction (up or down) from the starting layer. Figure 6-3 depicts the divide-and-conquer troubleshooting approach. If a layer is in good working condition, you inspect the layer above it. If a layer is not in good working condition, you inspect the layer below it. The layer that you ultimately select as the first targeted layer is the one that is faulty, and the layer below it is in good working condition. The particular layer at which you begin the divide-and-conquer approach is based on your experience level and the symptoms you have gathered about the problem. For example, if a user reports that he can't go to or has some trouble with a particular Web page but has no trouble going to or using other Web pages, you can safely decide that you do not need to begin troubleshooting at the physical, data link, or even the network layer. However, if many users report that they have problems accessing all resources on the Internet, you might start at the network layer and take the next step based on those findings.

**Figure 6-3**  *A Divide-and-Conquer Troubleshooting Approach*

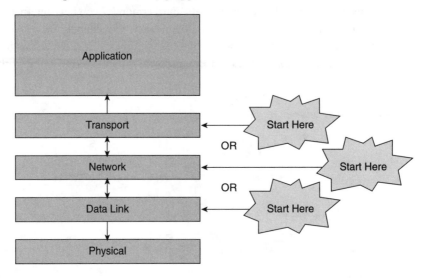

During the course of divide-and-conquer troubleshooting, if you can verify that a layer is functioning well, you can pretty safely assume that the layers below it are functioning as well. If a layer is not functioning at all or it is working intermittently or erroneously, you must immediately inspect the layer below it (with the exception of the physical layer, which does not have a layer below it). If the layer below the current layer is in good working condition, the culprit resides in the current layer. If the layer below is also malfunctioning, you should gather symptoms of the problem at that layer and work your way down.

# Selecting a Troubleshooting Approach

Selecting the most effective troubleshooting approach to solve a network problem allows you to resolve the problem in a quicker, more cost-effective manner. To select an effective troubleshooting approach, you must do the following:

1.  Determine the scope of the problem.

2.  Apply your experience.

3.  Analyze the symptoms.

*Determining the scope of the problem* means selecting the troubleshooting approach based on the perceived complexity of the problem. A bottom-up approach typically works better for complex problems. A top-down approach is typically best for simpler problems. Using a bottom-up approach for a simple problem might be wasteful and inefficient. Typically when users report symptoms, you should use a top-down approach because of the likelihood that the problem is upper-layer related.

If symptoms come from the network (such as through an SNMP trap, error log, or alarm), using a bottom-up approach will likely be more effective.

*Applying your experience* means that if you have troubleshot a particular problem (or a similar problem) previously, you might know of a way or a shortcut to expedite the troubleshooting process. If you are less experienced, you likely will implement a bottom-up approach regardless of the circumstances. In contrast, if you are skilled at troubleshooting, you might be able to get a head start by beginning at a different layer using the divide-and-conquer approach.

*Analyzing the symptoms* allows you to have a better chance of solving a problem if you know more about it. At times, you can immediately correct a problem simply by analyzing the symptoms and swiftly recognizing the culprit.

To make an example for the topic of selecting a troubleshooting approach, assume that you have identified two IP routers in your network that have connectivity but are not exchanging routing information. Before you attempt to solve the problem, select a troubleshooting approach. You have seen similar symptoms previously, which point to a likely protocol issue. Because connectivity exists between the routers, you know that it is not likely a problem at the physical or data link layers. Based on this knowledge and your past experience, you decide to use the divide-and-conquer approach, and you begin testing the TCP/IP-related functions at the network layer. Having chosen to start at the network layer, you decide to ping one router from the router on the other side. If the ping is fully successful, then the problem could be due to restrictive access lists or mismatched settings between the routing protocols at the opposite ends. Therefore, it is apparent that with the divide-and-conquer approach and utilizing your experience, you have arrived near the problem (and hopefully its solution) quickly. Now, again using your knowledge and expertise, you can analyze the symptoms and hopefully identify the culprit.

# Foundation Summary

The "Foundation Summary" section of each chapter lists the most important facts from that chapter. Although this section does not list every fact from the chapter that will be on your CCNP exam, a well-prepared CCNP candidate should at a minimum know all the details in each "Foundation Summary" before taking the exam.

**Table 6-2**  *Summary of Troubleshooting Approaches*

| Troubleshooting Approach | How It Operates | Cases It Is Suitable For | Advantages/ Disadvantages |
|---|---|---|---|
| Bottom-up | Always starts at the physical layer and works its way up until it finds a faulty layer. | More suited for complex cases. | It is a slow, but solid approach.<br><br>When the problem is application (or upper layer) related, this approach can take a long time. |
| Top-down | Always starts at the application layer and works its way down until it finds a faulty layer. | More suitable for simpler problems or those that are suspected to be application/user or upper-layer related. | If the problem turns out to be related to lower layers, you have wasted a lot of time and effort at the upper or application layers. |
| Divide-and-conquer | Based on the circumstances (reported issues) and your experience, you might decide to start at any layer and work up or down the OSI stack. | Most suitable when you are experienced and the problem has precise symptoms. | It approaches the layer of the culprit faster than the other approaches.<br><br>You need experience to use this approach effectively. |

# Q&A

As mentioned in the introduction, you have two choices for review questions. The questions that follow give you a bigger challenge than the exam because they use an open-ended question format. By reviewing now with this more difficult question format, you can exercise your memory better and prove your conceptual and factual knowledge of this chapter. You can find the answers to these questions in Appendix A.

For more practice with exam-like question formats, including questions that use a router simulator and multiple choice format, use the exam engine on the CD.

1. What is the benefit of following a method for troubleshooting?

2. What are the main troubleshooting approaches?

3. Which approach is best for complex cases?

4. Which approach is usually adapted for user-initiated and simple cases?

5. What are the drawbacks of the bottom-up approach?

6. What are the drawbacks of the top-down approach?

7. What are the guidelines for selecting the most effective troubleshooting approach?

8. What does it mean to determine the scope of the problem?

9. What does it mean to apply experience?

10. What is the main benefit of analyzing the symptoms?

11. At which layer of the OSI model does the bottom-up approach to troubleshooting begin?

12. You have isolated a problem to be an encapsulation type mismatch between point-to-point serial interfaces (data link layer). Given this problem, which troubleshooting approach would be the least effective to select?

13. A user has reported that a certain application does not run from his end system. You know that no filters are applied that would prevent the application from working. Running a **traceroute** command verifies that a connection exists between the end system of the user and the application server. Applying a layered approach to troubleshooting, which layer should you troubleshoot next?

14. If you know that a user can access some resources but not others, which layer is the least likely culprit?

15. When you learn that the users cannot browse the World Wide Web, you decide to first check the network layer and, based on your findings, decide what to troubleshoot next. Which approach have you adapted?

The following CIT exam topics are covered in this part. (To view the CIT exam outline, visit www.cisco.com/go/training.)

- Verify connectivity at all layers.

- Use Cisco IOS commands and applications to identify system problems at all layers.

- Isolate system problems to one or more specific layers.

- Resolve suboptimal system performance problems at Layers 2 through 7.

- Resolve local connectivity problems at Layer 1.

- Restore optimal baseline service.

- Work with external providers to resolve service provision problems.

- Work with system users to resolve network-related end-use problems.

# Part III: Resolving Problems at the Physical and Data Link Layers

## This chapter covers the following subjects:

- Identifying the symptoms of problems occurring at the physical layer

- Identifying the symptoms of problems occurring at the data link layer

- Analyzing commands and applications used to isolate problems occurring at the physical and data link layers

- Isolating a physical or data link problem

CHAPTER **7**

# Isolating a Problem at the Physical or Data Link Layer

In the course of troubleshooting, symptoms help narrow the possible problems to a single problem or a small set of related problems. Symptoms help direct or focus troubleshooting efforts. The physical and data link layers are closely related. This close relationship often makes isolating a problem difficult. This chapter shows you how to utilize certain characteristics and commands to isolate failures of media, devices, and software at the physical and data link layers of networks. All the upper layers of the Open System Interconnection (OSI) model depend on the media, devices, and software operating at the physical and data link layers to function. Therefore, it is vital to be able to isolate and correct failures and suboptimal conditions at the lower layers effectively.

## "Do I Know This Already?" Quiz

The purpose of the "Do I Know This Already?" quiz is to help you decide if you really need to read this entire chapter. If you already intend to read the entire chapter, you do not need to answer these questions now.

The 10-question quiz, derived from the major sections in the "Foundation Topics" portion of the chapter, helps you determine how to spend your limited study time.

Table 7-1 outlines the major topics discussed in this chapter and the "Do I Know This Already?" quiz questions that correspond to those topics.

**Table 7-1** *"Do I Know This Already?" Foundation Topics Section-to-Question Mapping*

| Foundation Topics Section | Questions Covered in This Section |
| --- | --- |
| "Identifying the Symptoms of Problems Occurring at the Physical Layer" | 2 |
| "Identifying the Symptoms of Problems Occurring at the Data Link Layer" | 2 |
| "Analyzing Commands and Applications Used to Isolate Problems Occurring at the Physical and Data Link Layers" | 4 |
| "Isolating a Physical or Data Link Problem" | 2 |

> **CAUTION**    The goal of self-assessment is to gauge your mastery of the topics in this chapter. If you do not know the answer to a question or are only partially sure of the answer, you should mark this question wrong for purposes of the self-assessment. Giving yourself credit for an answer you correctly guess skews your self-assessment results and might provide you with a false sense of security.

1.  Which command output would you most likely see if you had a problem at the physical layer?

    a. Neighbor 192.168.66.10 is down: holding time expired

    b. Ethernet1/1 is down, line protocol is down

    c. Serial 0/1 is up, line protocol is administratively down

    d. Invalid Routing Update—Ignored

2.  Which command output would you most likely see if you had a problem at the data link layer?

    a. Serial1/0 is down, line protocol is down

    b. Ethernet 0/0 is down, line protocol is down

    c. Interface Serial1/0, changed state to up

    d. Ethernet 0/0 is up, line protocol is down

3.  Which Cisco IOS command would you enter to view details about the Cisco IOS software and all installed hardware configurations?

    a. **show protocols**

    b. **show version**

    c. **show line**

    d. **show ip interface brief**

4.  You have been informed that a group of users lost its connection to the network due to a problem in either the physical or data link layer. You check the operational status, errors, and configuration of the affected interfaces. You still have not found the cause of the problem. Which guideline for isolating a problem at the physical and data link layers have you omitted?

    a. Verifying the IP address of the default gateway

    b. Checking cable configuration

    c. Disabling spanning tree

    d. Viewing TCP information on a host

5.  Which of the following is *not* a common symptom of physical layer problems?

    a.  Frame errors

    b.  Problems at the network layer but not at the data link layer

    c.  Line coding errors

    d.  Synchronization errors

6.  If the problem is at the data link layer and not the physical layer, then entering the **show interface** command indicates which of the following?

    a.  Interface is up; line protocol is up

    b.  Interface is up; line protocol is down

    c.  Interface is down; line protocol is up

    d.  Interface is down; line protocol is down

7.  Which of the following is *not* a general end system command to isolate physical and data link layer problems?

    a.  **ping**

    b.  **arp -a**

    c.  **netstat -rn**

    d.  **telnet**

8.  Which of the following are *not* Microsoft Windows commands to isolate physical and data link layer problems?

    a.  **ipconfig /all**

    b.  **traceroute**

    c.  **winipcfg**

    d.  **show interface**

9.  Which of the following is *not* a Cisco command to isolate physical layer problems?

    a.  **show ifconfig -a**

    b.  **show version**

    c.  **show interface**

    d.  **show controllers**

10. Which of the following is *not* a fit guideline for isolating problems at the physical and data link layers?

    a. Check operational status and data error rates of the interfaces and check proper interface configurations.

    b. Replace all cables.

    c. Check for bad cables or connections.

    d. Check for incorrect cables.

You can find the answers to the "Do I Know This Already?" quiz in Appendix A, "Answers to the 'Do I Know This Already?' Quizzes and 'Q&A' Sections." The suggested choices for your next step are as follows:

■ **8 or less overall score**—Read the entire chapter. This includes the "Foundation Topics" and "Foundation Summary" sections, as well as the "Q&A" section.

■ **9 or 10 overall score**—If you want more review on these topics, skip to the "Foundation Summary" section and then go to the "Q&A" section. Otherwise, move to the next chapter.

# Foundation Topics

The sections that follow discuss how to identify symptoms of problems occurring at the physical and data link layers. Following that, you will learn how to analyze the output of commands and applications. All those techniques serve to isolate problems occurring at the physical and data link layers.

## Identifying the Symptoms of Problems Occurring at the Physical Layer

Because the components of the OSI model's physical layer are tangible and can be inspected physically, this layer is somewhat unique relative to the other layers. Examples of the physical layer components include interfaces/ports, modules, cables, connectors, adapters, transceivers, and so on. Problems at the physical layer might cause complete or intermittent loss of data across a link, generating symptoms such as application failures or data transfers at lower than expected rates. If you log in to a device where, for example, a faulty link terminates, and you start gathering symptoms, you see that no network component above the physical layer is communicating with peer components on systems that are connected through the failed interface or media.

When you gather facts and symptoms of problems related to the physical layer, you might encounter errors relating to framing, line coding, and synchronization on the output of some **show** commands (such as **show interface**). Other symptoms of a physical layer problem that you might encounter include console and management messages and system log files. Example 7-1 displays one example of a console message after a router interface has failed.

**Example 7-1**  *A Console Message for a Failing Interface*

```
Feb 8 9:08:27: %LINEPROTO-5-UPDOWN: Line protocol on Interface Serial0/1,
    changed state to down
```

The LED of a particular component or port of a device usually provides reliable feedback on the operational status of the component it corresponds to. The LEDs of a failing device turn into a particular state (color or flashing) that is meant to inform the administrator about a failure or malfunction. The changed state of the LED could be off, flashing, or some variation in color (such as red).

A device might have a problem at the physical layer because more traffic is being directed to its interface(s) than it can serve. When troubleshooting this type of problem, you find that the interface under focus is operating at or near the maximum capacity and you might have an increase in the number of interface errors. When the physical layer problem is due to an actual breakdown of a piece of hardware such as a cable or connector, usually no data can move across that link.

As you gather information, a problematic interface reveals excessive runts, late collisions, loss of framing, or an increase in the number of buffer failures. In addition, the output from a utility such as ping or traceroute might report excessive packet loss or latency. The following list is a summary of some common symptoms of physical layer problems:

- No component on the failing interface appears to be functional above the physical layer.

- The network is functional, but it is operating either consistently or intermittently less than the baseline level.

- No connectivity on the interfaces is seen from the data link layer.

- Framing errors, line coding errors, and synchronization errors are present.

- LEDs are off, flashing, or in a state other than the expected state during normal operation.

- Utilization is excessive.

- The number of interface errors has increased.

- Console messages (reporting error) appear.

- System log file messages (reporting error) emerge.

- Management system alarms go off.

Assume that a router named SanFran has a serial connection (T1) to another router in a remote city. You are connected to the SanFran router's console port. As a demonstration for the symptoms of an interface problem (at the physical layer), Example 7-2 shows a console message that you might receive while configuring the SanFran router. The "line protocol down" message indicates that there is a problem with the interface serial 1/0 preventing it from functioning properly.

**Example 7-2**    *Console Message Showing a Symptom of a Physical Layer Problem*

```
SanFran(config)#interface serial 1/0
SanFran(config-if)#ip address 192.168.1.2 255.255.255.252
SanFran(config-if)#no shutdown
Aug 27 14:00:02: %LINK-3-UPDOWN: Interface Serial1/0, changed state to up
Aug 27 14:00:03: %LINEPROTO-5-UPDOWN: Line protocol on Interface Serial1/0,
    changed state to up
Aug 27 14:00:25: %LINEPROTO-5-UPDOWN: Line protocol on Interface Serial1/0,
    changed state to down
SanFran(config-if)#
```

Naturally, after you notice the console message shown in Example 7-2, you have to take the next step. Based on your responsibilities and expertise, you might have to investigate further or pass the problem to the person who is responsible for it. However, the purpose of Example 7-2 at this stage is just to provide a sample output showing you a symptom of physical layer problems. Later in this chapter, this example is repeated and analyzed further.

# Identifying the Symptoms of Problems Occurring at the Data Link Layer

When the data received from or sent to the network layer is not properly encapsulated into or de-encapsulated from data link layer frames, or when data link layer frames are not properly formed, transmitted, and received across working physical layer links, you have data link layer problem(s). Improper frame types (mismatched encapsulations), duplicate MAC addresses, and misbehaving Layer 2 devices such as switches or bridges (due to various configuration or hardware problems or limitations such as lack of unidirectional link detection, UDLD) might play a role in data link layer problems. When you have a data link layer problem across a link, the interfaces at either side of the link might display symptoms. Sometimes the symptom might merely be that Layer 3 (network layer) does not function across the link due to encapsulation failure, often requiring hardware reseating. Layer 2 and Layer 3 diagnostic tools such as Cisco Discovery Protocol (CDP), Protocol Analyzers, and ping can be helpful in detecting and verifying data link layer problems.

If the problem is at the data link layer, then console messages on the affected device usually warn that the line protocol on a particular interface is down (meaning it just went down). You can use CDP to verify the health of the data link layer. However, proper CDP operation does not guarantee that the data link layer is in perfect condition. For example, if your hardware (such as fastethernet removable interface) needs to be reseated, it might be able to transport CDP frames but fail to encapsulate IP packets in Layer 2 (such as Ethernet) frames. In that case, while the CDP neighbors receive each other's CDP messages, they cannot ping each other. When an interface is experiencing data link layer problems, entering the **show interfaces** command might indicate that the interface is up but the line protocol is down. Example 7-3 displays the type of messages you might see about failing interfaces on the output of the **show interfaces** command.

**Example 7-3**  *Data Link Layer Status as Reported by the Output of the* **show interface** *Command*

```
router1>show interfaces
Ethernet0/0 is up, line protocol is down
(rest of output is deleted/not shown)
router2>show interfaces
Serial0/0 is up, line protocol is down
(rest of output is deleted/not shown)
```

Sometimes the data link layer is not completely broken, but it experiences optimization problems. In those cases, even though the data link layer indicators do not show it as "down", the rate of data flow across the faulty link is substandard or below the baseline. These types of problems are tougher to diagnose and correct. Symptoms that might be present during the suboptimal performance of data link layer components include excessive errors such as cyclic redundancy check (CRC), frame, giants, runts, no buffer, ignore, abort, dribble condition, and so on. Through console messages, you might also discover large quantities of broadcast traffic (usually due to bridging loop) that indicate this type of problem. The following is a list of possible symptoms of data link layer problems:

- No component on the failing link appears to be functional above the data link layer.

- The link is functional, but it is operating either consistently or intermittently less than the baseline level.

- No connectivity on the link is seen from the network layer.

- Framing errors or encapsulation errors are present.

- Address resolution errors exist.

- Excessive CRC errors appear.

- Broadcast traffic emerges in large quantities.

- A MAC address is cycling between ports.

- Console messages (reporting error) appear.

- System log file messages (reporting error) pop up.

- Management system alarms indicate problems.

## Analyzing Commands and Applications Used to Isolate Problems Occurring at the Physical and Data Link Layers

This section covers commands that you use to isolate problems at the physical and data link layers. This section also demonstrates isolating problems at physical and data link layers through some examples.

Table 7-2 shows end system commands used to isolate problems at the physical and data link layers. The first part of this table lists general commands. The second section lists commands you enter at an end system running a version of the Windows operating system. In the third part of Table 7-2, commands shown are those you enter at an end system running a version of the UNIX or Mac OS X operating system. These commands display information about several networking layers. You use the output to isolate problems at the physical and data link layers.

**Table 7-2**   *End System Commands to Isolate Physical and Data Link Layer Problems*

| Command | Type | Description |
|---|---|---|
| **ping** {*host* \| *ip-address*} | General End System | Sends an echo request packet to an address and then waits for a reply. The {*host* \| *ip-address*} variable is the IP alias or IP address of the target system. |
| **arp –a** | General End System | Displays the current mappings of the IP address to the MAC address in the ARP table. |
| **Netstat [–rn]** | General End System | The **netstat** command displays active TCP/IP connections. The **–rn** option is for displaying the routing table in numerical format (without querying a Domain Name System [DNS] server). |
| **ipconfig /all** | Windows Command | Displays IP information for hosts that are running Windows NT/Windows 2000/Windows XP. |
| **Tracert [*destination*]** | Windows Command | Verifies connectivity (and displays a path) to a destination device for Windows hosts. The *destination* variable is the IP alias or IP address of the target system. |
| **Winipcfg** | Windows Command | Displays IP information for hosts that are running Windows 9x and Windows Me. |
| **ifconfig –a** | UNIX and Mac OS X | Displays IP information for UNIX and Mac OS X hosts. |
| **traceroute [*destination*]** | UNIX and Mac OS X | Identifies the path that a packet takes through the network. The *destination* variable is the host name or IP address of the target system. |

The commands listed in Table 7-3 are Cisco IOS commands that display information about several networking layers. Although you can use these commands to display information about several networking layers, these commands are also important for isolating problems at the physical and data link layers. Table 7-3 indicates which of the two layers each command is best for isolating according to the CIT student guide.

**Table 7-3**    *General Physical and Data Link Layer Isolation Cisco IOS Commands*

| Command | Description |
|---|---|
| **ping** {*host* | *ip-address* } | (User or Privileged) Sends an echo request packet to an address and then waits for a reply. The {*host* | *ip-address*} variable is the IP alias or IP address of the target system.<br><br>Best for isolating the physical and data link layers. |
| **traceroute** [*destination* ] | (User or Privileged) Identifies the path a packet takes through the network. The *destination*  variable is the IP alias or IP address of the target system.<br><br>Best for isolating the physical and data link layers. |
| **[no] debug ?** | Displays a list of options for enabling or disabling debugging events on a device.<br><br>Best for isolating the physical and data link layers. |
| **show version** | Displays the Cisco IOS software version and all installed hardware configurations.<br><br>Best for isolating the physical layer. |
| **show ip interface brief** | Displays a summary of the status of all interfaces on a device.<br><br>Best for isolating the physical layer. |
| **show interfaces** [*type number* ] | Displays the operational status of an interface as well as the amount and type of traffic being sent and received.<br><br>Best for isolating the physical layer. |

**Table 7-3**  *General Physical and Data Link Layer Isolation Cisco IOS Commands (Continued)*

| Command | Description |
|---|---|
| **show cdp neighbor detail** | Displays the device type and Cisco IOS version of neighboring devices.<br><br>Best for isolating the physical layer. |
| **show controllers** | Displays current internal status information for the interface controller cards.<br><br>Best for isolating the physical layer. |
| **debug [asynch \| ethernet-interface \| frame-relay \| isdn \| ppp \| serial]** | Captures events on physical interfaces.<br><br>Best for isolating the physical layer. |
| **show arp** | Displays entries in the ARP table.<br><br>Best for isolating the data link layer. |
| **debug [arp \| lapb \| stun]** | Captures events relating to data link layer protocols.<br><br>Best for isolating the data link layer. |

**NOTE**   The **show** command shows a snapshot of the current characteristics of the network device interface or protocol. **debug** shows you the events taking place from the time the command is entered until reporting is disabled. Using **debug** commands places more of a negative impact on the performance of a networking device than isolating a problem with **show** commands. Therefore, it is a good idea to isolate a problem using only **show** commands when possible. If the information returned from entering **show** commands does not help you isolate a problem, use **debug** commands that are targeted at what is the most likely cause of the problem.

Now look at some examples that demonstrate isolating problems at physical and data link layers using these commands.

Consider two routers—one named SanFran and the other named SanJose—that are located in different cities (see Figure 7-1). The routers are connected via a T1 link. (E1 is a similar service in Europe.)

**Figure 7-1** *T1 Connection (Similar to the European E1) Between Two Routers at Remote Branches*

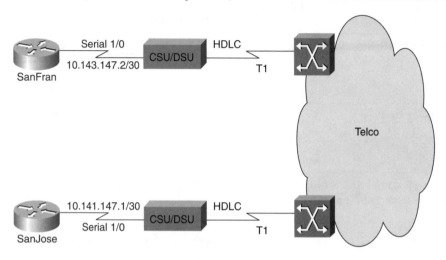

While you are configuring SanFran, you observe a console message that indicates a physical layer issue. To isolate the problem and confirm that the system message is not transient, you decide to use a Cisco **show** command that will display a summary of the status of the interface. Entering the **show ip interface brief** command shows that the interface named serial 1/0 is up, but the line protocol is down. (See the top portion of Example 7-4.)

**Example 7-4** *Gathering Information to Isolate a Physical Layer Problem on a Cisco Router*

```
SanFran#show ip interface brief
Interface          IP-Address      OK? Method Status Protocol
FastEthernet0/0    10.141.148.129  YES NVRAM  up      up
Serial1/0          10.141.147.2    YES manual up      down
SanFran#
SanJose#show ip interface brief
Interface       IP-Address    OK? Method Status      Protocol
FastEthernet0/0 10.141.141.1  YES NVRAM  up          up
Serial1/0       10.141.147.1  manual administratively down down
SanJose#
```

To continue with problem isolation, you use your dial-up modem to connect to the console session on the SanJose router. There you use the **show ip interface brief** command. The output of this command shows that interface Serial 1/0 on SanJose is administratively down, or that the interface is not configured to be active. The line protocol is also in the down state. (See the bottom portion of Example 7-4.) For Cisco routers, the default interface state is shutdown. Your associate forgot to activate the interface when it was configured. To fix this problem, you need to activate the interface using the **no shutdown** command.

As a second example, assume that you are the network engineer for a router named Orlando. Orlando uses Frame Relay to connect to a router named Daytona (see Figure 7-2).

**Figure 7-2**   *Frame Relay Connection Between the Remote Branches at Daytona and Orlando*

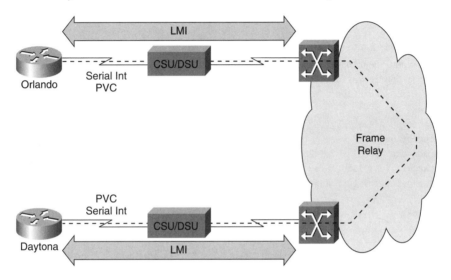

Now imagine that Network Operations calls to inform you that the link to Daytona is down. You ask if anyone had made changes to the configuration of Orlando. Network Operations says that it made no changes. Example 7-5 shows a console message that Network Operations says that it saw on Orlando during a check of the logs. The line protocol down message is an indication that there is a problem with the interface at the data link layer that prevents it from functioning properly. (Note that when the line protocol goes down, Enhanced Interior Gateway Routing Protocol (EIGRP) neighbor adjacencies time out.)

**Example 7-5**   *Console Message Showing a Symptom of a Data Link Layer Problem*

```
Orlando#
Aug 03 21:14:24: %LINEPROTO-5-UPDOWN: Line protocol on Interface Serial1/0,
    changed state to down
Aug 03 21:14:24: %DUAL-5-NBRCHANGE: IP-EIGRP 101: Neighbor 172.21.177.1
    (Serial1/0) is down: interface down
Orlando#
```

To start problem isolation, you connect into the console port on Orlando and use the **show ip interface brief** command to look for interface status. The output of this command shows that interface Serial 1/0 on Orlando is up, but the line protocol is down. (See the top portion of Example 7-6.)

**Example 7-6** *Gathering Information to Isolate a Data Link Layer Problem on a Cisco Router*

```
Orlando#show ip interface brief
Interface          IP-Address      OK? Method Status Protocol
FastEthernet0/0    172.21.178.129  YES NVRAM  up     up
Serial1/0          172.21.177.2    YES NVRAM  up     down
Orlando#


Orlando#show running-config interface serial 1/0
Building configuration...
Current configuration : 162 bytes
!
interface Serial1/0
 description Frame Relay link to Daytona
 ip address 172.21.177.2 255.255.255.252
 encapsulation frame-relay
 frame-relay lmi-type ansi
end
Orlando#
```

You call Network Operations in Daytona and ask your contact to use the **show ip interface brief** command to display the interface status and any recent console messages. Your contact at Network Operations reads a recent console message stating that the hold time for the EIGRP neighbor has expired. However, your contact at Network Operations tells you that the output of the **show ip interface brief** command on Daytona shows interface Serial 1/0 of Daytona is up and the line protocol is also up.

So far, the problem appears to be on your device; therefore, you return to your console session on Orlando for further problem isolation. You display specific interface configuration information with the **show running-config interface serial 1/0** command. (See the bottom portion of Example 7-6.) The configuration indicates that the interface has Frame Relay encapsulation and is expecting an American National Standards Institute (ANSI) Local Management Interface (LMI) type. This output matches your baseline configuration information. You decide to look for more information on the interface with the **show interface serial 1/0** command and see the results shown in Example 7-7. You notice that Orlando is sending LMI inquiries but not receiving the same number of LMI status packets from the Frame Relay service provider. You also notice a large number of input errors and carrier transitions.

**Example 7-7**  *Analyzing the Output of a* **show interface** *Command on a Cisco Router*

```
Orlando#show interface serial 1/0
Serial1/0 is up, line protocol is down
  Hardware is PowerQUICC Serial
  Description: Frame Relay link to Daytona
  Internet address is 172.21.177.2/30
  MTU 1500 bytes, BW 128 Kbit, DLY 20000 usec,
     reliability 254/255, txload 1/255, rxload 1/255
  Encapsulation FRAME-RELAY, loopback not set
  Keepalive set (10 sec)
  LMI enq sent  232, LMI stat recvd 73, LMI upd recvd 0, DTE LMI down
.
.
. (some output is deleted)
.
.
37 input errors, 0 CRC, 36 frame, 0 overrun, 0 ignored, 1 abort
     268 packets output, 10960 bytes, 0 underruns
     0 output errors, 0 collisions, 50 interface resets
     0 output buffer failures, 0 output buffers swapped out
     112 carrier transitions
     DCD=up  DSR=up  DTR=up  RTS=up  CTS=up
Orlando#
```

Finally, you begin to question what your Frame Relay carrier has done. You decide to enter the
**debug frame-relay lmi** command to gather some additional details. The results are shown in
Example 7-8.

**Example 7-8**  *Analyzing the Output of a* **debug frame-relay** *Command on a Cisco Router*

```
Orlando#debug frame-relay lmi
Frame Relay LMI debugging is on
Displaying all Frame Relay LMI data
Orlando#
Aug 03 21:43:13.655: Serial1/0(out): StEnq, myseq 174, yourseen 19, DTE down
Aug 03 21:43:13.655: datagramstart = 0x3B5BC14, datagramsize = 14
Aug 03 21:43:13.655: FR encap = 0x00010308
Aug 03 21:43:13.655: 00 75 95 01 01 00 03 02 AE 13
Aug 03 21:43:13.655:
Aug 03 21:43:23.656: Serial1/0(out): StEnq, myseq 175, yourseen 19, DTE down
Aug 03 21:43:23.656: datagramstart = 0x3999F54, datagramsize = 14
Aug 03 21:43:23.656: FR encap = 0x00010308
Aug 03 21:43:23.656: 00 75 95 01 01 00 03 02 AF 13
Aug 03 21:43:23.656:
Aug 03 21:43:33.656: Serial1/0(out): StEnq, myseq 176, yourseen 19, DTE down
Aug 03 21:43:33.656: datagramstart = 0x3B5BE94, datagramsize = 14
Aug 03 21:43:33.656: FR encap = 0x00010308
```

*continues*

**Example 7-8** *Analyzing the Output of a* **debug frame-relay** *Command on a Cisco Router (Continued)*

```
Aug 03 21:43:33.656: 00 75 95 01 01 00 03 02 B0 13
.
.
.
Orlando#undebug all
All possible debugging has been turned off
Orlando#
```

The result of the **debug frame-relay lmi** command helps you isolate the issue. If the Frame Relay service were working correctly, you would see an LMI reply from the switch for every LMI request the router sends to the switch. In addition, you should periodically see a full LMI status message from the switch that includes a description of the permanent virtual circuits (PVCs). This full LMI status message is sent in response to a status inquiry message that the router transmits after every six LMI keepalives. With the default keepalive of 10 seconds, you should see the full LMI status every minute. You should also see an incrementing counter in the yourseen field. In addition, the data terminal equipment (DTE) status should be up. Because everything used to work and no one changed anything on Orlando, you can pinpoint the issue to the Frame Relay carrier and the LMI encapsulation type. You have a defined LMI type in your interface configuration. If your service provider changed the LMI type that was offered to you, the line protocol would fail due to mismatched LMI types.

# Guidelines for Isolating a Physical or Data Link Problem

This section provides a set of guidelines for isolating problems at the physical and data link layers followed by an example that demonstrates how to use those guidelines effectively. The guidelines for isolating a physical or data link problem are as follows:

- **Check operational status and data error rates**—Use Cisco **show** commands to check for statistics such as collisions, input, and output errors. The characteristics of these statistics vary, depending on the protocols used on the network. Use **debug** commands for additional detail when you cannot get enough information to isolate the problem through the use of **show** commands.

- **Verify proper interface configurations**—Check that all switch or hub ports are configured for the correct VLAN or collision domain, and that spanning tree, speed, and duplex settings are correctly configured. Confirm that any active ports or interfaces are not in shutdown state.

- **Check cable configuration**—Check to make sure that all cables are connected to their correct ports or interfaces. All cross-connects should be properly patched to the correct location.

- **Check for bad cables or connections**—Verify that the cable from the source interface is properly connected and in good condition. If you doubt the integrity of a cable, exchange it with a known working cable. If you doubt that the connection is good, remove the cable, perform a physical inspection of both the cable and the interface, and then reconnect the cable. If a suspect cable is connected to a wall jack, use a cable tester to ensure that the jack is properly wired. A link light that is lit and displays the color that indicates proper operation is further evidence that the connection is successful.

- **Check for incorrect cables**—Verify that the proper cable is being used. A crossover or rollover cable might be required for direct connections between some devices.

As an example, imagine that a group of users has reported that their connection to the network has gone down. Examining the end system topology diagram for the network, you realize that all these affected users are connected to the same switch and hub combination. This situation leads you to continue isolating the problem at the common connection. You perform an on-site inspection of physical connection of the switch and the hub and note that all the link lights are lit and are showing a color that indicates correct operation. All cables appear to be of the correct type and pin out. After verifying that the physical connections are working, you decide to connect to the switch to check the port configurations. You note that the speed setting for one of the ports is set to 10 Mbps, when it should be set to 100 Mbps. This mismatch in speed is the likely source of your connection problem.

# Foundation Summary

The "Foundation Summary" section of each chapter lists the most important facts from that chapter. Although this section does not list every fact from the chapter that will be on your CCNP exam, a well-prepared CCNP candidate should at a minimum know all the details in each "Foundation Summary" before taking the exam.

## Symptoms of Physical Layer Problems

Following are some common symptoms of physical layer problems:

- No component on the failing interface appears to be functional above the physical layer.

- The network is functional, but it is operating either consistently or intermittently less than the baseline level.

- No connectivity on the interfaces is seen from the data link layer.

- Framing errors, line coding errors, and synchronization errors occur.

- LEDs are off, flashing, or in a state other than the expected state during normal operation.

- Utilization is excessive.

- Interface errors have increased.

- Console messages (reporting error) are present.

- System log file messages (reporting error) appear.

- Management system alarms indicate problems.

## Symptoms of Data Link Layer Problems

Following are some common symptoms of data link layer problems:

- No component on the failing link appears to be functional above the data link layer.

- The link is functional, but it is operating either consistently or intermittently less than the baseline level.

- No connectivity on the link is seen from the network layer.

- Framing errors occur.

- Encapsulation errors are present.

- Address resolution errors emerge.

- Excessive CRC errors and frame check sequence errors exist.

- Broadcast traffic has increased.

- A MAC address is cycling between ports.

- Console messages (reporting error) are present.

- System log file messages (reporting error) occur.

- Management system alarms indicate problems.

## End System Isolation Commands

Following are some of the useful end system commands to isolate physical and data link layer problems:

- General commands:

   — **ping**

   — **arp -a**

   — **netstat -rn**

- Windows commands:

   — **ipconfig**

   — **tracert**

   — **winipcfg**

- UNIX and Mac commands:

   — **Ifconfig -a**

   — **traceroute**

## Cisco IOS Isolation Commands

Following are some Cisco IOS commands to isolate physical and data link layer problems:

- **ping**

- **trace**

- **debug**

- **show version**

- **show ip int brief**

- **show interface**

- **show cdp neighbor detail**

- **show controllers**

## Guidelines for Isolating Problems at the Physical and Data Link Layers

Following are some useful guidelines for isolating problems at the physical and data link layers:

- Check operational status and data error rates.

- Verify proper interface configurations.

- Check cable configuration.

- Check for bad cables or connections.

- Check for incorrect cables.

# Q&A

As mentioned in the introduction, you have two choices for review questions. The questions that follow give you a bigger challenge than the exam because they use an open-ended question format. By reviewing now with this more difficult question format, you can exercise your memory better and prove your conceptual and factual knowledge of this chapter. You can find the answers to these questions in Appendix A.

For more practice with exam-like question formats, including questions that use a router simulator and multiple choice format, use the exam engine on the CD.

1. List at least four common symptoms of physical layer problems.

2. List at least four common symptoms of data link layer problems.

3. Name an end system command for isolating physical and data link layer problems.

4. What does the end system command **netstat –rn** do?

5. Name a Microsoft Windows command that is useful for isolating physical and data link layer problems.

6. Name a UNIX/Mac OS X command that is useful for isolating physical and data link layer problems.

7. List at least two Cisco IOS commands for isolating physical and data link layer problems.

8. Which Cisco IOS command would be useful for troubleshooting data link address resolution?

9. List at least two valid guidelines for isolating problems at the physical and data link layers.

## This chapter covers the following subjects:

- Commands and applications used to correct problems occurring at the physical and data link layers

- Physical and data link layer support resources

- Correcting a physical or data link layer problem

# CHAPTER 8

# Correcting a Problem at the Physical or Data Link Layer

After you determine the cause of the problem, you must correct it. This chapter discusses how to correct the isolated problems at the data link and physical layers. It also explains the commands necessary to configure physical and data link layer components. Correcting the problem is the ultimate goal of the troubleshooting process.

## "Do I Know This Already?" Quiz

The purpose of the "Do I Know This Already?" quiz is to help you decide if you really need to read this entire chapter. If you already intend to read the entire chapter, you do not need to answer these questions now.

The 10-question quiz, derived from the major sections in the "Foundation Topics" portion of the chapter, helps you determine how to spend your limited study time.

Table 8-1 outlines the major topics discussed in this chapter and the "Do I Know This Already?" quiz questions that correspond to those topics.

**Table 8-1**  *"Do I Know This Already?" Foundation Topics Section-to-Question Mapping*

| Foundation Topics Section | Questions Covered in This Section |
|---|---|
| "Commands and Applications Used to Correct Problems Occuring at the Physical and Data Link Layers" | 8 |
| "Physical and Data Link Layer Support Resources" | 1 |
| "Correcting a Physical or Data Link Layer Problem" | 1 |

**CAUTION**   The goal of self-assessment is to gauge your mastery of the topics in this chapter. If you do not know the answer to a question or are only partially sure of the answer, you should mark this question wrong for purposes of the self-assessment. Giving yourself credit for an answer you correctly guess skews your self-assessment results and might provide you with a false sense of security.

1. Which command is used at an end system to correct problems at the data link layer relating to resolving network and data link layer addresses?

   a. **shutdown**

   b. **interface**

   c. **clock rate**

   d. **arp -d**

2. Which of the following Cisco IOS global configuration commands enters interface configuration mode?

   a. **intconfig**

   b. **ifconfig**

   c. **winipcfg**

   d. **interface**

3. Which of the following Cisco IOS interface configuration commands activates an interface?

   a. **enable**

   b. **shut up**

   c. **no shutdown**

   d. **activate**

4. Which of the following Cisco IOS interface configuration commands configures an encapsulation type on an interface?

   a. **encapsulation type**

   b. **set encap**

   c. **encapsulation**

   d. **config encap**

5. Which of the following Cisco IOS interface configuration commands configures a clock rate on an interface?

   a. **clockrate**

   b. **clock rate**

   c. **set clockrate**

   d. **config clock**

**6.** Which of the following Cisco IOS global configuration commands enters controller configuration mode?

    **a.** **controller**

    **b.** **interface controller**

    **c.** **config controller**

    **d.** **set controller**

**7.** Which of the following Cisco IOS interface configuration commands configures Frame Relay LMI type on an interface?

    **a.** **config lmi**

    **b.** **set lmi**

    **c.** **interface lmi-type**

    **d.** **frame-relay lmi-type**

**8.** Which Web site would you most likely use to find the latest detailed technical documentation about the PPP protocol?

    **a.** www.ietf.org

    **b.** www.apple.com

    **c.** www.sniffers.com

    **d.** www.linux.org

**9.** Which of the following is *not* part of the procedure for correcting physical and data link layer problems?

    **a.** Evaluate and document the results of each change that you make.

    **b.** Verify that the changes you made actually fixed the problem without introducing new problems.

    **c.** Do not consult outside resources.

    **d.** Stop making changes when the original problem appears to be solved.

**10.** Which of the following is a valid Cisco IOS command to configure an interface for full duplex operation?

    **a.** **duplex full**

    **b.** **fulduplex**

    **c.** **duplexing full**

    **d.** **set duplex full**

You can find the answers to the "Do I Know This Already?" quiz in Appendix A, "Answers to the 'Do I Know This Already?' Quizzes and 'Q&A' Sections." The suggested choices for your next step are as follows:

- **8 or less overall score**—Read the entire chapter. This includes the "Foundation Topics" and "Foundation Summary" sections, as well as the "Q&A" section.

- **9 or 10 overall score**—If you want more review on these topics, skip to the "Foundation Summary" section and then go to the "Q&A" section. Otherwise, move to the next chapter.

# Foundation Topics

## Commands and Applications Used to Correct Problems Occurring at the Physical and Data Link Layers

The CIT course discusses certain commands with regards to correcting physical and data link problems. This section discusses those commands. Neither the CIT course nor this book imply by any means that you can fix all physical and data link layer problems by using these commands. The commands are listed and briefly described in Table 8-2. From there, a more detailed discussion of these controller and interface configuration commands is provided. The last part of this section gives examples on correcting physical or data link layer problems by using Cisco IOS interface configuration commands.

**Table 8-2**  *Commands Used to Correct Physical and Data Link Problems*

| Command | Description |
|---|---|
| **arp −d** *ip-address* | You use this command on end systems with Microsoft operating systems (Windows) to delete a specific entry or the entire contents of the Address Resolution Protocol (ARP) table. |
| | You can clear the entire content of the ARP cache on a Cisco router by using the **clear arp-cache** command. |
| **interface** | This Cisco IOS command enters interface configuration mode (from global configuration mode). When you are in interface configuration mode, you can enter commands such as **encapsulation**, **ip address**, **clock rate**, **speed**, **duplex**, and **no shutdown**. |
| **no shutdown** | This Cisco IOS command activates an interface that is inactive (shut down). You enter this command while in interface configuration mode. |
| **encapsulation** | This command configures an encapsulation type on an interface (such as serial). You enter this command while in interface configuration mode. The choice of encapsulation type is interface dependent. For example, you have the **hdlc**, **ppp**, **frame-relay**, and other options on a serial interface, but you don't have those options on an Ethernet interface. |
| **clock rate** | This is a Cisco IOS interface configuration command. It configures a clock rate on an interface (serial interface with the DCE end of the cable plugged in it). You enter this command while in interface configuration mode. |

*continues*

**Table 8-2** *Commands Used to Correct Physical and Data Link Problems (Continued)*

| Command | Description |
|---|---|
| **controller** | This command enters controller configuration mode. You enter it while in global configuration mode. Controller configuration mode is usually entered for T1/E1 controllers. |
| **duplex {full \| half \| auto}** <br><br> or <br><br> **full-duplex** <br><br> **half-duplex** | A router interface or a switch port might be capable of operating in half-duplex or in full-duplex. (Some can negotiate it with the connected device on the opposite end of the cable.) This is an interface or a port configuration command, and its exact syntax varies based on the device. Two different versions of this command are presented here. |
| **speed {10 \| 100 \| auto}** | A router interface or a switch port might be capable of operating at a speed of 10 or 100 Mbps. (Some can negotiate it with the connected device on the opposite end of the cable.) This is an interface or a port configuration command. |

You enter the **controller** command, as specified in Table 8-2, while in global configuration mode. Controller configuration mode is usually entered for T1/E1 controllers. For example, to enter the controller configuration mode to configure a T1 or E1 controller on the Cisco MC3810, use the **controller** global configuration command as follows:

```
TEST-ROUTER(config)#controller {t1 | e1} number
```

Note that *number* is the controller unit number. For Cisco MC3810, enter **0** for the multiflex trunk module (MFT) and **1** for the digital voice module (DVM). Some of the configuration commands for the T1/E1 controllers are presented in Table 8-3. These commands configure the access interface ports that are attached to the T1/E1 controllers.

**Table 8-3** *Common Commands Used to Correct T1/E1 Controller Problems*

| T1/E1 Controller Configuration Command | Description |
|---|---|
| **channel-group** *channel-no* **timeslots** *timeslot-list* **speed {56 \| 64}** | Configures a list of timeslots for voice channels on the T1 or E1 controller. <br><br> *channel-no* is the ID number to identify the channel group. The valid range is 0 to 31. <br><br> *timeslot-list* is the timeslots (DS0s) to include in this channel group. The valid timeslots are 1 to 24 for T1 and 1 to 15 and 17 to 31 for E1. |

**Table 8-3**   *Common Commands Used to Correct T1/E1 Controller Problems (Continued)*

| T1/E1 Controller Configuration Command | Description |
|---|---|
| **clock source** {**line** \| **internal**} | Configures the clock source for a T1/E1 controller. |
| | **line** is used so that the controller recovers the external clock from the line and provides the recovered clock to the internal (system) clock generator. The line value is the default clock source for the MFT. |
| | **internal** is used so that the controller synchronizes itself to the internal (system) clock. The internal value is the default clock source for the DVM. |
| For T1 lines: **framing** {**sf** \| **esf**} For E1 lines: **framing** {**crc4** \| **no-crc4**} [**australia**] | Sets the frame type for the E1 or T1 data line: **sf**—Super frame. **esf**—Extended super frame. **crc4**—CRC4 frame. **australia**—E1 frame type used in Australia. |
| For T1 lines: **linecode** {**ami** \| **b8zs**} For E1 lines: **linecode** {**ami** \| **hdb3**} | Sets the line-code type for a T1 or E1 line: **ami**—Alternate mark inversion (AMI) line-code type. **b8zs**—B8ZS line-code type. **hdb3**—High-density bipolar 3 (HDB3) line-code type. |
| **pri-group** [**timeslots** *range*] | Specifies ISDN Primary Rate Interface (PRI) on a channelized T1 or E1 controller. **timeslots** *range*—Specifies a single range of values from 1 to 23 for channelized T1 and from 1 to 31 for channelized E1. |

You can fix a typical physical or data link layer problem whose remedy is configuration changes from within the interface configuration mode. The commands you can enter while in interface configuration mode are of two classes:

■   Those that can be entered on all kinds of interfaces (serial, Ethernet, and so on), such as the **IP** command

■   Those that are interface hardware-specific, such as the **clock rate** command, which is entered on serial interfaces (while the DCE end of the serial cable is connected to it)

Example 8-1 shows a sample of the types of commands that are available from within the interface configuration mode. The example was generated for a serial interface. As mentioned earlier, depending on the type of interface, the types and number of commands available vary.

**Example 8-1**    *Sample Interface (Serial) Configuration Commands (C2600 Software, Version 12.2(2)T)*

```
TEST-ROUTER#configure terminal
Enter configuration commands, one per line.  End with CNTL/Z.
TEST-ROUTER(config)#interface serial0/0
TEST-ROUTER(config-if)#?
Interface configuration commands:
  access-expression         Build a bridge boolean access expression
  apollo                    Apollo interface subcommands
  appletalk                 Appletalk interface subcommands
  arp                       Set arp type (arpa, probe, snap) or timeout
  asp                       ASP interface subcommands
  autodetect                Autodetect Encapsulations on Serial interface
  backup                    Modify backup parameters
  bandwidth                 Set bandwidth informational parameter
  bridge-group              Transparent bridging interface parameters
  bsc                       BSC interface subcommands
  bstun                     BSTUN interface subcommands
  carrier-delay             Specify delay for interface transitions
  cdp                       CDP interface subcommands
  clns                      CLNS interface subcommands
  clock                     Configure serial interface clock
  custom-queue-list         Assign a custom queue list to an interface
  dce-terminal-timing-enable Enable DCE terminal timing
  decnet                    Interface DECnet config commands
  default                   Set a command to its defaults
  delay                     Specify interface throughput delay
  description               Interface specific description
  dialer                    Dial-on-demand routing (DDR) commands
  dialer-group              Assign interface to dialer-list
  diffserv                  diffserv (Provisioning)
  dlsw                      DLSw Interface Subcommands
  down-when-looped          Force looped serial interface down
  dspu                      Down Stream PU
  dxi                       ATM-DXI configuration commands
  encapsulation             Set encapsulation type for an interface
  exit                      Exit from interface configuration mode
  fair-queue                Enable Fair Queuing on an Interface
  frame-relay               Set frame relay parameters
  fras                      DLC Switch Interface Command
  full-duplex               Configure full-duplex operational mode
  h323-gateway              Configure H323 Gateway
  half-duplex               Configure half-duplex and related commands
  help                      Description of the interactive help system
  hold-queue                Set hold queue depth
  idle-character            Set idle character type
  ignore                    ignore signals
  ignore-dcd                ignore dcd
  invert                    Serial invert modes
```

**Example 8-1**    *Sample Interface (Serial) Configuration Commands (C2600 Software, Version 12.2(2)T) (Continued)*

```
ip                      Interface Internet Protocol config commands
ipv6                    IPv6 interface subcommands
ipx                     Novell/IPX interface subcommands
isis                    IS-IS commands
iso-igrp                ISO-IGRP interface subcommands
keepalive               Enable keepalive
lan-name                LAN Name command
lat                     LAT commands
llc2                    LLC2 Interface Subcommands
load-interval           Specify interval for load calculation for an
                        interface
locaddr-priority        Assign a priority group
logging                 Configure logging for interface
loopback                Configure internal loopback on an interface
mac-address             Manually set interface MAC address
map-group               Configure static map group
max-reserved-bandwidth  Maximum Reservable Bandwidth on an Interface
mop                     DEC MOP server commands
mpls                    Configure MPLS interface parameters
mpoa                    MPOA interface configuration commands
mtu                     Set the interface Maximum Transmission Unit (MTU)
multilink-group         Put interface in a multilink bundle
netbios                 Use a defined NETBIOS access list or enable
                        name-caching
no                      Negate a command or set its defaults
nrzi-encoding           Enable use of NRZI encoding
ntp                     Configure NTP
ppp                     Point-to-Point Protocol
priority-group          Assign a priority group to an interface
pulse-time              Force DTR low during resets
random-detect           Enable Weighted Random Early Detection (WRED) on
                        an Interface
rate-limit              Rate Limit
roles                   Specify roles (by entering roles mode)
sap-priority            Assign a priority group
sdllc                   Configure SDLC to LLC2 translation
serial                  serial interface commands
service-policy          Configure QoS Service Policy
shutdown                Shutdown the selected interface
smds                    Modify SMDS parameters
smrp                    Simple Multicast Routing Protocol interface
                        subcommands
sna                     SNA pu configuration
snapshot                Configure snapshot support on the interface
snmp                    Modify SNMP interface parameters
source                  Get config from another source
```

*continues*

**Example 8-1**   *Sample Interface (Serial) Configuration Commands (C2600 Software, Version 12.2(2)T) (Continued)*

```
stun                      STUN interface subcommands
tag-switching             Tag Switching interface configuration commands
tarp                      TARP interface subcommands
timeout                   Define timeout values for this interface
traffic-shape             Enable Traffic Shaping on an Interface or
                          Sub-Interface
transmit-interface        Assign a transmit interface to a receive-only
                          interface
trunk-group               Configure interface to be in a trunk group
tx-ring-limit             Configure PA level transmit ring limit
vines                     VINES interface subcommands
xns                       XNS interface subcommands

TEST-ROUTER(config-if)#
```

The output displayed in Example 8-2 was generated so that you could further explore the **encapsulation** and the **clock rate** interface configuration commands. Note that both of these commands are hardware specific, are not available for all types of interfaces, and might not work the same way for all interface types. As you can see in Example 8-2, a serial interface was chosen to generate the output. The **encapsulation** command, when used on serial interfaces, allows you to set the serial encapsulation type (serial protocol frame type such as **ppp** and **frame-relay**). You use the **clock rate** command on a serial interface when the DCE end of a DCE-DTE cable (such as a V.35 DCE-DTE pair) is plugged into it, connecting this interface to another serial interface (usually of another router).

**Example 8-2**   *Configuration Options for Cisco IOS Interface Configuration Commands:* **clock rate** *and* **encapsulation**

```
TEST-ROUTER#configure terminal
Enter configuration commands, one per line.  End with CNTL/Z.
TEST-ROUTER(config)#interface serial0/0
TEST-ROUTER(config-if)#clock rate ?
      Speed (bits per second)
  1200
  2400
  4800
  ... (output deleted)
  2000000
  4000000
  8000000

  <300-4000000>    Choose clockrate from list above

TEST-ROUTER(config-if)#encapsulation ?
  atm-dxi         ATM-DXI encapsulation
  bstun           Block Serial tunneling (BSTUN)
```

**Example 8-2** *Configuration Options for Cisco IOS Interface Configuration Commands:* **clock rate** *and* **encapsulation** *(Continued)*

```
    frame-relay     Frame Relay networks
    hdlc            Serial HDLC synchronous
    lapb            LAPB (X.25 Level 2)
    ppp             Point-to-Point protocol
    sdlc            SDLC
    sdlc-primary    SDLC (primary)
    sdlc-secondary  SDLC (secondary)
    smds            Switched Megabit Data Service (SMDS)
    stun            Serial tunneling (STUN)
    x25             X.25
TEST-ROUTER(config-if)#end
TEST-ROUTER#
5d04h: %SYS-5-CONFIG_I: Configured from console by console
```

In the first example on using the commands listed in Table 8-2, assume that you find a problem with an interface (serial0/1) of a router named SanJose (see Figure 8-1).

**Figure 8-1** *Network Topology Diagram for the HDLC Connection Between the SanJose Router and the SanFran Router*

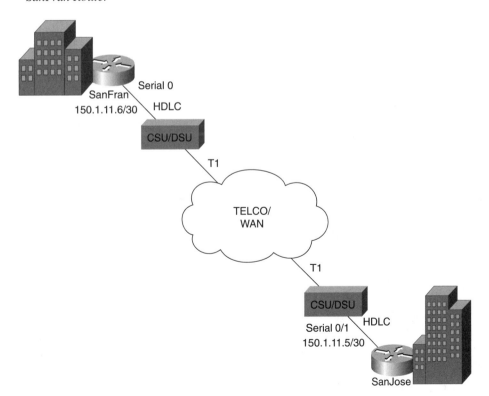

After observing the output of the **show ip interface brief** command, you notice that the serial0/1 interface is administratively down. Therefore, you need to enter a Cisco IOS command to activate the interface Serial0/1. To accomplish this, you enter interface configuration mode and apply the **no shutdown** command. The console messages report that interface Serial0/1 has gone into active state. Example 8-3 displays the commands entered and the messages indicating that the state of interface serial0/1 has changed to up. To continue with the task at hand, enter the **show ip interface brief** command on the SanJose router to verify the interface status. The results are shown in the last part of Example 8-3. The line status is up on the SanJose router's serial 0/1 interface.

**Example 8-3** *Correcting the Inactive Interface on a Router*

```
SanJose#show ip interface brief
Interface              IP-Address       OK? Method Status                Protocol
Ethernet0/0            192.168.22.1     YES manual up                    up
Serial0/0              unassigned       YES unset  up                    up
Serial0/0.1            192.168.1.18     YES manual up                    up
Serial0/0.2            192.168.1.21     YES manual up                    up
Serial0/0.4            150.1.12.1       YES manual up                    up
Serial0/1              150.1.11.5       YES manual administratively down down
Loopback0              192.168.1.2      YES manual up                    up
SanJose#configure terminal
Enter configuration commands, one per line.  End with CNTL/Z.
SanJose(config)#interface serial0/1
SanJose(config-if)#no shutdown
SanJose(config-if)#end
SanJose#
5d06h: %SYS-5-CONFIG_I: Configured from console by vty0 (192.168.1.22)
SanJose#
5d06h: %LINK-3-UPDOWN: Interface Serial0/1, changed state to up
5d06h: %LINEPROTO-5-UPDOWN: Line protocol on Interface Serial0/1, changed state
to up
SanJose#show ip interface brief
Interface              IP-Address       OK? Method Status                Protocol
Ethernet0/0            192.168.22.1     YES manual up                    up
Serial0/0              unassigned       YES unset  up                    up
Serial0/0.1            192.168.1.18     YES manual up                    up
Serial0/0.2            192.168.1.21     YES manual up                    up
Serial0/0.4            150.1.12.1       YES manual up                    up
Serial0/1              150.1.11.5       YES manual up                    up
Loopback0              192.168.1.2      YES manual up                    up
SanJose#
```

Next, you must check the status of the serial 0 interface on the SanFran router (see Figure 8-1 again), which connects to the SanJose router via a T1 link. Example 8-4 shows the resulting output after the **show ip interface brief** command was entered on the SanFran router. As a final validation effort, use the **ping** command to verify connectivity across the link between the SanFran and SanJose routers. The **ping** test is successful (see the bottom of Example 8-4), which validates physical and data link layers between those routers. You have corrected the problem.

**Example 8-4**  *Verifying the Correct Operation of Physical and Data Link Layers on a Link Between Two Cisco Routers*

```
SanFran#show ip interface brief
Interface              IP-Address      OK? Method Status                 Protocol
Ethernet0              201.1.2.1       YES manual up                     up
Ethernet1              unassigned      YES unset  administratively down  down
Loopback0              201.1.0.2       YES manual up                     up
Serial0                150.1.11.6      YES manual up                     up
Serial1                unassigned      YES unset  administratively down  down
SanFran#ping 150.1.11.5
Type escape sequence to abort.
Sending 5, 100-byte ICMP Echos to 150.1.11.5, timeout is 2 seconds:
!!!!!
Success rate is 100 percent (5/5), round-trip min/avg/max = 36/39/52 ms
SanFran#
```

In this second example on usage of the commands listed in Table 8-2, imagine that you have isolated a problem believed to be an encapsulation mismatch on the serial 0 interface of a router called Orlando currently configured for HDLC encapsulation. You have discovered from the documentation that Orlando is connected to SanJose via a Frame Relay PVC using DLCI 211 (not an HDLC connection), as shown in Figure 8-2, and the service provider uses the ANSI LMI.

**Figure 8-2**  *Network Diagram Displaying the Connection Between Orlando and SanJose*

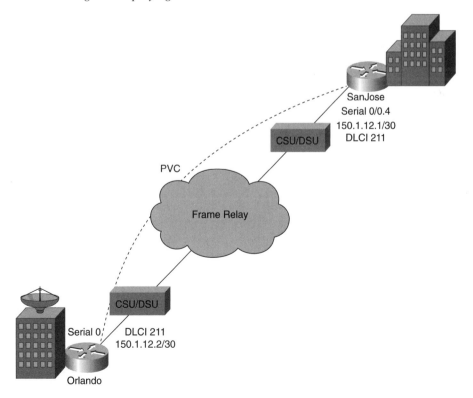

You can see correction done on the encapsulation type, setting the Frame Relay LMI type, and configuring the point-to-point Frame Relay subinterface with the appropriate DLCI number in Example 8-5. After the corrections are made, the line protocol on the serial 0 interface of the Orlando router goes up for a few seconds but then goes down again shortly after. To confirm the event, type the **show ip interface brief** command. You see once again that the line protocol on serial 0 is down.

**Example 8-5** *Correcting the Encapsulation Error on the Serial 0 Interface of Orlando*

```
Orlando#show ip interface serial 0
Serial0 is up, line protocol is down
  Internet protocol processing disabled
Orlando#configure terminal
Enter configuration commands, one per line.  End with CNTL/Z.
Orlando(config)#interface Serial0
Orlando(config-if)# encapsulation frame-relay
Orlando(config-if)# frame-relay lmi-type ansi
Orlando(config-if)# no shut
Orlando(config-if)# exit
Orlando(config)#interface Serial0.1 point-to-point
Orlando(config-subif)# description *** Link to SanJose ***
Orlando(config-subif)# frame-relay interface-dlci 211
Orlando(config-fr-dlci)# ip address 150.1.12.2 255.255.255.252
Orlando(config-if)# end
Orlando#
5d19h: %LINEPROTO-5-UPDOWN: Line protocol on Interface Serial0, changed state to up
5d19h: %SYS-5-CONFIG_I: Configured from console by console
Orlando#
5d19h: %LINEPROTO-5-UPDOWN: Line protocol on Interface Serial0, changed state to down
Orlando#show ip interface brief
Interface            IP-Address     OK? Method Status               Protocol
Ethernet0            201.2.1.1      YES manual up                    up
Ethernet1            unassigned     YES unset  administratively down down
Loopback0            201.2.0.1      YES manual up                    up
Serial0              unassigned     YES unset  up                    down
Serial0.1            150.1.12.2     YES manual down                  down
Serial1              unassigned     YES unset  administratively down down
Orlando#
```

At this point, you decide to investigate the issue by using the **show interface** and the **show frame-relay lmi** commands. The results are shown in Example 8-6. Based on the fact that the outputs of both commands display that Orlando is sending LMIs but it is not receiving LMIs (see the shaded lines in Example 8-6), you suspect that the ANSI LMI type that Orlando is using does not match the LMI type currently used by the service provider's local switch.

**Example 8-6**  *Investigating the State of the Serial 0 (Frame Relay) Interface Using the* **show interface** *and* **show frame-relay lmi** *Commands*

```
Orlando#show interface serial 0
Serial0 is up, line protocol is down
  Hardware is HD64570
  MTU 1500 bytes, BW 1544 Kbit, DLY 20000 usec,
     reliability 255/255, txload 1/255, rxload 1/255
  Encapsulation FRAME-RELAY, loopback not set
  Keepalive set (10 sec)
  LMI enq sent  196, LMI stat recvd 0, LMI upd recvd 0, DTE LMI down
  LMI enq recvd 0, LMI stat sent  0, LMI upd sent  0
  LMI DLCI 0  LMI type is ANSI Annex D  frame relay DTE
  ... (output text deleted)


Orlando#show frame-relay lmi
LMI Statistics for interface Serial0 (Frame Relay DTE) LMI TYPE = ANSI
  Invalid Unnumbered info 0          Invalid Prot Disc 0
  Invalid dummy Call Ref 0           Invalid Msg Type 0
  Invalid Status Message 0           Invalid Lock Shift 0
  Invalid Information ID 0           Invalid Report IE Len 0
  Invalid Report Request 0           Invalid Keep IE Len 0
  Num Status Enq. Sent 200           Num Status msgs Rcvd 0
  Num Update Status Rcvd 0           Num Status Timeouts 199
Orlando#
```

Therefore, you decide to test the validity of the ANSI LMI type by removing the **frame-relay lmi-type ansi** command and relying on the LMI auto-sensing feature of the Cisco serial interface (available as of IOS version 11.2). Example 8-7 displays removal of the **frame-relay lmi-type ansi** command, along with the console message indicating that the line protocol on interface serial0 has changed state to up.

**Example 8-7**  *Removing the* **frame-relay lmi-type** *Command and Relying on the LMI Auto-Sensing Feature of the Cisco Serial Interfaces Configured with the Frame Relay Encapsulation*

```
Orlando#configure terminal
Enter configuration commands, one per line.  End with CNTL/Z.
Orlando(config)#interface serial 0
Orlando(config-if)#no frame-relay lmi-type ansi
Orlando(config-if)#end
Orlando#
5d21h: %SYS-5-CONFIG_I: Configured from console by console
Orlando#
5d21h: %LINEPROTO-5-UPDOWN: Line protocol on Interface Serial0, changed state to up
Orlando#show ip interface brief
Interface            IP-Address      OK? Method Status                Protocol
Ethernet0            201.2.1.1       YES manual up                    up
Ethernet1            unassigned      YES unset  administratively down down
```
                                                                              *continues*

**Example 8-7** *Removing the **frame-relay lmi-type** Command and Relying on the LMI Auto-Sensing Feature of the Cisco Serial Interfaces Configured with the Frame Relay Encapsulation (Continued)*

```
Loopback0             201.2.0.1        YES manual up                          up
Serial0               unassigned       YES unset  up                          up
Serial0.1             150.1.12.2       YES manual up                          up
Serial1               unassigned       YES unset  administratively down down
Orlando#
```

Although you saw the line protocol going up on the serial 0 interface (and on the point-to-point serial 0.1 interface), you decide to test the link at the network layer by pinging Orlando's counterpart on the Frame Relay connection (that is, SanJose). The results are shown in Example 8-8. The 100 percent success rate of the **ping** command assures you that the link is in good condition. You have corrected the data link layer problem between Orlando and SanJose by fixing the encapsulation type (switching from HDLC to Frame Relay) and setting the Frame Relay LMI type to be auto-sensed (rather than fixated to ANSI) on Orlando's serial 0 interface. Out of curiosity, you then decide to find out what the LMI type used by the service provider is after all (that is, what your router auto-sensed). After the **ping** command, you type **show interface serial 0** on Orlando and find out that the service provider is now using the Cisco LMI type (see Example 8-8). You need to correct your documentation, and you need to find out why the news about the service provider changing its LMI type was not received and implemented on your side.

**Example 8-8** *Testing the Frame Relay Link Between Orlando and SanJose Using **ping***

```
Orlando#ping 150.1.12.1
Type escape sequence to abort.
Sending 5, 100-byte ICMP Echos to 150.1.12.1, timeout is 2 seconds:
!!!!!
Success rate is 100 percent (5/5), round-trip min/avg/max = 60/60/60 ms
Orlando#
Orlando#show interface serial 0
Serial0 is up, line protocol is up
  Hardware is HD64570
  MTU 1500 bytes, BW 1544 Kbit, DLY 20000 usec,
     reliability 255/255, txload 1/255, rxload 1/255
  Encapsulation FRAME-RELAY, loopback not set
  Keepalive set (10 sec)
  LMI enq sent  839, LMI stat recvd 390, LMI upd recvd 0, DTE LMI up
  LMI enq recvd 0, LMI stat sent  0, LMI upd sent  0
  LMI DLCI 1023  LMI type is CISCO  frame relay DTE
... (output text deleted)
Orlando#
```

For the third example on correcting problems at the physical and data link layers, imagine that you are assigned to troubleshoot the connection problem between the Toronto router and the Buffalo6000 switch (see Figure 8-3).

**Figure 8-3**  *Partial Network Diagram Showing the Connection Between the Toronto Router and the Buffalo6000 Switch*

Buffalo6000

Fa3/1

Fa0

Toronto

Your troubleshooting efforts (partially shown in Example 8-9) reveal the following to you:

■  Based on the output of the **show interface FastEthernet0** command showing this interface administratively down, you need to enable the interface using the **no shut** command.

■  After the **no shut** command, the line protocol stays down showing no carrier, so you conclude that the connection of the cable to the interface is bad, loose, or it needs reseating.

**Example 8-9**  *Initial Corrective Actions on the Toronto Router*

```
Toronto#show interface fa0
FastEthernet0 is administratively down, line protocol is down
  Hardware is DEC21140, address is 00e0.1eef.8b40 (bia 00e0.1eef.8b40)
  MTU 1500 bytes, BW 100000 Kbit, DLY 100 usec,
     reliability 128/255, txload 1/255, rxload 1/255
  Encapsulation ARPA, loopback not set
  Keepalive set (10 sec)
  Full-duplex, 100Mb/s, 100BaseTX/FX
  ... (output text deleted)
Toronto#configure terminal
Enter configuration commands, one per line.  End with CNTL/Z.
Toronto(config)#interface fastethernet0
Toronto(config-if)#no shutdown
Toronto(config-if)#end
Toronto#
Toronto#show interface fastethernet0
FastEthernet0 is up, line protocol is down
  Hardware is DEC21140, address is 00e0.1eef.8b40 (bia 00e0.1eef.8b40)
  MTU 1500 bytes, BW 100000 Kbit, DLY 100 usec,
     reliability 128/255, txload 1/255, rxload 1/255
  Encapsulation ARPA, loopback not set
  Keepalive set (10 sec)
```

*continues*

**Example 8-9**    *Initial Corrective Actions on the Toronto Router (Continued)*

```
  Full-duplex, 100Mb/s, 100BaseTX/FX
... (output text deleted)
     121 packets output, 8578 bytes, 0 underruns(0/116/0)
     116 output errors, 116 collisions, 1 interface resets
     0 babbles, 0 late collision, 0 deferred
     116 lost carrier, 0 no carrier
     0 output buffer failures, 0 output buffers swapped out
Toronto#
```

After you reseat the loose cable to the fastethernet0 interface on the Toronto router, your colleagues send you e-mails reporting that a message about a duplex mode mismatch is displayed on the Buffalo6000 switch:

```
%CDP-4-DUPLEXMISMATCH:Full/half-duplex mismatch detected o1
```

The Cisco Discovery Protocol (CDP) creates this message, not the 802.3 auto-negotiation protocol. CDP can report problems it discovers. A duplex mismatch might or might not result in an error message. Another indication of a duplex mismatch is rapidly increasing frame check sequence (FCS) and alignment errors on the half-duplex side and runts on the full-duplex side of a duplex-mismatching connection. Knowing that the connection between the Toronto router and the Buffalo6000 switch must be at 100 Mbps and full-duplex (according to baseline), you configure the Buffalo6000 switch based on these settings, as shown in Example 8-10. The commands shown in Example 8-10 apply to the following types of switch products: Catalyst 2900XL, 3500XL, 2950, 3550, 2948G-L3, 4908G-L3, Catalyst 4000 running Cisco IOS (Supervisor III), and the Catalyst 6000 running Cisco IOS (Native) software.

**Example 8-10**    *Setting the Speed and Duplex on a Catalyst 6000 Running Native IOS*

```
Buffalo6000#show interface fastEthernet 3/1 status

Port    Name            Status      Vlan      Duplex Speed Type
Fa3/1                   notconnected routed    a-half a-100 10/100BaseTX

Buffalo6000#
Buffalo6000#configure terminal
Enter configuration commands, one per line.  End with CNTL/Z.
Buffalo6000(config)#interface fastEthernet3/1
Buffalo6000(config-if)#duplex full

Duplex will not be set until speed is set to non-auto value

Buffalo6000(config-if)#speed 100
Buffalo6000(config-if)#duplex full
Buffalo6000(config-if)#^Z
Buffalo6000#show interfaces fastEthernet 3/1 status
```

**Example 8-10**    *Setting the Speed and Duplex on a Catalyst 6000 Running Native IOS (Continued)*

```
Port    Name                Status    Vlan    Duplex Speed Type
Fa3/1                       connected routed  full   100   10/100BaseTX


Buffalo6000#
```

Finally, you decide to recheck the status of the fastEthernet0 interface on the Toronto router to be confident that the problem is corrected. Example 8-11 displays the results. Note that the line protocol is up, keepalive is set, the interface is operating in full-duplex at 100 Mbps, and there is no lost carrier, late collision, output errors, and so on. This troubleshooting task required corrections done at both the physical and data link layers.

**Example 8-11**    *Showing the Status of the FastEthernet0 Interface on the Toronto Router*

```
Toronto#show interfaces fastethernet 0
FastEthernet0 is up, line protocol is up
  Hardware is DEC21140, address is 00e0.1eef.8b40 (bia 00e0.1eef.8b40)
  MTU 1500 bytes, BW 100000 Kbit, DLY 100 usec,
     reliability 255/255, txload 1/255, rxload 1/255
  Encapsulation ARPA, loopback not set
  Keepalive set (10 sec)
  Full-duplex, 100Mb/s, 100BaseTX/FX
  ARP type: ARPA, ARP Timeout 04:00:00
  .
  . (output text deleted)
  .
     21021 packets output, 1387934 bytes, 0 underruns
     0 output errors, 0 collisions, 0 interface resets
     0 babbles, 0 late collision, 0 deferred
     0 lost carrier, 0 no carrier, 0 PAUSE output
     0 output buffer failures, 0 output buffers swapped out

Toronto#
```

# Physical and Data Link Layer Support Resources

During the course of troubleshooting, you can run out of ideas and essentially feel stuck at a dead end. Many resources are available. In addition to colleagues, certified Cisco consultants and Cisco Technical Assistance Center personnel are valuable resources. Cisco Connection Online (CCO) has information on various legacy and new technologies, configuration and troubleshooting of Cisco devices, design and migration solutions, and so on. The following is a list of online resources that Cisco Systems offers:

■ **Cisco Systems Technical Assistance Center**—www.cisco.com/TAC/

■ **Cisco Connection Online**—www.cisco.com

- **Internetwork Troubleshooting Guide**—www.cisco.com/univercd/cc/td/doc/cisintwk/itg_v1/

- **Cisco Systems Technologies Reference (online documentation)**—www.cisco.com/univercd /home/home.htm

In addition, several standards bodies control research, development, and maintenance of standards that are related to specific technologies. Examples of those bodies and their Web sites, which are valuable sources of information and troubleshooting resources, include the following:

- **Internet Engineering Task Force (IETF)**—www.ietf.org

- **International Telecommunications Union (ITU-T)**—www.itu.int/home

- **Frame Relay Forum**—www.frforum.com

- **ATM Forum**—www.atmforum.com

# Correcting a Physical or Data Link Layer Problem

The following are suggested steps for correcting an isolated problem at the physical and data link layers:

1. Ensure that you have a valid saved configuration for any device on which you intend to modify the configuration. This provides for eventual recovery to a known initial state.

2. Make initial hardware and software configuration changes. If the correction requires more than one change, make only one change at a time.

3. Evaluate and document the changes and the results of each change that you make. If you perform your problem-solving steps and the results are unsuccessful, immediately undo the changes. If the problem is intermittent, you might need to wait to see if the problem occurs again before you can evaluate the effects of your changes.

4. Verify that the changes you make actually fix the problem without introducing new problems. The network should be returned to the baseline operation, and no new or old symptoms should be present. If the problem is not solved, undo all your changes. If you discover new or additional problems while you are correcting, step back and modify your correction plan.

5. Continue making changes until the original problem appears to be solved.

6. If necessary, get input from outside resources. If none of your attempts to correct the problem is successful, take the problem to another person. This might be a co-worker, consultant, or Cisco's Technical Assistance Center. On rare occasions, you might need to perform a core dump, which creates output that a specialist at Cisco Systems can analyze.

7. After you solve the problem, document the solution.

# Foundation Summary

The "Foundation Summary" section of each chapter lists the most important facts from that chapter. Although this section does not list every fact from the chapter that will be on your CCNP exam, a well-prepared CCNP candidate should at a minimum know all the details in each "Foundation Summary" before taking the exam.

**Table 8-4**   *Commands Used to Correct Physical and Data Link Problems*

| Command | Description |
|---|---|
| **arp –d** *ip-address* | You use this command on end systems with Microsoft operating systems (Windows) to delete a specific entry or the entire contents of the ARP table. You can clear the entire content of the arp-cache on a Cisco router by using the command **clear arp-cache**. |
| **interface** | This Cisco IOS command enters interface configuration mode (from global configuration mode). After you are in interface configuration mode, you can enter such commands as **encapsulation**, **ip address**, **clock rate**, **speed**, **duplex**, and **no shutdown**. |
| **no shutdown** | This Cisco IOS command activates an interface that is inactive (shut down). You enter this command while in interface configuration mode. |
| **encapsulation** | This command configures an encapsulation type on an interface (such as serial). You enter this command while in interface configuration mode. The choice of encapsulation type is interface dependent. For example, you have the **hdlc**, **ppp**, **frame-relay**, and other options on a serial interface, but you don't have those options on an Ethernet interface. |
| **clock rate** | This is a Cisco IOS interface configuration command. It configures a clock rate on an interface (serial interface with the DCE end of the cable plugged into it). You enter this command while in interface configuration mode. |
| **controller** | This command enters controller configuration mode. You enter it while in global configuration mode. Controller configuration mode is usually entered for T1/E1 controllers. |
| **duplex {full \| half \| auto}** <br> or: <br> **full-duplex** <br> **half-duplex** | A router interface or a switch port might be capable of operating in half-duplex or in full-duplex. (Some can negotiate it with the connected device on the opposite end of the cable). This is an interface or a port configuration command, and its exact syntax varies based on the device. Two different versions of this command are presented here. |
| **speed {10 \| 100 \| auto}** | A router interface or a switch port might be capable of operating at a speed of 10 or 100 Mbps. (Some can negotiate it with the connected device on the opposite end of the cable.) This is an interface or a port configuration command. |

The following list presents the online resources that Cisco Systems offers:

- **Cisco Systems Technical Assistance Center**—www.cisco.com/TAC/

- **CCO**—www.cisco.com

- **Internetwork Troubleshooting Guide**—www.cisco.com/univercd/cc/td/doc/cisintwk/itg_v1/

- **Cisco Systems Technologies Reference**—www.cisco.com/univercd/home/home.htm

Several standards bodies control research, development, and maintenance of standards related to specific technologies. Following are examples of those bodies and their Web sites:

- **IETF**—www.ietf.org

- **ITU-T**—www.itu.int/home

- **Frame Relay Forum**—www.frforum.com

- **ATM Forum**—www.atmforum.com

The following are guidelines for correcting physical and data link layer problems:

1. Ensure that you have a valid saved configuration for any device on which you intend to modify the configuration. This provides for eventual recovery to a known initial state.

2. Make initial configuration changes.

3. Evaluate and document the results of each change that you make.

4. Verify that the changes you make actually fix the problem without introducing new problems.

5. Continue making changes until the original problem appears to be solved.

6. If necessary, get input from outside resources.

7. After you have solved the problem, document the solution.

# Q&A

As mentioned in the introduction, you have two choices for review questions. The questions that follow give you a bigger challenge than the exam because they use an open-ended question format. By reviewing now with this more difficult question format, you can exercise your memory better and prove your conceptual and factual knowledge of this chapter. You can find the answers to these questions in Appendix A.

For more practice with exam-like question formats, including questions that use a router simulator and multiple choice format, use the exam engine on the CD.

1. Which Cisco IOS commands allow you to deactivate and activate a Cisco router's interface? In which configuration mode can you do that?

2. Which Cisco IOS command displays the status of all router interfaces along with their IP addresses (if the interface has one) in a brief table format?

3. Specify the Cisco IOS commands (in sequence) that you need to enter to 1) go from privileged mode to global configuration mode; 2) get into interface configuration mode for serial1/0; 3) set the clock rate to 64000 on serial 1/0.

4. Which Cisco IOS command allows you to test connectivity to an IP host or device?

5. Name the Cisco IOS command that allows you to set the encapsulation type on a router interface. Specify the mode in which the command must be entered.

6. Which command allows you to change the Frame Relay LMI type on an interface?

7. When troubleshooting physical and data link layers, what support resources are available to you?

8. Before you modify the configuration of a Cisco device, what is the first thing you must ensure?

9. Name at least two guidelines that are important to follow when you have isolated a problem and are ready to correct it.

10. What is CCO's Web (HTTP) address?

The following CIT exam topics are covered in this part. (To view the CIT exam outline, visit www.cisco.com/go/training.)

- Verify connectivity at all layers.

- Use Cisco IOS commands and applications to identify system problems at all layers.

- Isolate system problems to one or more specific layers.

- Resolve suboptimal system performance problems at Layers 2 through 7.

- Restore optimal baseline service.

- Work with external providers to resolve service provision problems.

- Work with system users to resolve network-related end-use problems.

# Part IV: Resolving Problems at the Network Layer

## This chapter covers the following subjects:

- The symptoms of problems occurring at the network layer

- End system commands and applications used to isolate problems occurring at the network layer

- Analyzing Cisco command and application output to isolate problems occurring at the network layer

- Isolating a problem occurring at the network layer

# CHAPTER 9

# Isolating a Problem at the Network Layer

This chapter first discusses and identifies the symptoms of problems that occur at the network layer. As you will see, with physical and data link layers in good working condition, erroneous addressing or routing configurations cause most network layer problems. Next, this chapter presents the end system commands and applications that are used to isolate network layer problems. You analyze the output of those commands and applications to isolate the problems occurring at this layer. Finally, this chapter discusses the general guidelines for isolating network layer problems.

## "Do I Know This Already?" Quiz

The purpose of the "Do I Know This Already?" quiz is to help you decide if you really need to read this entire chapter. If you already intend to read the entire chapter, you do not need to answer these questions now.

The 10-question quiz, derived from the major sections in the "Foundation Topics" portion of the chapter, helps you determine how to spend your limited study time.

Table 9-1 outlines the major topics discussed in this chapter and the "Do I Know This Already?" quiz questions that correspond to those topics.

**Table 9-1**  *"Do I Know This Already?" Foundation Topics Section-to-Question Mapping*

| Foundation Topics Section | Questions Covered in This Section |
| --- | --- |
| "The Symptoms of Problems Occurring at the Network Layer" | 2 |
| "End System Commands and Applications Used to Isolate Problems Occurring at the Network Layer" | 3 |
| "Analyzing Cisco Command and Application Output to Isolate Problems Occurring at the Network Layer" | 3 |
| "Isolating a Problem Occurring at the Network Layer" | 2 |

> **CAUTION** The goal of self-assessment is to gauge your mastery of the topics in this chapter. If you do not know the answer to a question or are only partially sure of the answer, you should mark this question wrong for purposes of the self-assessment. Giving yourself credit for an answer you correctly guess skews your self-assessment results and might provide you with a false sense of security.

1. Users in a segment of your company LAN are complaining that access to devices on the network is much slower than usual. You check the network topology diagram to determine which devices are routing packets to that network segment. Which of the following symptoms would be present if this problem were located at the network layer?

   a. A particular application consistently crashes.

   b. No devices are reachable.

   c. CRC/FCS errors are excessive.

   d. Traffic is taking a path other than the expected path recorded in the baseline.

2. Which of the following commands would you enter at a Windows NT end system to display the current IP routing table for a device?

   a. **ipconfig /all**

   b. **ifconfig –a**

   c. **route print**

   d. **arp -a**

3. A network interface card on an end system was faulty and replaced. However, the end system still cannot connect beyond the local network. Examine the following snippet of the configuration for the default gateway for the end system and then choose a command that might solve the problem using the information given.

   ```
   interface Ethernet0
   ip address 192.168.1.254 255.255.255.0
   no ip directed-broadcast
   arp timeout 0
   ```

   a. **clear interface Ethernet10**

   b. **clear arp-cache**

   c. **ip directed-broadcasts**

   d. **debug ip packet detail**

4.  A group of users on a large Ethernet LAN report that their connection to the network is much slower than usual. You determine which two routers are closest to the source (the users) and the destination devices. You know that there is connectivity, so you run a trace instead of pinging between the devices. Running a trace from the source to the destination indicates that there is significant latency at a few of the hops along the path. You reverse the trace and verify that there is latency from the destination to the source as well. You recognize that this latency is the cause of the problem, but you are not sure why it is happening. Which guideline for isolating problems at the network layer should you practice next?

    a.  Perform a loopback test to verify that the TCP/IP stack is loaded and functional.

    b.  Disable spanning tree on the destination device but not the source device.

    c.  Refer to the network diagram to verify that the devices are connecting across the expected path.

    d.  Visually inspect the serial connection between the devices.

5.  Which of the following is not a symptom of network layer problems?

    a.  No component on the failing link appears to be functional above the network layer.

    b.  The network is functional but is operating either consistently or intermittently at a lower capacity (speed, response, or throughput) than the baseline level.

    c.  Connectivity on the link as seen from the transport layer seems to be functional.

    d.  Pings succeed only a percentage of the time.

    e.  The routing tables are empty, inconsistent, or incomplete.

6.  Which of the following is not an end system command to isolate network layer problems?

    a.  **ping**

    b.  **arp -a**

    c.  **show cdp neighbor**

    d.  **ipconfig**

    e.  **route print**

7.  Which of the following commands displays IP information for hosts that are running Windows NT/2000/XP?

    a.  **netstat -rn**

    b.  **route print**

    c.  **ifconfig -a**

    d.  **traceroute /d** [*destination*]

    e.  **ipconfig /all**

**8.** During the course of troubleshooting and isolating problems occurring at the network layer, analyzing the packet forwarding behavior of a router might be necessary. Select the command that displays the contents of a table most appropriate for this purpose.

   a. **show ip protocols**

   b. **show ip bgp**

   c. **show ip traffic**

   d. **show ip route**

   e. **show ip interfaces brief**

**9.** If you identify a single pair of problematic source and destination devices during a troubleshooting assignment, which of the following would be the most logical step to take next?

   a. Test the connectivity between the two devices.

   b. Try to identify more problematic devices.

   c. Contact Cisco Technical Assistance Center.

   d. Change/fix the configuration of those devices.

   e. Use the network diagram and run loopback tests.

**10.** Which of the following Cisco IOS commands displays the list of BGP peers along with the status of the relationship with each of them?

   a. **show ip bgp**

   b. **show ip bgp summary**

   c. **show bgp neighbors**

   d. **show bgp flap-statistics**

   e. **debug ip bgp**

You can find the answers to the "Do I Know This Already?" quiz in Appendix A, "Answers to the 'Do I Know This Already?' Quizzes and 'Q&A' Sections." The suggested choices for your next step are as follows:

■ **8 or less overall score**—Read the entire chapter. This includes the "Foundation Topics" and "Foundation Summary" sections, as well as the "Q&A" section.

■ **9 or 10 overall score**—If you want more review on these topics, skip to the "Foundation Summary" section and then go to the "Q&A" section. Otherwise, move to the next chapter.

# Foundation Topics

## The Symptoms of Problems Occurring at the Network Layer

When the network layer or higher experiences symptoms or difficulties, it might be difficult to determine exactly at which layer the root problem is located. The reason is that the symptom or problem might also have sprung from physical or data link layer failures. If troubleshooting efforts show that the physical and data link layers are problem free, then you have a concrete indication that your problem resides at the network layer or higher. Following are some common symptoms of network layer problems:

- No component on the failing link appears to be functional above the network layer.

- The network is functional but is operating either consistently or intermittently at a lower capacity (speed, response, or throughput) than the baseline level.

- No connectivity on the link is seen from the transport layer.

- Pings succeed only part of the time.

- Routing tables are empty, inconsistent, or incomplete.

- Routing behavior is unexpected.

- Packets are delivered to incorrect destinations.

- Various console messages report failures and problems.

- System log-file messages report failures/problems.

- Management system alarms indicate problems/failures.

When the network is functional but is operating either consistently or intermittently less than the baseline level, the problem might be an optimization issue. In these situations, users report that data transfer is slow, sporadic, or inconsistent with the usual data transfer rate. As the list of common symptoms of network layer problems indicates, not all network layer problems present the same symptoms. These symptoms can range from the system displaying console messages to misrouted packets (connectivity problems).

Example 9-1 shows a console message that you might see if the router detects a duplicate IP address on the network. Ping failures and "ICMP Unreachable" messages are common symptoms of network layer failures. Alarms from the network management system or accumulation of failure messages in the system logs are other possible symptoms of network layer problems.

**Example 9-1** *System Message Indicating Duplicate IP Address*

```
Feb 08 98:08:08: %IP-4-DUPADDR: Duplicate address 172.16.118.1 on
    FastEthernet0/1, sourced by 0000.0c12.3456
```

# End System Commands and Applications Used to Isolate Problems Occurring at the Network Layer

Table 9-2 describes some general end system commands, some commands specific to Microsoft Windows operating systems, and some UNIX/Mac OS X commands that you can use to isolate problems at the network layer. Although many such commands also display information that concerns the data link layer, they are noteworthy at the network layer because they highlight problems in the interface between the data link and network layers.

**Table 9-2** *End System Commands to Isolate Network Layer Problems*

| System | Command | Description |
|---|---|---|
| General | **ping** {*host* \| *ip-address*}<br><br>Useful options:<br><br>[**-t**]<br><br>[**-a**]<br><br>[**-n** *count* ]<br><br>[**-l** *size* ]<br><br>[**-f**]<br><br>[**-i** *TTL* ]<br><br>[**-v** *TOS* ]<br><br>[**-r** *count* ]<br><br>[**-s** *count* ]<br><br>[[**-j** *host-list* ] \| [**-k** *host-list*] ]<br><br>[**-w** *timeout* ]<br><br>*destination-list* | Sends an echo request packet to an address and then waits for a reply. The {*host* \| *ip-address*} variable is the IP alias or IP address of the target system.<br><br>To take full advantage of the command in real troubleshooting cases, you should become familiar with the optional parameters/switches that are available with this command:<br><br>**-t**—Ping the specified host until stopped. To see statistics and continue, press **Ctrl-Break**; To stop, press **Ctrl-C**.<br><br>**-a**—Resolve addresses to host names.<br><br>**-n** *count* —Number of echo requests to send.<br><br>**-l** *size* —Send buffer size.<br><br>**-f**—Set Don't Fragment flag in packet.<br><br>**-i** *TTL* —Time To Live.<br><br>**-v** *TOS* —Type Of Service.<br><br>**-r** *count* —Record route for count hops.<br><br>**-s** *count* —Timestamp for count hops.<br><br>**-j** *host-list* —Loose source route along *host-list* .<br><br>**-k** *host-list* —Strict source route along *host-list* .<br><br>**-w** *timeout* —Timeout in milliseconds to wait for each reply. |
| | **arp –a** | Displays the current mappings of the IP addresses to MAC addresses in the Address Resolution Protocol (ARP) table. |

**Table 9-2**   *End System Commands to Isolate Network Layer Problems (Continued)*

| System | Command | Description |
|---|---|---|
| General | **Netstat** [**-a**] [**-e**] [**-n**] [**-s**] [**-p** *proto*] [**-r**] *interval* | Displays protocol statistics and current TCP/IP network connections.<br><br>**-a**—Displays all connections and listening ports.<br><br>**-e**—Displays Ethernet statistics. This might be combined with the -s option.<br><br>**-n**—Displays addresses and port numbers in numerical form.<br><br>**-p** *proto*—Shows connections for the protocol specified by *proto*; *proto* might be TCP or UDP. If used with the -s option to display per-protocol statistics, proto might be TCP, UDP, or IP.<br><br>**-r**—Displays the routing table.<br><br>**-s**—Displays per-protocol statistics. By default, statistics are shown for TCP, UDP, and IP; the **-p** option might be used to specify a subset of the default.<br><br>*interval* —Redisplays selected statistics, pausing interval seconds between each display. Press **Ctrl-C** to stop redisplaying statistics. If omitted, **netstat** prints the current configuration information once. |
| Windows | **route print** | Displays the current IP routing table. |
|  | **ipconfig** [**/all**] | Displays IP information for hosts that are running Windows NT/2000/XP. |
|  | **tracert** [**-d**] [**-h** *maximum-hops* ] [**-j** *host-list* ] [**-w** *timeout* ] [*destination* ] | Verifies connectivity to a destination device for Windows hosts. The *destination* variable is the IP alias or IP address of the target system.<br><br>**-d**—Do not resolve addresses to host names without querying a DNS server.<br><br>**-h** *maximum-hops* —Maximum number of hops to search for target.<br><br>**-j** *host-list* —Loose source route along host-list.<br><br>**-w** *timeout* —Wait timeout milliseconds for each reply. |
|  | **Winipcfg** [**/all**] | Displays IP information for hosts that are running Windows 9x and Windows Me. |

*continues*

**Table 9-2** *End System Commands to Isolate Network Layer Problems (Continued)*

| System | Command | Description |
|---|---|---|
| UNIX/Mac OS X | **ifconfig –a** | Displays IP information for UNIX and Mac OS X hosts. |
| | **traceroute** [*destination* ] | Identifies the path that a packet takes through the network. The *destination* variable is the host name or IP address of the target system. |
| | **route -n** | Displays the content of the IP routing table for the local device. |

# Analyzing Cisco Command and Application Output to Isolate Problems Occurring at the Network Layer

This section describes several important Cisco IOS commands that display information that is useful for isolating network layer problems (see Table 9-3). Following that, a scenario-style example demonstrates how you can use the commands listed in Table 9-3 to help isolate a realistic network layer problem.

The first few commands listed in Table 9-3 are marked as general commands because they might reveal issues related to many aspects of configuration at the network layer (addressing, routing, optimization, symmetry, and so on). The next few commands concentrate on the ARP and IP routing table's contents and operations (through **show** and **debug**) and IP interfaces. The list of BGP **show** and **debug** commands makes a useful set for isolating problems that might spring from BGP configuration errors. IP traffic statistics, Internet Control Message Protocol (ICMP) messages, IP packet handling, and contents of active access lists are the focus of the last set of commands presented in Table 9-3.

**Table 9-3** *Cisco Commands to Isolate Network Layer Problems*

| Focus | Command | Description |
|---|---|---|
| General | **ping** {*host* | *ip-address*} | Sends an echo request packet to an address and then waits for a reply. The {*host* | *ip-address*} variable is the IP alias or IP address of the target system. |
| | **trace** [*destination* ] | Runs a trace. Displays the list of IP nodes between the local device and the destination IP address (IP host). |
| | [**no**] **debug ?** | Displays a list of options for enabling or disabling debugging events on a device. |
| | **show running-config** | Displays the current configuration of the Cisco device. (You might call it the currently running configuration file.) |

**Table 9-3**  *Cisco Commands to Isolate Network Layer Problems (Continued)*

| Focus | Command | Description |
|---|---|---|
| ARP | **show ip arp** | Displays all ARP table entries in cache. |
| | **debug arp** | Displays information about ARP transactions. |
| Routing table (IP) | **show ip route** | Displays the current content of the routing table. |
| | **debug ip routing** | Displays information on routing table updates and route-cache updates. |
| IP interface | **show ip interface [brief]** | Displays the list of local router's interfaces, their IP addresses, their physical and logical status, and so on. Adding the **brief** keyword displays a summary table showing all interfaces, their IP addresses (even those that are unassigned), and status.<br><br>You can inspect one particular interface at a time by typing the interface ID after this command. For example,<br><br>**show ip interface Ethernet 0** |
| BGP (exterior routing) | **show ip bgp** | Displays the content of the BGP table (entries). |
| | **show ip bgp summary** | Displays the list and status of all BGP connections (peers). |
| | **show ip bgp neighbors** | Displays information about the TCP and BGP connections to neighbors. |
| | **show ip bgp flap-statistics** | Displays information about BGP route flapping. |
| | **debug ip bgp [dampening \| events \| keepalives \| updates]** | Displays information that is related to BGP processing. |
| IP traffic | **show ip traffic** | Displays statistics about IP traffic, such as format errors, bad hops, encapsulation failures, unknown routes, and probe proxy requests. |
| | **debug ip icmp** | Displays information about ICMP transactions. |
| | **debug ip packet** | Displays general IP debugging information and IP Security Option (IPSO) security transactions. |
| IP access lists | **show ip access-lists** [*access-list-number* \| *access-list-name* ] | Displays the content of all IP access lists or a specified numbered or named IP access list. |

Now imagine that you are a network engineer at a corporation with offices in Washington, Baltimore, and Columbia. The networking devices at each location are named after the city in which they reside. You have console access to the router in Washington, which gives you IP connectivity to all devices in your network (see Figure 9-1).

**Figure 9-1** *Partial Network Diagram Showing the Connections Among Columbia (Access), Baltimore (Distribution), and Washington (Core) and Their Dual Connection to the Corporate Core (Lenexa and Elmhurst)*

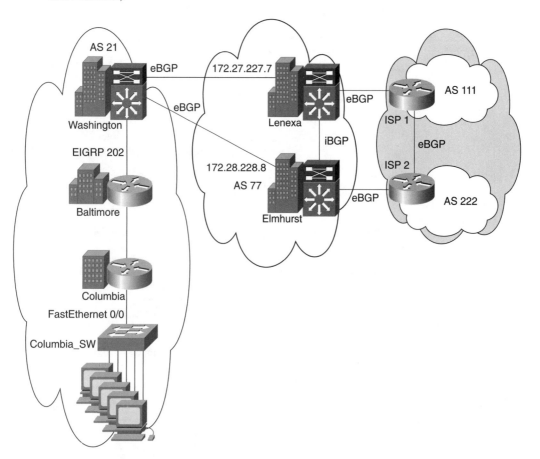

You have determined that even though the prefix 198.133.219.0/24 (a network associated to Cisco Systems) is supposed to be in the routing tables of all the devices you manage, it is not present in any of them. To help isolate the problem, you first review the status of the current routing protocols on the router named Washington using the command **show ip protocols**. (See the output displayed in Example 9-2.) The output reveals that process EIGRP 202 is running and is redistributing BGP 21, which is also an active process on the Washington router and has neighbor relationships with 172.27.227.7 and 172.28.228.8.

**Example 9-2**  *Output of the Cisco IOS* **show ip protocols** *Command*

```
Washington>show ip protocol
Routing Protocol is "eigrp 202"
.
.
  Redistributing: static, eigrp 202, bgp 21
.
.
  Routing Protocol is "bgp 21"
.
.
  Routing Information Sources:
    Gateway        Distance      Last Update
    (this router)       200      4d15h
    172.28.128.8         20      4d15h
    172.27.227.7         20      4d15h
  Distance: external 20 internal 200 local 200
Washington>
```

The route to Cisco's 198.133.219.0 can only be learned from Lenexa or Elmhurst through BGP. You decide to connect to Lenexa, a corporate core device, at 172.27.227.7 (one of Washington's BGP peers from Example 9-2) and check for the presence of the 198.133.219.0 prefix using the **show ip route** command (see Example 9-3). Lenexa's IP routing table (shown in Example 9-3) includes the 198.133.219.0 prefix.

**Example 9-3**  *Output of the Cisco IOS* **show ip route** *Command*

```
Lenexa>show ip route
.
.
    172.17.0.0/30 is subnetted, 1 subnets
C      172.17.12.0 is directly connected, FastEthernet0/13
B    172.22.0.0/16 [20/0] via 172.27.227.2, 00:06:04
.
.
B    172.26.0.0/16 [20/0] via 172.27.227.6, 4d22h
     172.27.0.0/27 is subnetted, 1 subnets
C      172.27.227.0 is directly connected, Vlan27
     172.28.0.0/28 is subnetted, 1 subnets
C      172.28.128.0 is directly connected, Vlan28
.
.
B    198.133.219.0/24 [20/0] via 172.17.12.1, 4d16h
B    213.173.185.0/24 [20/0] via 172.17.12.1, 4d16h
B    216.239.33.0/24 [20/0] via 172.17.12.1, 4d16h
S*   0.0.0.0/0 [1/0] via 172.17.12.1
Lenexa>
```

After you verify that the 198.133.219.0/24 route is on at least one of the corporate core devices (Lenexa), you can return to the console on Washington and examine its BGP routing table using the **show ip bgp** command (see Example 9-4). You discover that the 198.133.219.0/24 prefix is not in Washington's BGP table.

**Example 9-4**    *Output of the Cisco IOS **show ip bgp** Command*

```
Washington>show ip bgp
BGP table version is 27, local router ID is 172.22.129.1
Status codes: s suppressed, d damped, h history, * valid, > best, i - internal
Origin codes: i - IGP, e - EGP, ? - incomplete

    Network          Next Hop          Metric LocPrf Weight Path
*> 172.21.0.0        172.28.128.1                      0 77 11  i
*> 172.22.0.0        0.0.0.0                        32768      i
s> 172.22.121.0/26  0.0.0.0           3850240        32768      i
s> 172.22.122.0/26  0.0.0.0           3850240        32768      i
s> 172.22.123.0/26  0.0.0.0           3850240        32768      i
 .
 .
 .
s> 172.22.129.0/26  0.0.0.0                 0        32768      i
*   172.23.0.0       172.27.227.3                      0 77 31  i
*>                   172.28.128.3                      0 77 31  i
*   172.24.0.0       172.27.227.4                      0 77 41  i
*>                   172.28.128.4                      0 77 41  i
*   172.25.0.0       172.27.227.5                      0 77 51  i
*>                   172.28.128.5                      0 77 51  i
*   172.26.0.0       172.27.227.6                      0 77 61  i
*>                   172.28.128.6                      0 77 61  i
Washington>
```

Having observed that the 198.133.219.0/24 prefix (BGP) is present in the Lenexa router (which is a peer of Washington) but absent from the Washington router, you decide to re-examine the status of the routing protocols on the Washington router using the **show ip protocols** command (see Example 9-5). You notice that a distribute list named CIT is applied to inbound routes from the BGP neighbors of Washington. You realize that you were not observant enough the first time because you did not notice this filter.

**Example 9-5**    *Output of the Cisco IOS Command **show ip protocols** Showing a Distribute List Applied to the Inbound Updates Received from BGP Peers*

```
Washington>show ip protocols
Routing Protocol is "eigrp 202"
 .
 .
 .
```

**Example 9-5**  *Output of the Cisco IOS Command* **show ip protocols** *Showing a Distribute List Applied to the Inbound Updates Received from BGP Peers (Continued)*

```
  Neighbor(s):
    Address           FiltIn FiltOut DistIn DistOut Weight RouteMap
    172.27.227.7                     CIT
    172.28.128.8                     CIT
  Maximum path: 1
  Routing for Networks:
  Routing Information Sources:
    Gateway         Distance      Last Update
    (this router)       200       4d15h
    172.28.128.8         20       4d15h
    172.27.227.7         20       4d15h
  Distance: external 20 internal 200 local 200

Washington>
```

You then use the Cisco IOS **show access-lists** command to review the content of the access list named CIT (see Example 9-6). You know that networks (prefixes) that are not explicitly permitted by an access list are implicitly denied. You see that the access list named CIT does not permit the prefix 198.133.219.0/24 (Cisco Systems network). Therefore, the issue has been isolated to the missing network address in this access list.

**Example 9-6**  *Output of the Cisco IOS* **show access-lists** *Command*

```
Washington>show access-lists
Standard IP access list 21
    permit 172.28.128.7
    permit 172.28.128.8
    permit 172.27.227.7
    permit 172.27.227.8
    permit 172.22.0.0, wildcard bits 0.0.255.255
Standard IP access list CIT
    permit 172.21.0.0, wildcard bits 0.0.255.255 (5 matches) check=200
    permit 172.23.0.0, wildcard bits 0.0.255.255 (8 matches) check=192
    permit 172.24.0.0, wildcard bits 0.0.255.255 (12 matches) check=180
    permit 172.25.0.0, wildcard bits 0.0.255.255 (10 matches) check=170
    permit 172.26.0.0, wildcard bits 0.0.255.255 (10 matches) check=160
Extended IP access list dhcp_glean_acl (per-user)
    permit udp any eq bootpc host 255.255.255.255 eq bootps
Washington>
```

The following example demonstrates how system log messages can help isolate network layer problems. While still in charge of the network displayed in Figure 9-1, assume that one day Network Operations calls you to report that it can't ping or Telnet into the access switch named Columbia_SW from Washington. Network Operations does not recall changing any of the configurations. Observe Figure 9-2, which focuses on the local devices of the network examined in the previous example.

**Figure 9-2** *Network Diagram Displaying Columbia Access Router, Columbia_SW Access Switch, and the End Devices*

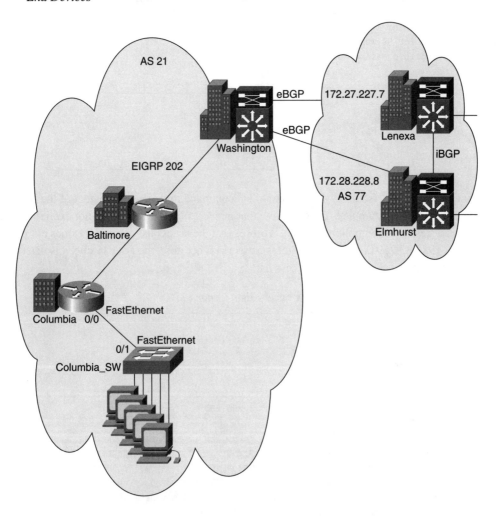

To help isolate the problem, you decide to review the current interface status on Columbia using the Cisco IOS **show ip interface brief** command. You see that the link providing connectivity to Columbia_SW—namely interface FastEthernet 0/0—is up. (See the top portion of Example 9-7.) You then check for the Columbia router's CDP neighbors with the **show cdp neighbor detail** command. (See the bottom portion of Example 9-7.) You observe that CDP packets are being received from Columbia_SW; nevertheless, you notice another fact that you suspect is the cause of the current issues and decide to show it to Network Operations.

**Example 9-7**  *Output of the* **show ip interfaces brief** *and* **show cdp neighbors detail** *Cisco IOS Commands*

```
Columbia>show ip interface brief
Interface              IP-Address      OK? Method Status        Protocol
Virtual-Access1        unassigned      YES unset  up            up
FastEthernet0/0        unassigned      YES manual up            up
FastEthernet0/0.1      172.22.121.1    YES manual up            up
FastEthernet0/0.2      172.22.122.1    YES manual up            up
FastEthernet0/0.3      172.22.123.1    YES manual up            up
Serial1/0              172.22.127.1    YES manual up            up
Serial1/1              172.22.127.129  YES manual up            up
.
.
.
Columbia>show cdp neighbors detail
.
.
.
Device ID: Columbia_SW
Entry address(es):
  IP address: 172.22.121.1
Platform: cisco WS-C2950T-24,  Capabilities: Switch IGMP
Interface: FastEthernet0/0,  Port ID (outgoing port): FastEthernet0/1
.
.
.
Columbia>
```

You call back Network Operations in Columbia and ask whether it has seen error messages on the console of Columbia or Columbia_SW. Network Operations tells you that it hasn't seen any. You ask it to input the Cisco IOS command **show logging** on Columbia to help isolate the issue. (You enter the command on Columbia as well so that you can discuss those results.) The results are shown in Example 9-8. You ask Network Operations to look at the output and see if console logging is reported as enabled or disabled. Your default practice is to have console logging enabled because console messages can provide useful information. Obviously, someone has disabled console logging (the first deviation from the baseline). You then suggest that Network Operations scan the output for reoccurring messages. Network Operations finally notices that there is a message reporting a duplicate IP address 172.22.121.1 on FastEthernet 0/0.1. This is indeed a network layer problem. You know from the baseline that Columbia should have an IP address 172.22.121.1 on FastEthernet 0/0.1, and Columbia_SW should use 172.22.121.2. If logging had been enabled, the isolation problem would have been trivial and noticed much earlier.

**Example 9-8**  *Output of the* **show logging** *Cisco IOS Command*

```
Columbia>show logging
Syslog logging: enabled (0 messages dropped, 1 messages rate-limited,
    0 flushes, 0 overruns)
    Console logging: disabled
.
.
```

*continues*

**Example 9-8**  *Output of the* **show logging** *Cisco IOS Command (Continued)*

```
Log Buffer (65536 bytes):
.
.
Dec 17 15:33:29: %IP-4-DUPADDR: Duplicate address 172.22.121.1 on
    FastEthernet0/0.1, sourced by 000a.8a44.de40
.
.
Columbia>
```

# Isolating a Problem Occurring at the Network Layer

The guidelines for isolating problems at the network layer are presented here. The goal of the following guidelines is to equip you with a set of effective and systematic techniques that elevate the chance of swift and successful network layer problem isolation:

- **Identify a single pair of problematic source and destination devices**—When you have identified the two devices that are the most likely source of the connectivity problem, test the connectivity between the two devices.

- **Ping a device across the connection**—Pinging a device verifies that the problem is at the network layer. If the ping fails (completely), check both the physical and data link layers. If the **ping** command is fully successful, the physical and data link layers are most likely functioning properly; the problem probably resides in the upper layers. Intermittent and partial success in **ping** results might be indicative of circuits going up and down, routes flapping, routing loops, and so on. Further investigation is necessary. Also, successful **ping** does not guarantee optimal network performance.

- **Test connectivity at each hop of a connection**—Every hop between the source and the destination has a potential for problems. Therefore, it is important that you test connectivity at each hop to determine where a problem exists.

- **Troubleshoot in both directions along an IP path**—A packet can have a working path in one direction (such as from the source to the destination) but not have a working path in the opposite direction. This situation happens because IP does not store path information in its packets. To prevent overlooking an error, perform all troubleshooting steps in both directions of an IP path.

> **NOTE**  The discussion on how asymmetric IP paths are formed and how/why this is the nature of IP routing is beyond the scope of this book; however, this asymmetric nature is important to remember and consider during the course of troubleshooting. Remember that just because Node X can send a packet to Node Y does not necessarily mean that Node Y can send a packet to Node X. Routing and QoS policies, management and security rules, and many other factors contribute to this phenomenon.

■ **Use a network diagram**—Use a network diagram to understand the path that the traffic should take. Compare the path that the traffic should have taken to the path that it is actually taking. This task is especially important when you are troubleshooting a problem across large networks. Traceroute is an invaluable tool for examining the path a packet takes. Beware of load-sharing paths and their effects on the traceroute results.

To illustrate how the provided guidelines can assist in a real network layer problem isolation scenario, assume that a group of users on an Ethernet LAN has reported that its connection to the Internet has gone down. Examining the topology diagram for the network, you determine which networking devices are the possible problematic ones. You use Cisco diagnostic commands to narrow the problem to a particular path involving multiple routers. You enter the **ping** command from the source router that the users have been attempting to connect through to the destination router. As expected, this test fails. You then enter the **ping** command from the destination router to the source router. The ping works. You test the connectivity between the source and destination routers at the physical and data link layers and determine that both layers are functioning correctly. The results indicate that you have a problem at the network layer. You execute appropriate **show** and **debug** commands on the path and discover that an erroneous static route in the routing table of one of the routers in the path is the cause of the problem.

# Foundation Summary

The "Foundation Summary" section of each chapter lists the most important facts from that chapter. Although this section does not list every fact from the chapter that will be on your CCNP exam, a well-prepared CCNP candidate should at a minimum know all the details in each "Foundation Summary" before taking the exam.

Following are some common symptoms of network layer problems:

- No component on the failing link appears to be functional above the network layer.

- The network is functional but is operating either consistently or intermittently at a lower capacity (speed, response, or throughput) than the baseline level.

- No connectivity on the link is seen from the transport layer.

- Pings succeed only part of the time.

- Routing tables are empty, inconsistent, or incomplete, and routing behavior is unexpected.

- Various console or system log messages report failures and problems.

- Management system alarms indicate problems/failures.

The following is a set of general end system commands to isolate network layer problems:

- **ping**

- **arp -a**

- **netstat -rn**

- **netstat -a**

- **traceroute /d** [*destination*]

The following are Windows commands to isolate network layer problems:

- **ipconfig /all** (on Windows NT/2000/XP)

- **route print**

- **tracert** [*destination*]

- **Winipcfg /all** (on Windows 9x/Me)

The following are UNIX/Mac OS X commands to isolate network layer problems:

■ **ifconfig -a**

■ **traceroute** [*destination*]

■ **route -n**

Following are some of the important general Cisco IOS commands that display/reveal information that is useful for isolating network layer problems:

■ **ping** {*host* | *ip-address*}

■ **traceroute** {*destination*}

■ **show running-config**

■ **[no] debug ?**

The following Cisco IOS ARP-related commands are useful for isolating address resolution-related issues:

■ **show ip arp**

■ **debug arp**

You can utilize the following Cisco IOS commands when isolating IP routing and interface problems:

■ **show ip route**

■ **debug ip routing**

■ **show ip interface [brief]**

You can facilitate BGP problem isolation by analyzing the output of the following Cisco IOS commands:

■ **show ip bgp**

■ **show ip bgp summary**

■ **show ip bgp neighbors**

■ **show ip bgp flap-statistics**

■ **debug ip bgp [dampening | events | keepalives | updates]**

Other useful commands for isolating IP traffic and access list problems are as follows:

■    **show ip traffic**

■    **debug ip icmp**

■    **debug ip packet**

■    **show ip access-lists** [*access-list-number* | *access-list-name*]

Use an effective and systematic technique to successfully isolate a problem at the network layer. Follow these guidelines to isolate network layer problems:

■    Identify a single pair of problematic source and destination devices.

■    Ping a device across the connection.

■    Test connectivity at each hop of a connection.

■    Troubleshoot in both directions along an IP path.

■    Use a network diagram.

# Q&A

As mentioned in the introduction, you have two choices for review questions. The questions that follow give you a bigger challenge than the exam does because they use an open-ended question format. By reviewing now with this more difficult question format, you can exercise your memory better and prove your conceptual and factual knowledge of this chapter. You can find the answers to these questions in Appendix A.

For more practice with exam-like question formats, including questions that use a router simulator and multiple choice format, use the exam engine on the CD.

1. Is it possible to have network layer problems while the addresses are correct and routing is operational and functional?

2. Is it possible to have a network layer problem—such as a router's address being duplicated by another router or device—but see no log messages on the console? Explain.

3. Is it possible that only a percentage of ping messages sent to an IP address succeed? Explain.

4. What does the command **route print** do? Is it an end system or a Cisco IOS command?

5. Provide three commands—one for Windows NT/2000/XP, one for Windows 9x/Me, and one for UNIX/MAC OS X—that display information about that device's IP settings (address and other information).

6. Which two Cisco IOS commands display and clear the content of the ARP cache table?

7. Which Cisco IOS command displays the list of local router interfaces, their IP addresses, and their physical and logical status?

8. List two Cisco IOS commands that display all BGP neighbors (peers) and the status of their peering with the local router. (One provides more detail than the other.)

9. Which Cisco IOS command displays the content of the BGP table?

10. It is important to use an effective and systematic technique to successfully isolate a problem at the network layer. Provide at least two of the recommended guidelines for isolating network layer problems.

## This chapter covers the following subjects:

- Cisco commands used to correct problems occurring at the network layer

- End system commands and applications used to correct problems occurring at the network layer

- Examples that demonstrate correction of network layer problems

- Network layer support resources

- Correcting problems occurring at the network layer

# CHAPTER 10

# Correcting a Problem at the Network Layer

The previous chapter covered isolating a problem at the network layer. After you have determined the most likely cause of the problem, the next stage of the general troubleshooting process is to correct the problem. This chapter's focus is correcting network layer problems using the appropriate and relevant commands and applications. This will complete your objective of resolving the network layer problems. You must use the tools and resources that Cisco IOS and your end systems' operating systems provide to configure the properties of your network.

## "Do I Know This Already?" Quiz

The purpose of the "Do I Know This Already?" quiz is to help you decide if you really need to read this entire chapter. If you already intend to read the entire chapter, you do not need to answer these questions now.

The 10-question quiz, derived from the major sections in the "Foundation Topics" portion of the chapter, helps you determine how to spend your limited study time.

Table 10-1 outlines the major topics discussed in this chapter and the "Do I Know This Already?" quiz questions that correspond to those topics.

**Table 10-1** *"Do I Know This Already?" Foundation Topics Section-to-Question Mapping*

| Foundation Topics Section | Questions Covered in This Section |
|---|---|
| "Cisco Commands Used to Correct Problems Occurring at the Network Layer" | 4 |
| "End System Commands and Applications Used to Correct Problems Occurring at the Network Layer" | 2 |
| "Network Layer Support Resources" | 2 |
| "Correcting Problems Occurring at the Network Layer" | 2 |

> **CAUTION** The goal of self-assessment is to gauge your mastery of the topics in this chapter. If you do not know the answer to a question or are only partially sure of the answer, you should mark this question wrong for purposes of the self-assessment. Giving yourself credit for an answer you correctly guess skews your self-assessment results and might provide you with a false sense of security.

1. Which of the following is a Cisco IOS command used to correct a problem directly related to the BGP routing protocol?

   a. **passive-interface** {*interface-type number*}

   b. **neighbor** {*ip-address | peer-group-name*} **update-source** *interface*

   c. **ip route** *prefix mask address* [*distance*]

   d. **ip mroute-cache**

2. Which end system command do you use to release or renew the leased IP information on a Windows 98 machine?

   a. **ipconfig**

   b. **arp**

   c. **winipcfg**

   d. **route delete**

3. Which Web site would you most likely use to read the latest detailed technical documentation about the EIGRP protocol?

   a. www.itu.int/home

   b. www.atmforum.com

   c. www.frforum.com

   d. www.cisco.com

4. While correcting a problem with a misconfigured access list, you notice that the problem is not solved despite the numerous changes you have made. Instead of making additional configuration changes, you wisely undo all your previous changes. Which step of the recommended procedure for correcting problems at the network layer are you performing?

   a. Make initial configuration changes.

   b. Stop making changes when the original problem appears to be solved.

   c. After the problem is solved, document the solution.

   d. Verify that the changes you make actually fix the problem without introducing new problems.

**5.** Select the Cisco IOS command that enables/disables the IP DNS-based host name-to-address translation.

  **a.** [no] **ip redirects**

  **b.** **bandwidth** *kilobits*

  **c.** [no] **ip proxy-arp**

  **d.** [no] **ip mroute-cache**

  **e.** [no] **ip domain-lookup**

**6.** Which of the following Cisco IOS commands applies an access list to an interface?

  **a.** **ip access-list**

  **b.** **ip access-group**

  **c.** **access-list**

  **d.** **distribute-list**

  **e.** **ip distribute-list**

**7.** Select the Cisco IOS command that enables/disables the sending of routing updates on a specific interface.

  **a.** [no] **passive-interface** *interface-type number*

  **b.** [no] **ip redirects**

  **c.** [no] **ip split-horizon**

  **d.** [no] **ip route-cache**

  **e.** [no] **ip mroute-cache**

**8.** Which of the following adds an entry to the IP routing table of an end system (running Windows 9x, for example)?

  **a.** **arp -d**

  **b.** **route add**

  **c.** **ipconfig**

  **d.** **winipcfg**

  **e.** **ifconfig**

9. Which of the following provides the correct URL for CCO?

    a. www.atmforum.com

    b. www.frforum.com

    c. www.cisco.com

    d. www.itu.int

    e. www.ietf.org

10. Which of the following should be the first step in correcting problems at the network layer?

    a. Make initial configuration changes.

    b. Stop making changes when the original problem appears to be solved.

    c. After the problem is solved, document the solution.

    d. Verify that the changes you make actually fix the problem without introducing new problems.

    e. Verify that you have a valid saved configuration for the device whose configuration you intend to modify.

You can find the answers to the "Do I Know This Already?" quiz in Appendix A, "Answers to the 'Do I Know This Already?' Quizzes and 'Q&A' Sections." The suggested choices for your next step are as follows:

- **8 or less overall score**—Read the entire chapter. This includes the "Foundation Topics" and "Foundation Summary" sections, as well as the "Q&A" section.

- **9 or 10 overall score**—If you want more review on these topics, skip to the "Foundation Summary" section and then go to the "Q&A" section. Otherwise, move to the next chapter.

# Foundation Topics

# Cisco Commands Used to Correct Problems Occurring at the Network Layer

This section lists a collection of Cisco IOS commands. These commands are used to correct different types of network layer problems and can be categorized as follows:

- General/global

- IP interface

- IP access list

- IP routing

A brief explanation is provided for each Cisco IOS command.

## General Command

The following command enables or disables (with the **no** form of the command) the ability of the router to generate a request for name to IP address resolution. If you are using the **ip name-server** *ip-address* global configuration command, an address for the name server is specified. A unicast request is sent to the name server (DNS server); otherwise, the request is sent using a User Datagram Protocol (UDP)-based broadcast. You enter this general IP command from the global configuration mode.

```
router(config)# [no] ip domain-lookup
```

## IP Interface Commands

The following command switches the prompt mode from the global configuration mode to the interface configuration mode (the particular interface name and number that was entered). In interface configuration, you can enter commands such as **bandwidth**, **ip address**, [no] **shut**, **encapsulation**, [no] **ip proxy-arp**, **ip access-group**, and so on.

```
Router(config)# interface type number
```

The following command sets the IP address and subnet mask of the interface. If the keyword **secondary** is used, the existing IP addresses remain, while this new address is added to the existing set of IP addresses on the interface. Based on the IP address and subnet mask of each of the interfaces, the IP routing process computes what networks the router is connected to.

```
Router(config-if)# ip address ip-address mask [secondary]
```

The following command enables or disables the sending of redirect messages on the local interface.

```
Router(config-if)# [no] ip redirects
```

Assume that S, R, and D are on the same IP subnet. If a router's IP interface (R) receives a packet (in a frame sent by S) and believes that packet must be forwarded to another IP device (D) on the local subnet, the IP interface (R) sends a redirect message to S and advises it to send the packet directly to D. (See the top of Figure 10-1.)

**Figure 10-1** *IP Redirects*

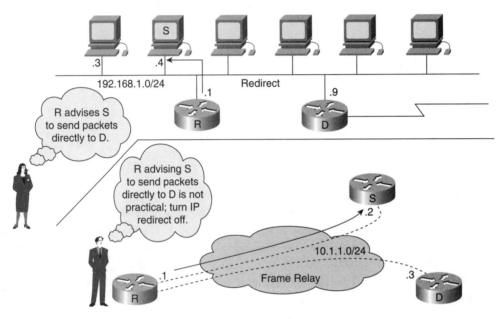

In some cases, you might need to turn off this feature. For example, if a Frame Relay multipoint connection is set up over a single IP subnet, you might need to turn off the IP redirects on the hub device. That is because the spokes in the hub and spoke setup do not have a direct link between them; therefore, advising one to send a packet directly to the other is not practical. (See the bottom of Figure 10-1.)

The following command specifies the value that you should use as the bandwidth of this interface for the purpose of computing the load/utilization of the interface. Some routing protocols, such as Open Shortest Path First (OSPF) and Enhanced Interior Gateway Routing Protocol (EIGRP), make use of this value to calculate routing metrics.

```
Router(config-if)# bandwidth kilobits
```

The following interface configuration command enables/disables the proxy Address Resolution Protocol (ARP) behavior on the interface. Proxy ARP is enabled by default; the router replies to an ARP request for an address other than its own, as long as the address is reachable via another one of its interfaces. If an IP interface of a router is connected to a segment in which some IP hosts rely on the proxy ARP behavior, keeping this command, which is the default setting on Cisco (router) IP interfaces, is crucial to the ability of those IP hosts to communicate with devices outside their subnet.

```
Router(config-if)# [no] ip proxy-arp
```

The following interface configuration command configures the interface to watch for UDP broadcasts (usually sent by Dynamic Host Configuration Protocol [DHCP], Network Time Protocol [NTP], Terminal Access Controller Access Control System [TACACS] clients, and so on) and send their request in the form of IP unicast to the server address that is specified. Because the requests that clients send are broadcasts, they cannot reach servers that are in other networks. The **helper-address** command ensures that the client request is sent to the address specified and that the server's reply goes back to the segment that the client request originated from. When the router sends a client request to the server, it actually specifies the network address from which the request originated. Based on that information, a server such as a DHCP knows from which address range to choose an IP lease and furnish it to the interested/requesting client.

```
Router(config-if)# ip helper-address address
```

The following command enables or disables IP multicast route caching on an interface.

```
Router(config-if)# [no] ip mroute-cache
```

## IP Access List Commands

The following command defines an extended IP access list. The access list number must be between 100 and 199.

```
Router(config)# access-list {access-list-number} {deny | permit}
    protocol source source-wildcard destination
    destination-wildcard [log]
```

The following command defines a standard or extended named IP access list.

```
Router(config)# ip access-list {standard | extended} {access-list-name}
```

The following command applies an access list to the interface. The keywords **in** and **out** specify whether the access list should be applied to the interface in the inbound or in the outbound direction. (The default is outbound.)

```
Router(config-if)# ip access-group {access-list-number | access-list-name} [in | out]
```

## IP Routing Commands

The following command configures a static route on the router. A static route has an administrative distance value of 0 if it points to an interface as the egress interface. A static route has an administrative distance value of 1 if it points to an IP address as the next hop. However, you can also specify an administrative distance that suits your needs for the static route.

```
Router(config)# ip route prefix mask {address | interface-type} [admin-distance]
```

The following command configures a manual static default (gateway of last resort) route on the router.

```
Router(config)# ip route 0.0.0.0 0.0.0.0 {address | interface-type} [distance]
```

The following interface command enables or disables use of fast-switching cache on the particular interface. A router that has fast switching enabled (default) forwards packets more quickly by routing the first packet in a packet train and building a cache entry and then switching the following packets using the cache entry created during the processing of the first packet. This feature must be left on unless it is in conflict with another required feature/technology. The fast-switching cache is kept in shared memory. As you can see, this feature is turned off for some interfaces (and selected protocols) but left on for others.

```
Router(config-if)# [no] ip route-cache
```

The following interface configuration command enables or disables IP split horizon on the particular interface. This command is applicable to distance vector protocols (IGRP and RIP). However, it is seldom used. One place that you can use this command might be on a hub that has a multipoint connection (such as with Frame Relay) to two or more spoke sites. This hub might want to pass (send out) routes learned from one spoke site to the other spoke site(s). On a multipoint interface, this means that the route learned from an interface is sent out the same interface it was learned from, thereby breaking the split-horizon rule of distance-vector routing protocols.

```
Router(config-if)# [no] ip split-horizon
```

The following command configures a particular routing process (such as RIP and (E)IGRP) to *not* send updates out of a particular interface.

```
Router(config-router)# passive-interface interface-type number
```

The **network** command configures a particular interior routing process (such as RIP, (E)IGRP, or OSPF) to determine and go active on all those local interfaces whose IP addresses match this statement. The routing process advertises the networks that are connected via those interfaces as its locally connected networks (links). The **network** command, when used within a BGP process, has a different role/effect: It makes the BGP process advertise the mentioned prefix as a local network, provided that the network is present in the IP forwarding table (reachable).

For RIP and IGRP:

```
Router(config-router)# network classful-address
```

For EIGRP:

```
Router(config-router)# network address [wildcard-mask]
```

For OSPF:

```
Router(config-router)# network address inverted-mask area area-number
```

For BGP:

```
Router(config-router)# network network-number [mask network-mask]
```

# End System Commands and Applications Used to Correct Problems Occurring at the Network Layer

This section identifies a group of end system commands and applications that you can use to correct problems at the network layer.

The following command allows you to delete an entry from the end system's ARP table.

```
arp -d
```

The next command adds a static IP route to the end system's routing table.

```
route add
```

The following command allows you to check, release, or renew the end system's IP address lease. This command is available on systems that are running Windows NT, Windows 2000, and Windows XP operating systems.

```
ipconfig
```

The next command allows you to check, release, or renew the end system's IP address lease. This command is available on systems that are running Windows 9x and Windows Me operating systems.

```
winipcfg
```

The following command configures IP information on hosts that are running Mac OS X and UNIX.

```
ifconfig
```

# Examples That Demonstrate Correction of Network Layer Problems

So that you can practice correcting a network layer problem that has already been isolated, this section continues and corrects the two cases that were started in the previous chapter. To refresh your memory, both cases begin with the background information.

## Correcting an Access List to Stop a Router from Rejecting a Prefix Sent from a BGP Peer

You are the second-level network engineer responsible for sites in Washington, Baltimore, and Columbia. (The routers in each city are named after the city names.) The devices are arranged and connected as shown in Figure 10-2.

**Figure 10-2** *Network You Are Responsible For, and Connections to ISP1 and ISP2*

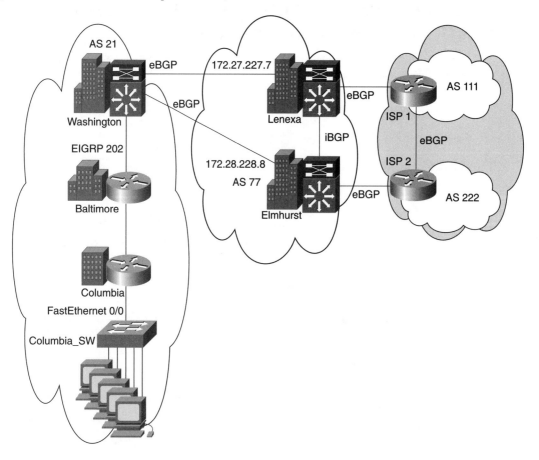

You have determined that the route 198.133.219.0/24 that belongs to Cisco Systems is not in the routing tables for any of your devices. This prefix is supposed to be in the routing table for all devices. As a result of your investigation and review of the access lists on Washington, you have discovered that the Cisco network 198.133.219.0/24 is not permitted by the access list called CIT. The access list CIT is applied to the BGP neighbors of Washington in the inbound direction using the **distribution-list in** command. To correct the problem, you need to expand the CIT access list to permit 198.133.219.0/24. You go into configuration mode and update the access list. (See the top of Example 10-1.) You then verify that the access list was updated. (See the bottom of Example 10-1.)

**Example 10-1**  *Adding a Statement to an Existing Access List and Verifying the Access List*

```
Washington(config)#ip access-list standard CIT
Washington(config-std-nacl)# remark Include Cisco network as well
Washington(config-std-nacl)# permit 198.133.219.0 0.0.0.255
Washington(config-std-nacl)#exit
Washington#
Oct 27 14:19:48: %SYS-5-CONFIG_I: Configured from console by console
Washington#show access-lists
Standard IP access list 21
    permit 172.28.128.7
    permit 172.28.128.8
    permit 172.27.227.7
    permit 172.27.227.8
    permit 172.22.0.0, wildcard bits 0.0.255.255
Standard IP access list CIT
    permit 172.21.0.0, wildcard bits 0.0.255.255 (4 matches) check=158
    permit 172.23.0.0, wildcard bits 0.0.255.255 (6 matches) check=152
    permit 172.24.0.0, wildcard bits 0.0.255.255 (10 matches) check=142
    permit 172.25.0.0, wildcard bits 0.0.255.255 (8 matches) check=134
    permit 172.26.0.0, wildcard bits 0.0.255.255 (8 matches) check=126
    permit 198.133.219.0, wildcard bits 0.0.0.255
Washington#
```

You now check to see if the Cisco Systems route is in the BGP table on Washington. The network 198.133.219.0 is not yet present. You need to clear the BGP session when you change the inbound or outbound policy for the session. Changing the inbound access list changes the inbound policy for a BGP session. You use the **debug ip routing** command to watch for routing updates and then clear the BGP session with the corporate core neighbors in AS 77. (See the top of Example 10-2.) You know that the 198.133.219.0 route has been added when you see the line "RT: Nexthop for 198.133.219.0/24 updated." Now you verify that the Cisco Systems route is in the BGP table on Washington. (See the middle of Example 10-2.) You verify that the Cisco Systems address is also in the IP routing table by entering the **show ip route** command. (See the bottom of Example 10-2.) The 198.133.219.0 route is now present in the routing table on Washington.

**Example 10-2** *Output of* **debug ip routing**, **show ip bgp**, *and* **show ip route** *After Clearing the BGP Session*

```
Washington#debug ip routing
Washington#clear ip bgp 77
Oct 27 14:23:46: %BGP-5-ADJCHANGE: neighbor 172.27.227.7 Down User reset
Oct 27 14:23:46: %BGP-5-ADJCHANGE: neighbor 172.28.128.8 Down User reset
.

.
Oct 27 14:24:05: %BGP-5-ADJCHANGE: neighbor 172.27.227.7 Up
Oct 27 14:24:05.475: RT: Nexthop for 198.133.219.0/24 updated
Washington#no debug all
All possible debugging has been turned off
Washington#
Washington#show ip bgp
BGP table version is 38, local router ID is 172.22.129.1
Status codes: s suppressed, d damped, h history, * valid, > best, i - internal
Origin codes: i - IGP, e - EGP, ? - incomplete
   Network          Next Hop          Metric LocPrf Weight Path
*> 172.21.0.0       172.28.128.1                       0 77 11 i
.

.
*  198.133.219.0    172.28.128.8                       0 77 222 111 i
*>                  172.27.227.7                       0 77 111 i
Washington#
Washington#show ip route
Codes: C - connected, S - static, I - IGRP, R - RIP, M - mobile, B - BGP
       D - EIGRP, EX - EIGRP external, O - OSPF, IA - OSPF inter area
       N1 - OSPF NSSA external type 1, N2 - OSPF NSSA external type 2
       E1 - OSPF external type 1, E2 - OSPF external type 2, E - EGP
       i - IS-IS, L1 - IS-IS level-1, L2 - IS-IS level-2, ia - IS-IS inter area
       * - candidate default, U - per-user static route, o - ODR
       P - periodic downloaded static route
.

.
B    172.26.0.0/16 [20/0] via 172.27.227.6, 00:03:15
     172.28.0.0/28 is subnetted, 1 subnets
C       172.28.128.0 is directly connected, Vlan28
B    198.133.219.0/24 [20/0] via 172.27.227.7, 00:03:15
S*   0.0.0.0/0 [1/0] via 172.28.128.8
Washington#
```

As a final validation that the network layer issue has been resolved, you use the **show ip route** command on Baltimore and Columbia to verify that those routers also have the 198.133.219.0/24 route in their routing table (see Example 10-3). The Cisco Systems route has been restored to all your devices. You have resolved the network layer issue and restored your baseline configuration.

**Example 10-3**  *Checking Routing Tables of Baltimore and Columbia*

```
Baltimore> show ip route
 .
 .
 .
D EX 172.25.0.0/16 [170/284160] via 172.22.128.130, 00:05:06, FastEthernet0/0
D EX 172.24.0.0/16 [170/284160] via 172.22.128.130, 00:05:06, FastEthernet0/0
D EX 172.26.0.0/16 [170/284160] via 172.22.128.130, 00:05:06, FastEthernet0/0
D EX 198.133.219.0/24 [170/284160] via 172.22.128.130, 00:05:06, FastEthernet0/0
D*EX 0.0.0.0/0 [170/28416] via 172.22.128.130, 3d22h, FastEthernet0/0
Baltimore>

Columbia> show ip route
 .
 .
 .
D EX 172.25.0.0/16 [170/3873280] via 172.22.126.2, 00:06:48, Serial0/0:0
D EX 172.24.0.0/16 [170/3873280] via 172.22.126.2, 00:06:48, Serial0/0:0
D EX 172.26.0.0/16 [170/3873280] via 172.22.126.2, 00:06:48, Serial0/0:0
D EX 198.133.219.0/24 [170/3873280] via 172.22.126.2, 00:06:48, Serial0/0:0
D*EX 0.0.0.0/0 [170/3847936] via 172.22.126.2, 3d22h, Serial0/0:0
Columbia>
```

## Correcting a Duplicate IP Address Problem

Moving on to the second case from Chapter 9, assume that you are the second-level network engineer for the offices of a corporation that has locations in Washington, Baltimore, and Columbia. The routers at each location are named after the cities in which they reside. One day, Network Operations calls to report that it can't ping or Telnet into the access switch named Columbia_SW from Washington. Network Operations does not recall changing any of the configurations. Figure 10-3 focuses on the local devices of the network examined in the previous example.

You have determined that a duplicate IP address 172.22.121.1 exists on the FastEthernet between Columbia and Columbia_SW. You know from the baseline that Columbia should have an IP address of 172.22.121.1/26 on FastEthernet 0/0.1 and Columbia_SW should use 172.22.121.2/26. To correct the problem, Network Operations needs to modify the IP address on Columbia_SW. As a good practice, it should also restore console logging. Network Operations goes into configuration mode and tries to update the IP address on FastEthernet 0/1 on Columbia_SW. Network Operations calls you back, stating that it cannot configure the IP address on FastEthernet 0/1 because it is a switched interface (see Example 10-4).

**Figure 10-3** *Network Diagram Displaying the Columbia Access Router, the Columbia_SW Access Switch, and the End Devices*

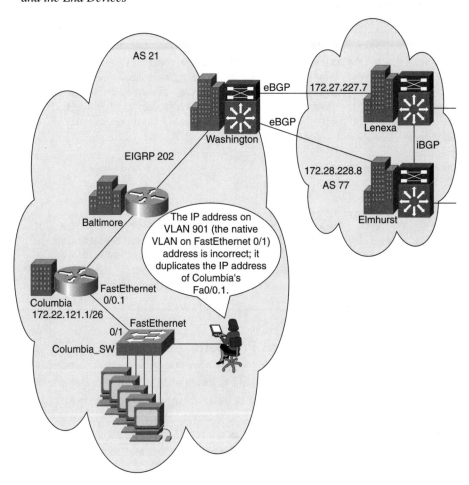

**Example 10-4** *Attempt to Configure the IP Address on a Layer 2 (Switching) Interface of a Switch*

```
Columbia_SW>enable
Columbia_SW#configure terminal
Enter configuration commands, one per line.  End with CNTL/Z.
Columbia_SW(config)#interface fastethernet 0/1
Columbia_SW(config-if)#ip address 172.22.121.2 255.255.255.192

% IP addresses may not be configured on L2 links.

Columbia_SW(config-if)#exit
Columbia_SW(config)#logging console
Oct 27 17:33:43: %IP-4-DUPADDR: Duplicate address 172.22.121.1 on Vlan901,
    sourced by 0007.8580.a157
```

You ask Network Operations to enter the **show running-config interface FastEthernet 0/1** command from the Privileged Exec mode and look for the native VLAN for the 2950 switch. The results (see the top of Example 10-5) tell you that the interface FastEthernet 0/1 is a switch port in trunk mode and its native VLAN is vlan 901. You then ask Network Operations to enter the **show ip interface brief** command and confirm that this interface (vlan 901) is active. (See the middle of Example 10-5.) Finally, you direct Network Operations to change the IP address on the vlan 901 interface. (See the bottom of Example 10-5.)

**Example 10-5**   *Output of* **show running-config** *and* **show ip interface brief commands** *and Changing the IP Address of a VLAN Interface*

```
Columbia_SW#show running-config interface fastEthernet 0/1
Building configuration...

Current configuration : 310 bytes
!
interface FastEthernet0/1
 switchport trunk native vlan 901
 switchport mode trunk
 no ip address
 duplex full
 speed 100
 storm-control broadcast level 1.00 0.50
 storm-control multicast level 10.00 5.00
 storm-control unicast level 10.00 5.00
 storm-control action shutdown
 storm-control action trap
end
Columbia_SW#

Columbia_SW#show ip interface brief
Interface               IP-Address      OK? Method Status                Protocol
Vlan1                   unassigned      YES manual administratively down down
Vlan901                 172.22.121.1    YES manual up                    up
FastEthernet0/1         unassigned      YES unset  up                    up
.
.
Columbia_SW#

Columbia_SW#configure terminal
Columbia_SW(config)#interface vlan901
Columbia_SW(config-if)#ip address 172.22.121.2 255.255.255.192
Columbia_SW(config-if)#end
Columbia_SW#
.Oct 27 17:33:58: %SYS-5-CONFIG_I: Configured from console by console
```

To test that the new configuration will work, Network Operations verifies that Columbia_SW can reach Columbia. (See the top of Example 10-6.) You then verify that Columbia and Washington routers can reach Columbia_SW. (See the bottom of Example 10-6.) The duplicate IP address has been replaced with the proper IP address. You have resolved the network layer issue and restored your baseline configuration.

**Example 10-6**  *Verifying Connectivity Between Routers Using* **ping**

```
Columbia_SW>ping columbia
Type escape sequence to abort.
Sending 5, 100-byte ICMP Echos to 172.22.125.1, timeout is 2 seconds:
!!!!!
Success rate is 100 percent (5/5), round-trip min/avg/max = 1/2/4 ms
Columbia_SW>

Columbia>ping columbia_SW
Type escape sequence to abort.
Sending 5, 100-byte ICMP Echos to 172.22.121.2, timeout is 2 seconds:
!!!!!
Success rate is 100 percent (5/5), round-trip min/avg/max = 1/2/4 ms
Columbia>

Washington>ping columbia_sw
Type escape sequence to abort.
Sending 5, 100-byte ICMP Echos to 172.22.121.2, timeout is 2 seconds:
!!!!!
Success rate is 100 percent (5/5), round-trip min/avg/max = 28/32/36 ms
Washington>
```

# Network Layer Support Resources

Despite the level of your knowledge and experience about networking protocols, tools, and commands, sometimes you will need to consult an outside resource. These support resources are commonly used as reference materials for commands and configuration procedures, as well as research for technology-specific information and industry standards. Given the ability to use online support resources for effective research, you save yourself time that you might have otherwise spent on the phone with a support professional and money you would have committed to hiring a consultant.

For command and configuration references, go to the source. The Cisco Systems Web site has one of the largest collections of networking information on the Internet. Visit the Technical Assistance Center, Cisco Connection Online (CCO), and technology reference pages to find information for troubleshooting Cisco Systems products. To learn more about industry standards, visit the Internet Engineering Task Force (IETF), International Telecommunications Union (ITU-T), Frame Relay Forum, and ATM Forum. These sites contain detailed documentation about a wide array of networking technologies.

Table 10-2 provides the Web addresses for all these sites.

**Table 10-2**  *Support Resources to Correct Network Layer Problems*

| Internet Web Site | URL |
|---|---|
| Cisco Systems Technical Assistance Center | www.cisco.com/tac/ |
| CCO | www.cisco.com |
| Cisco Systems Technologies Reference | www.cisco.com/univercd/home/home.htm |
| IETF | www.ietf.org |
| ITU-T | www.itu.int/home |
| Frame Relay Forum | www.frforum.com |
| ATM Forum | www.atmforum.com |

# Correcting Problems Occurring at the Network Layer

This section provides a step-by-step procedure that you can use to correct isolated problems at the network layer:

1. Ensure that you have a valid saved configuration for the device whose configuration you intend to modify. This provides for eventual recovery to a known initial state.

2. Make initial hardware and software configuration changes. If the correction requires more than one change, make only one change at a time.

3. Evaluate and document the changes and the results of each change that you make. If you perform your problem-solving steps and the results are unsuccessful, immediately undo the changes. If the problem is intermittent, you might need to wait to see if the problem occurs again before you can evaluate the effect of your changes.

4. Verify that the changes you make actually fix the problem without introducing new problems. The network should be returned to the baseline operation, and no new or old symptoms should be present. If the problem is not solved, undo all your changes. If you discover new or additional problems while you are correcting, step back and modify your correction plan.

5. Continue making changes until the original problem appears to be solved.

6. If necessary, get input from outside resources. If none of your attempts to correct the problem is successful, take the problem to another person. This might be a co-worker, consultant, or Cisco's Technical Assistance Center. On rare occasions, you might need to perform a core dump, which creates output that a specialist at Cisco Systems can analyze.

7. After you resolve the problem, document the solution.

# Foundation Summary

The "Foundation Summary" section of each chapter lists the most important facts from that chapter. Although this section does not list every fact from the chapter that will be on your CCNP exam, a well-prepared CCNP candidate should at a minimum know all the details in each "Foundation Summary" before taking the exam.

**Table 10-3**  *Cisco IOS Commands to Correct Network Layer Problems*

| Focus | Command | Description |
|---|---|---|
| General | **[no] ip domain-lookup** | Enables the IP Domain Name System (DNS)-based host name-to-address translation. To disable, enter the **no** form of this command. |
| Interface configuration | **interface** {*interface-type number* } | Accesses a specified interface while in global configuration mode. |
| | **ip address** *ip-address mask* [**secondary**] | Specifies a primary or secondary IP address for an interface. |
| | **[no] ip redirects** | Enables (**no** disables) the sending of redirect messages through the same interface on which they were received. |
| | **bandwidth** *kilobits* | Communicates the bandwidth value of an interface to the higher-level protocols. |
| | **[no] ip proxy-arp** | Enables proxy ARP on an interface. (**no** disables it.) |
| | **[no] ip mroute-cache** | Enables IP multicast fast or multicast distributed switching. (**no** disables it.) |
| Access list | **access-list** {*access-list-number* } {**deny** \| **permit**} *protocol source source-wildcard destination destination-wildcard* [**log**] | Defines an extended access list. |
| | **ip access-list** {**standard** \| **extended**} {*access-list-name* } | Defines a standard or extended named access list. |
| | **ip access-group** {*access-list-number* \| *access-list-name* } [**in** \| **out**] | Applies an access list to an IP interface in the inbound or outbound (default) direction. |

**Table 10-3**  *Cisco IOS Commands to Correct Network Layer Problems (Continued)*

| Focus | Command | Description |
|---|---|---|
| IP routing | **ip route** *prefix mask address* [*distance* ] | Configures a static route. |
| | **ip route 0.0.0.0 0.0.0.0** {*ip-address* \| *interface-type number*  } [*distance* ] | Configures a default route (gateway of last resort). |
| | **ip route-cache** | Enables the use of a fast-switching cache for an interface. |
| | **ip split-horizon** | Enables split horizon. |
| | [**no**] **passive-interface** {*interface-type number*  } | Enables and disables the sending of routing updates on a specific interface. |
| | For RIP and IGRP:<br><br>Router(config-router)# **network** *classful-address*<br><br>For EIGRP:<br><br>Router(config-router)# **network** *address* [*wildcard-mask* ]<br><br>For OSPF:<br><br>Router(config-router)# **network** *address inverted-mask*  **area** *area-number*<br><br>For BGP:<br><br>Router(config-router)# **network** *network-number*  [**mask** *network-mask* ] | The **network** command configures a particular interior routing process (such as RIP, (E)IGRP, or OSPF) to determine and go active on all those local interfaces whose IP addresses match this statement. The routing process advertises the networks that are connected via those interfaces as its locally connected networks (links). The **network** command, when used within a BGP process, has a different role/effect: It makes the BGP process advertise the mentioned prefix as a local network, provided that the network is present in the IP forwarding table (reachable). |

**Table 10-4**  *End System Commands to Correct Problems at the Network Layer*

| Type/OS Category | Command | Description |
|---|---|---|
| General | **arp –d** | Deletes entries from an ARP table |
| | **route add** | Adds static routes to a routing table |
| Windows NT/2000/XP | **ipconfig** | Configures IP information on hosts that are running Windows NT/2000/XP |

*continues*

**Table 10-4**    *End System Commands to Correct Problems at the Network Layer (Continued)*

| Type/OS Category | Command | Description |
|---|---|---|
| Windows 98/Me | **winipcfg** | Configures IP information on hosts that are running Windows 98 and Windows Me |
| UNIX/Mac OS X | **ifconfig** | Configures IP information on hosts that are running Mac OS X and UNIX |

**Table 10-5**    *Support Resources for Correcting Network Layer Problems*

| Internet Web Site | URL |
|---|---|
| Cisco Systems Technical Assistance Center | www.cisco.com/tac/ |
| CCO | www.cisco.com |
| Cisco Systems Technologies Reference | www.cisco.com/univercd/home/home.htm |
| IETF | www.ietf.org |
| ITU-T | www.itu.int/home |
| Frame Relay Forum | www.frforum.com |
| ATM Forum | www.atmforum.com |

**Table 10-6**    *Correcting Network Layer Problems*

| Step | Description |
|---|---|
| **Step 1** | Verify that you have a valid saved configuration for the device whose configuration you intend to modify. |
| **Step 2** | Make initial configuration changes. |
| **Step 3** | Evaluate and document the results of each change that you make. |
| **Step 4** | Verify that the changes you make actually fix the problem without introducing new problems. |
| **Step 5** | Continue making changes until the original problem appears to be solved. |
| **Step 6** | If necessary, get input from outside resources. |
| **Step 7** | After you have solved the problem, document the solution. |

# Q&A

As mentioned in the introduction, you have two choices for review questions. The questions that follow give you a bigger challenge than the exam because they use an open-ended question format. By reviewing now with this more difficult question format, you can exercise your memory better and prove your conceptual and factual knowledge of this chapter. You can find the answers to these questions in Appendix A.

For more practice with exam-like question formats, including questions that use a router simulator and multiple choice format, use the exam engine on the CD.

1. Explain the effect of the command **ip address 192.168.1.20 255.255.255.0 secondary**.

2. What will the command **interface Ethernet 0** do?

3. Explain the purpose of *distance* in the command **ip route** *prefix mask address* [*distance*].

4. What end system command allows you to configure IP information on hosts that are running UNIX?

5. Which Cisco IOS command enables or disables console logging?

6. Which Cisco IOS command can you use to display the configured access lists on a router?

7. What is the URL for Cisco Systems' Technical Assistance Center?

8. What is the last task that you should perform after correcting a problem?

9. List the seven recommended steps for correcting problems at the network layer.

The following CIT exam topics are covered in this part. (To view the CIT exam outline, visit www.cisco.com/go/training.)

- Verify connectivity at all layers.

- Use Cisco IOS commands and applications to identify system problems at all layers.

- Isolate system problems to one or more specific layers.

- Resolve suboptimal system performance problems at Layers 2 through 7.

- Restore optimal baseline service.

- Work with external providers to resolve service provision problems.

- Work with system users to resolve network-related end-use problems.

# Part V: Resolving Problems at the Transport and Application Layers

## This chapter covers the following subjects:

- Symptoms of problems occurring at the transport layer

- Symptoms of problems occurring at the application layer

- Commands and applications used to isolate problems occurring at the transport layer

- Commands and applications used to isolate problems occurring at the application layer

- Guidelines for isolating a problem occurring at the transport or application layer

# Isolating a Problem at the Transport or Application Layer

To isolate problems at the transport and application layers, you use the general troubleshooting process for analyzing the gathered symptoms. The troubleshooting approach at these layers is similar to the processes presented in the previous chapters for the lower OSI layers. At the transport and application layers, issues usually revolve around whether the application is running at the target device, whether name resolution operates with success, whether router access lists permit flow of application data, and so on. This chapter first identifies the symptoms of problems occurring at the transport and application layer. Next, this chapter lists useful commands for isolating problems at the transport and application layers and explains their output. Finally, this chapter presents a set of guidelines for isolating a problem at the transport or application layer.

## "Do I Know This Already?" Quiz

The purpose of the "Do I Know This Already?" quiz is to help you decide if you really need to read this entire chapter. If you already intend to read the entire chapter, you do not need to answer these questions now.

The 10-question quiz, derived from the major sections in the "Foundation Topics" portion of the chapter, helps you determine how to spend your limited study time.

Table 11-1 outlines the major topics discussed in this chapter and the "Do I Know This Already?" quiz questions that correspond to those topics.

**Table 11-1** *"Do I Know This Already?" Foundation Topics Section-to-Question Mapping*

| Foundation Topics Section | Questions Covered in This Section |
|---|---|
| "Symptoms of Problems Occurring at the Transport Layer" | 2 |
| "Symptoms of Problems Occurring at the Application Layer" | 2 |
| "Commands and Applications Used to Isolate Problems Occurring at the Transport Layer" | 2 |

*continues*

**Table 11-1** *"Do I Know This Already?" Foundation Topics Section-to-Question Mapping (Continued)*

| Foundation Topics Section | Questions Covered in This Section |
|---|---|
| "Commands and Applications Used to Isolate Problems Occurring at the Application Layer" | 2 |
| "Guidelines for Isolating a Problem Occurring at the Transport or Application Layer" | 2 |

**CAUTION** The goal of self-assessment is to gauge your mastery of the topics in this chapter. If you do not know the answer to a question or are only partially sure of the answer, you should mark this question wrong for purposes of the self-assessment. Giving yourself credit for an answer you correctly guess skews your self-assessment results and might provide you with a false sense of security.

1.  Select the answer that best describes symptoms of failure problems at the transport layer.

    a.  Layers 1 and 2 have connectivity problems.

    b.  All applications and protocols except the upper layers function properly.

    c.  All layers up to and including the network layer are operating as per baseline; nothing above that is.

    d.  An excessive number of CRC errors has been logged.

    e.  Routers boot into ROMMON.

2.  A user has reported that the network is slow, there is partial or intermittent connectivity, and some behavior on the network is erratic. Which of the following might be the cause?

    a.  Transport layer protocol windowing problems

    b.  Long round-trip times

    c.  Retransmissions

    d.  Fragmentation or duplicates

    e.  All of the above

3.  A user complains of a particular network application problem, while stating that he can ping devices as usual. Which of the following would indicate that the problem is related to the application?

    a.  Other applications that use the same transport layer protocol as the failing application are functioning properly. No other problems have been reported.

    b.  Other applications that use the same transport layer protocol are experiencing problems as well.

    c.  There are also problems at the network layer.

    d.  The network is slower than usual.

    e.  All of the above.

4.  An application layer problem is indicated by a network problem that occurs at which of the following OSI layers? (Select all that apply.)

    a.  Transport layer

    b.  Session layer

    c.  Presentation layer

    d.  Application layer

    e.  Security layer

5.  Which of the following IP host (Windows 9x/2000/XP) commands lists the remote machine's name table (NetBIOS) given its IP address?

    a.  **netstat –r** *ip-address*

    b.  **nbtstat –A** *ip-address*

    c.  **ns-lookup** *ip-address*

    d.  **print name-table** *ip-address*

    e.  **show netbios all**

6.  Which of the following commands is useful for isolating TCP problems?

    a.  **show ip access-lists**

    b.  **show ip traffic**

    c.  **telnet** {*ip-address* | *host*} [*port*]

    d.  **show running-config**

    e.  All of the above

7. Which command can you use to test the functionality of the Simple Mail Transfer Protocol (SMTP) protocol?

   a. **test smtp**

   b. **debug udp**

   c. **telnet** *ip-address* **80**

   d. **telnet** *ip-address* **25**

   e. **show ip SMTP-server**

8. Which of the following are not considered directly useful for isolating file management problems? (Select two.)

   a. **nslookup** {*domain-name*}

   b. **copy tftp flash**

   c. **telnet** {*ip-address* | *host*} **21**

   d. **debug tftp**

   e. **debug ntp events**

9. A group of users from a common LAN segment has reported File Transfer Protocol (FTP) problems, whereas other users have not reported problems. Those users who are having FTP problems do have IP connectivity and can send e-mail. You have verified that the FTP server is up by Telnetting into it. What is the next best thing for you to do?

   a. Reboot the Dynamic Host Configuration Protocol (DHCP) server that serves these users.

   b. Investigate the users' default gateway.

   c. Turn debug on all routers and start analyzing.

   d. Tell users to keep trying to connect; the problem will go away.

   e. Refer to the RFCs related to FTP and learn about FTP port numbers, FTP session setup, and so on.

10. Which of the following are useful guidelines for isolating problems at the transport and application layers?

    a. Inspect the physical layer first because all layers depend on it.

    b. First establish whether IP connectivity exists between the source and the destination.

    c. If you are troubleshooting e-mail problems, make sure you test sending and receiving e-mail functions together.

    d. Thoroughly check the configuration of the routing protocols on the routers.

    e. Avoid using Telnet and debug commands because they are extremely detrimental to routers' behavior.

You can find the answers to the "Do I Know This Already?" quiz in Appendix A, "Answers to the 'Do I Know This Already?' Quizzes and 'Q&A' Sections." The suggested choices for your next step are as follows:

- **8 or less overall score**—Read the entire chapter. This includes the "Foundation Topics" and "Foundation Summary" sections, as well as the "Q&A" section.

- **9 or 10 overall score**—If you want more review on these topics, skip to the "Foundation Summary" section and then go to the "Q&A" section. Otherwise, move to the next chapter.

# Foundation Topics

The primary responsibility of the upper layers of the OSI model is providing services such as e-mail and file transfer. Upper layers must also handle transportation of the data used by applications to the lower layers. If a problem arises at these layers, the result is that the data is not delivered to the destination. Alternatively, the performance might be so slow that it affects productivity, and administrators will likely hear complaints from the users. To avoid extended or periodic losses in the ability to transmit data or degradation in performance, you should be able to effectively isolate problems at the transport and application layers.

## Symptoms of Problems Occurring at the Transport Layer

When the transport layer has problems, you can observe the symptoms at the application layer. Session layer protocols and network applications rely on the correct operation and services that the transport layer provides. With transport layer problems, users notice a lack of connectivity to network resources or network applications that do not function. The main transport layer protocols of the TCP/IP suite are Transmission Control Protocol (TCP) and User Datagram Protocol (UDP). (Real-Time Transport Protocol also has become a main player in recent years.) Familiarity with the TCP and UDP port numbers that application layer protocols use certainly facilitates problem isolation, especially when analyzing the IP access lists that are applied to router interfaces. Typical symptoms of a failure/problem at the transport layer can include one or more of the following:

- Unreachable resources and connectivity problems are an issue, while the physical, data link, and network layers are functional.

- The network is operating either consistently or intermittently less than the baseline level.

- Applications generate error messages; they might report link or connectivity problems (as they perceive it).

- Users complain that the network is slow or report of intermittent connectivity or erratic behavior.

- Console messages report abnormal events; unexpected events are observed in system log messages.

- Management system alarms indicate problems.

- Partial or intermittent connectivity or erratic performance results from TCP windowing problems, long round-trip times, excess retransmissions, and so on.

## Symptoms of Problems Occurring at the Application Layer

The application layer of the TCP/IP suite maps to the session (Layer 5), presentation (Layer 6), and application (Layer 7) layers of the OSI model. Therefore, issues that are related to any of these layers should be referred to as application layer problems within the TCP/IP framework. You can categorize a problem as a pure application layer problem if you can prove that all the lower layers up to the transport layer are in good working condition. Application layer problems might be rooted at the application server devices, client hosts, firewalls, routers, or multilayer switches. Typical symptoms of a failure/problem at the application layer can include one or more of the following:

- Resources are unreachable or unusable, while the physical, data link, network, and transport layers are functional.

- Operation of a network service or application does not meet a user's normal expectations.

- Applications generate error messages or report lack of functionality.

- Users complain that the network is slow or that their network applications are not functioning, are unavailable, or are too slow.

- Console messages indicate abnormal events; system log file messages report errors.

- Management system alarms deliver unexpected news.

You can observe some of these symptoms when the problem actually springs from the layers below the application layer. However, the fact remains that problems sourced at different layers of the OSI model can indeed yield similar symptoms. Therefore, it is your responsibility to isolate the problem, correct it, and document the results.

## Commands and Applications Used to Isolate Problems Occurring at the Transport Layer

To ascertain that a problem is rooted at the transport layer rather than at a layer below it, you must use proper tools and commands. You can test the operability of Layers 1, 2, and 3 by using the Windows commands **ping**, **tracert**, **netstat**, and **nbtstat**. If the results prove that the lower layers (physical, data link, and network) are in good working order, you can focus your attention on Layer 4-related issues such as filters, policies, quality of service (QoS) tools, and so on. You can use the commands in this section to isolate the problems at the transport layer and identify whether they are TCP or UDP related.

The following command displays protocol statistics and current TCP/IP network connections on an IP host (Windows 9x/2000/XP):

```
netstat [-a] [-e] [-n] [-s] [-p proto] [-r]
```

The elements of this command are as follows:

[**-a**]—Displays all connections and listening ports.

[**-e**]—Displays Ethernet statistics. You can combine this with the **–s** option.

[**-n**]—Displays addresses and port numbers in numerical form.

[**-s**]—Displays per-protocol statistics. By default, statistics are shown for TCP, UDP, and IP; you can use the **-p** option to specify a subset of the default.

[**-p** *proto*]—Shows connections for the protocol specified by *proto*; *proto* can be **TCP** or **UDP**. If *proto* is used with the **-s** option to display per-protocol statistics, it can be **TCP**, **UDP**, or **IP**.

[**-r**]—Displays the routing table.

> **NOTE**  NetBIOS over TCP (NBT) is a session layer protocol that provides three services: name service, session service, and datagram service. A few years ago, NetBIOS ran on top of the nonroutable protocol NetBEUI. Indeed, NetBIOS was considered an extension of the NetBEUI protocol. Many applications were written to run on top of NetBIOS/NetBEUI. Those applications took advantage of NetBIOS's name, session, and datagram service. Later, when routable protocols such as IPX/SPX and TCP/IP became popular, the NetBIOS protocol was enhanced to run on additional protocols besides NetBEUI. NBT is a result of those efforts.

The following command displays protocol statistics and current TCP/IP connections using NBT on an IP host (Windows 9x/2000/XP):

```
nbtstat [ [-a RemoteName] [-A IP-address] [-c] [-n]
         [-r] [-R] [-RR] [-s] [-S] ]
```

The elements of this command are as follows:

[**-a**]—Lists the remote machine's name table given its name

[**-A**]—Lists the remote machine's name table given its IP address

[**-c**]—Lists NBT's cache of remote (machine) names and their IP addresses

[**-n**]—Lists local NetBIOS names

[**-r**]—Lists names resolved by broadcast and via WINS

[**-R**]—Purges and reloads the remote cache name table

[**-RR**]—Sends name release packets to WINS and starts refresh

[**-s**]—Lists sessions table converting destination IP addresses to computer NetBIOS names

[**-S**]—Lists sessions table with the destination IP

The following Cisco IOS command displays all IP access lists that are configured on a router at the present time. Extended access lists, if used, can influence a router's behavior by referencing source/destination port numbers:

```
show ip access-lists
```

The following command displays various IP-related statistics. Examples of the displayed statistics are format errors, bad hops, encapsulation failures, unknown routes, and probe proxy requests:

```
show ip traffic
```

> **NOTE**   This example describes one of the pieces of useful information that the **show ip traffic** command yields. In one of the Trouble Ticket labs in the previous version of the CIT course, the global configuration command **no ip forward-protocol udp** was typed on the student router while **ip helper-address** *ip-address* was left on the router interface(s). The **no ip forward-protocol udp** command renders the **ip helper-address** *ip-address* interface configuration command useless. As a result, many applications such as DHCP clients failed because the router would not forward requests for leased IP addresses to the DHCP server(s). Most students got stuck on this problem because they had to isolate problems using the Cisco IOS **show** commands and avoid using the **show running-config** and the **show startup-config** commands on the routers. The students would then ask which **show** command they could have used to help them isolate the problem. The answer was always **show ip traffic**.
>
> **show ip traffic** displays various IP-related statistics. One of the statistics shown that can lead to isolating the aforementioned problem is the number of "UDP: no port" cases. When you enter the **no ip forward-protocol udp** global configuration command on a router, the router always notices a related request, such as a DHCP request. The router fails to forward the request and increment that counter, so the counter continues to grow. The **[no] ip forward-protocol udp** [*port*] command gives you the option of specifying the port number; however, if you do not specify a port, this command turns off/on forwarding for eight UDP ports (NetBIOS Name, Network Time Protocol [NTP], Terminal Access Controller Access Control System [TACACS], DHCP).

You can test the functionality of any TCP port by using the Telnet application as follows and referring to a desired port number:

```
telnet host [port]
```

You can examine the contents of a router's IP route caching table using the following command. The keyword **flow** specifies that the output should include the netflow cache:

```
show ip cache [flow]
```

Note that if Cisco Express Forwarding (CEF) is enabled on a router (at least on some interfaces), it builds and maintains the IP Forwarding Table. You can display the IP Forwarding Table (some people merely call it the IP CEF table) by using the following command:

```
show ip cef
```

The following Cisco IOS command displays the local router's QoS policy maps:

```
show policy-map
```

The following IOS command displays the current queueing configuration on the local router (such as custom, fair, priority, and random-detect):

```
show queueing
```

## Examples Demonstrating Transport Layer Problem Isolation Commands

So that you can practice isolating problems at the transport layer, this section presents a case along with a series of example outputs and results.

You are the second-level network engineer for the AMIRACAN Corporation. You have console access to the router named Toronto and the access switch named Toronto_SW, as well as IP connectivity to all other devices in your division. You are told that users cannot access the database server named CIT DB. The users report that they cannot even connect to the distribution router named Ottawa from their PCs. You know from your base configuration information that the end users connect over Toronto_SW to the Toronto router. Toronto and Toronto_SW are connected via a 100-Mbps FastEthernet link. Figure 11-1 is a simplified network diagram displaying your territory of responsibility, which includes the access layer (Toronto switch and router), the distribution layer router (Ottawa), and the connection to the core layer (Guelph).

**Figure 11-1**  *Baseline Network Diagram for AMIRACAN Corporation*

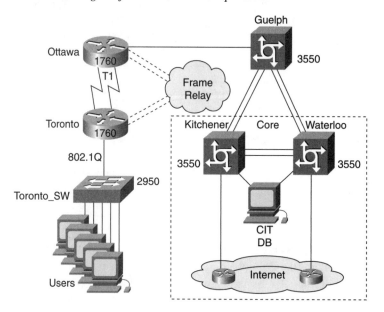

You connect to the console port on Toronto_SW and attempt to Telnet to the Toronto router. You can connect to Toronto from Toronto_SW, so there appears to be no issues between these two devices. (See the top part of Example 11-1.) You close the Telnet session to Toronto and try to connect to

Ottawa from Toronto_SW. The Telnet session from Toronto_SW cannot be opened on Ottawa. (See the middle part of Example 11-1.) To help isolate the problem, you check to see whether Toronto_SW can ping Ottawa. You see that Toronto_SW can ping Ottawa, so it appears that the physical, data link, and network layers among these devices are working. (See the bottom part of Example 11-1.) This makes you suspect that the issue is with an access list.

**Example 11-1**  *Output for* **ping** *and* **telnet** *from Toronto_SW to the Toronto and Ottawa Routers*

```
Toronto_SW>telnet Toronto
Trying Toronto (172.22.125.1)... Open
************************************************************
  Toronto:    A Distribution Workgroup Router at AMIRACAN
************************************************************
User Access Verification
Password:
Toronto>
Toronto>exit
[Connection to Toronto closed by foreign host]

Toronto_SW>telnet Ottawa
Trying Ottawa (172.22.128.1)...
% Destination unreachable; gateway or host down
Trying Ottawa (172.22.128.129)...
% Destination unreachable; gateway or host down
Trying Ottawa (172.22.127.2)...
% Destination unreachable; gateway or host down
Trying Ottawa (172.22.127.130)...
% Destination unreachable; gateway or host down
Toronto_SW>

Toronto_SW>ping Ottawa
Type escape sequence to abort.
Sending 5, 100-byte ICMP Echos to 172.22.128.1, timeout is 2 seconds:
!!!!!
Success rate is 100 percent (5/5), round-trip min/avg/max = 16/18/20 ms
Toronto_SW>
```

Next, you try to open a Telnet session from Toronto to Ottawa. You see that Toronto can open a Telnet session to Ottawa, so you know that Ottawa is not blocking all inbound Telnet traffic. (See the top part of Example 11-2.) You look for signs of recent configuration changes on Ottawa by entering the **show logging** and **show clock** commands. You see that no configuration changes have been made on Ottawa for several days, so you return to the console session on Toronto and hunt for signs of recent configuration changes on Toronto with the **show logging** and **show clock** commands. You notice that someone was at least in configuration mode on Toronto in the past few hours. (See the bottom part of Example 11-2.)

**Example 11-2** *Output for Telnet Attempt from Toronto to Ottawa and for the* **show logging** *and* **show clock**
*Commands on Toronto*

```
Toronto>telnet Ottawa
Trying Ottawa (172.22.128.1)... Open
**********************************************************
  Ottawa:      an AMIRACAN Distribution Workgroup Router
**********************************************************
User Access Verification
Password:
Ottawa>exit
[Connection to Ottawa closed by foreign host]

Toronto>show logging
Syslog logging: enabled (0 messages dropped, 1 messages rate-limited,
    0 flushes, 0 overruns)
    Console logging: level debugging, 115 messages logged
    Monitor logging: level debugging, 0 messages logged
    Buffer logging: level debugging, 155 messages logged
    Logging Exception size (4096 bytes)
    Count and timestamp logging messages: disabled
    Trap logging: level informational, 186 message lines logged
        Logging to 172.27.227.9, 139 message lines logged
Log Buffer (65536 bytes):
Dec 19 12:19:15: %SYS-5-CONFIG_I: Configured from console by vty0 (172.22.126.2)
Dec 19 13:03:06: %SYS-5-CONFIG_I: Configured from console by vty0 (172.22.126.2)
Dec 19 13:21:07: %SYS-5-CONFIG_I: Configured from console by vty0 (172.22.126.2)
Toronto>
Toronto>show clock
15:53:22.258 EST Thu Dec 19 2002
Toronto>
```

You did not have upgrades planned, but you need to review the details of the access lists on Toronto. Because pings to Ottawa from Toronto_SW are successful, you suspect the problem is probably with an extended access list filtering too much traffic. You use the **show access-lists** command to review the current access lists that are configured on Toronto. The **show ip access-lists** command that was mentioned previously displays the IP access lists only; the **show access-lists** command displays all access lists. Of course, in the absence of other access lists (such as IPX, AppleTalk, and so on), both commands will yield the same output.

The only extended access list is called Traffic. It explicitly permits Internet Control Message Protocol (ICMP), FTP, World Wide Web (WWW), and Trivial File Transfer Protocol (TFTP) traffic. However, the implicit deny at the end of the list blocks Telnet traffic that comes from Toronto_SW from being forwarded to Ottawa. (See the top part of Example 11-3.) You can also use **show ip route** to determine which interface is being used to forward traffic to Ottawa. You see that traffic for Ottawa is sent across the interface named Serial0/0:0. (See the middle part of Example 11-3.)

Finally, you must find out whether an access list is actually applied to the serial 0/0:0 interface. Therefore, you enter the **show ip interface serial 0/0:0** command. The results (output of the command) are shown in the bottom part of Example 11-3.

**Example 11-3**  *Output for the* **show access-lists**, **show ip route**, *and* **show ip interface** *Commands on Toronto*

```
Toronto>show access-lists
Standard IP access list Admin
    permit 172.22.121.0, wildcard bits 0.0.0.255 (95 matches)
    permit 172.22.125.0, wildcard bits 0.0.0.255
Standard IP access list END_USERS
    permit 172.22.124.0, wildcard bits 0.0.0.255
    permit 172.22.122.0, wildcard bits 0.0.1.255
Extended IP access list Traffic
    Remark Allow ICMP, Telnet Outbound, FTP, TFTP, and WWW
    permit icmp any any (15 matches)
    permit tcp 172.22.0.0 0.0.255.255 any eq ftp-data
    permit tcp 172.22.0.0 0.0.255.255 any eq ftp
    permit tcp 172.22.0.0 0.0.255.255 any eq www
    permit udp 172.22.0.0 0.0.255.255 any eq tftp
Toronto>

Toronto>show ip route
.
.
.
Gateway of last resort is 172.22.126.2 to network 0.0.0.0

D EX 172.21.0.0/16 [170/3873280] via 172.22.126.2, 2d00h, Serial0/0:0
D EX 172.23.0.0/16 [170/3873280] via 172.22.126.2, 2d00h, Serial0/0:0
        172.22.0.0/16 is variably subnetted, 13 subnets, 2 masks
D         172.22.128.0/26 [90/3973120] via 172.22.126.2, 6d00h, Serial0/0:0
D         172.22.129.0/26 [90/3975680] via 172.22.126.2, 6d00h, Serial0/0:0
C         172.22.126.128/26 is directly connected, Serial0/0:1
C         172.22.127.128/26 is directly connected, Serial1/1
D EX      172.22.0.0/16 [170/3873280] via 172.22.126.2, 2d02h, Serial0/0:0
D         172.22.128.128/26 [90/3847680] via 172.22.126.2, 6d00h, Serial0/0:0
C         172.22.122.0/26 is directly connected, FastEthernet0/0.2
C         172.22.123.0/26 is directly connected, FastEthernet0/0.3
C         172.22.121.0/26 is directly connected, FastEthernet0/0.1
C         172.22.126.0/26 is directly connected, Serial0/0:0
C         172.22.127.0/26 is directly connected, Serial1/0
C         172.22.124.0/26 is directly connected, FastEthernet0/0.4
C         172.22.125.0/26 is directly connected, Loopback0
D EX 172.25.0.0/16 [170/3873280] via 172.22.126.2, 2d00h, Serial0/0:0
D EX 172.24.0.0/16 [170/3873280] via 172.22.126.2, 2d00h, Serial0/0:0
D EX 172.26.0.0/16 [170/3873280] via 172.22.126.2, 2d00h, Serial0/0:0
```

*continues*

**Example 11-3** *Output for the* **show access-lists**, **show ip route**, *and* **show ip interface** *Commands on Toronto (Continued)*

```
D EX 198.133.219.0/24 [170/3873280] via 172.22.126.2, 2d00h, Serial0/0:0
D*EX 0.0.0.0/0 [170/3847936] via 172.22.126.2, 6d00h, Serial0/0:0
Toronto>

Toronto>show ip interface serial 0/0:0
Serial0/0:0 is up, line protocol is up
  Internet address is 172.22.126.1/26
  Broadcast address is 255.255.255.255
  Address determined by setup command
  MTU is 1500 bytes
  Helper address is not set
  Directed broadcast forwarding is disabled
  Multicast reserved groups joined: 224.0.0.10
  Outgoing access list is Traffic
  Inbound  access list is not set
  .
  .
  .
Toronto>
```

You have isolated the issue. The outbound access list named Traffic does not include a permit statement for Telnet. All Telnet traffic from the access switch and the end users is being filtered. The remark statement for the access list Traffic states that it should support TCP outbound.

# Commands and Applications Used to Isolate Problems Occurring at the Application Layer

This section presents a set of commands that you can use to isolate problems at the application layer. First, it introduces a set of commands used on end systems. Next, it discusses a set of Cisco IOS commands that display information related to host table, e-mail (Post Office Protocol 3 [POP3], SMTP, Internet Message Access Protocol [IMAP]), network management (Simple Network Management Protocol [SNMP], NTP), file management (FTP, TFTP), Telnet, and DHCP.

The **ifconfig –a** command is a useful command that is supported on UNIX and Max OS X hosts. This command displays IP information about the end system. **cat /etc/resolv.conf** (**cat** is the UNIX catalog command) displays the identity of the name server from hosts that are running UNIX. The UNIX machine also supports the **traceroute** command; you can use it to test connectivity to other hosts and discover the path (hops) between the two hosts along the current best network path:

```
UnixTerm% cat /etc/resolv.conf
UnixTerm% ifconfig –a
UnixTerm% traceroute {ip-address | host}
```

On end systems that are running Windows operating systems, **ipconfig** or **winipcfg**, **tracert**, **nslookup**, and **ping** are among the useful commands that can help you isolate application layer problems. The **winipcfg** command displays IP information for hosts that are running Windows 9x and Windows Me, whereas its counterpart, **ipconfig**, displays the same information on hosts that are running Windows NT/2000/XP. The **tracert** command works on all Microsoft operating systems; it verifies connectivity to an IP address or host and displays the path to that destination based on current best network path. The **nslookup** command allows you to discover the IP address of an IP host using its name, or to discover the host name for an IP address with the help of a name server. **ping** allows you to test connectivity to another IP host:

```
C:\> winipcfg /all (Windows 9X and Me command)
C:\> ipconfig /all (Windows NT/2000/XP command)
C:\> tracert {ip-address | ip host}
C:\> nslookup
```

**ping** is a command that you can use on all IP devices (end systems, routers, and switches) to test reachability to another host/IP address. This command is an important IP troubleshooting tool that helps you test health of the network layer:

```
ping {ip-address | host}
```

To test functionality of e-mail applications on an IP host, try to Telnet to the host (name or IP address), but specify the port number of the e-mail application:

```
telnet {ip-address | host} [port-number]
```

Telnet to port 25 tests functionality of the SMTP protocol, and Telnet to ports 110 and 143 tests functionality of Post Office Protocol (POP) and IMAP protocols, respectively. These tests are useful for isolating e-mail problems.

You can display the contents of the local device's (Cisco) host table by using the **show host** command. The contents are name-to-IP address mappings. The entries can be static, or they can be learned dynamically. **show host** also reveals the style of name lookup (for example, using a DNS server) and the default domain name for the device:

```
Router# show host
```

The following Cisco IOS commands display information about network management applications. You can use the information from these commands to isolate problems at the application layer that are related to the SNMP and NTP protocols:

```
show snmp
debug snmp requests
debug ntp events
```

The **show snmp** command displays the status of the SNMP communications, and the **debug snmp requests** command displays information about every SNMP request that the SNMP manager makes. The **debug ntp events** command displays information about the events/operation of NTP.

You can isolate file management problems by using commands that put the functionality of file transfer applications into test or debug their operation. FTP and TFTP are the main file transfer applications of the TCP/IP suite:

```
copy tftp flash
copy flash tftp
debug tftp
telnet {ip-address | host} 21
```

You can test the functionality of the TFTP application by trying to copy the IOS file from the flash memory of the local router to a TFTP server on the network using the **copy flash tftp** command. To observe the TFTP activity/operation, enter the **debug tftp** command. You can test FTP protocol's functionality on an IP host by attempting to Telnet to that host's IP address and referring to port 21, as shown.

Availability and functionality of the Telnet application in a network is particularly important. Telnet is the most significant application used for in-band network troubleshooting, monitoring, and management. You can use/test the Telnet application in its usual format, or you can specify the source interface whose address is to be used for the Telnet communication purposes. (See the following syntax.) As in other applications, you can debug the Telnet application and observe the negotiation process and events on the output:

```
telnet {ip-address | host} /source-interface interface
debug telnet
```

The usage of Dynamic Host Configuration Protocol (DHCP) is growing in popularity; therefore, troubleshooting and isolating problems related to this protocol are important. The DHCP server application is often active on a server/IP host. However, you can now set up your router to act as a DHCP server, too. You can investigate the DHCP-related issues and obtain useful information from the output of the following commands:

```
show ip dhcp binding
show dhcp lease
debug ip dhcp server [events | packets]
```

The **show ip dhcp binding** command displays address bindings on a DHCP server, and the **show dhcp lease** command lists the addresses leased from a server. The **debug ip dhcp server events** command reports DHCP server events, such as address assignments and database updates (the router is the DHCP server), and the **debug ip dhcp server packets** command reports on packet activities.

# Guidelines for Isolating a Problem Occurring at the Transport or Application Layer

The following guidelines help to isolate problems that are rooted at the transport and application layers:

- Establish that the problem is not at the network or lower layers by testing and proving IP connectivity between two points of interest.

- If you are troubleshooting e-mail–related problems, beware of the fact that sending and receiving e-mail utilize and depend on different protocols and might involve multiple components; therefore, you must test those functions separately.

- You might have to research the related RFCs to discover the detail of a particular transport or application layer protocol. Certain protocols/applications embed information such as addresses. Other applications might have special control, handshake, or authentication requirements.

# Foundation Summary

The "Foundation Summary" section of each chapter lists the most important facts from that chapter. Although this section does not list every fact from the chapter that will be on your CCNP exam, a well-prepared CCNP candidate should at a minimum know all the details in each "Foundation Summary" before taking the exam.

The following are common symptoms of transport layer problems:

- Unreachable resources and connectivity problems are an issue, while the physical, data link, and network layers are functional.

- The network is operating either consistently or intermittently less than the baseline level.

- Applications generate error messages; they might report link or connectivity problems (as they perceive it).

- Users complain that the network is slow.

- Console messages report abnormal events; unexpected events are observed in system log messages.

- Management system alarms indicate problems.

- Partial or intermittent connectivity or erratic performance results from TCP windowing problems, long round-trip times, excess retransmissions, and so on.

The following are common symptoms of application layer problems:

- Unreachable or unusable resources are an issue, while the physical, data link, network, and transport layers are functional.

- Operation of a network service or application does not meet the normal expectations of a user.

- Applications generate error message or report lack of functionality.

- Users complain that the network is slow or that their network applications are not functioning, are unavailable, or are too slow.

- Console messages indicate abnormal events; system log file messages report errors.

- Management system alarms deliver unexpected news.

The following are guidelines for isolating problems at the transport and application layers:

■   Establish that the problem is not at the network or lower layers by testing and proving IP connectivity between two points of interest.

■   If you are troubleshooting e-mail–related problems, beware of the fact that sending and receiving e-mail utilize and depend on different protocols and might involve multiple components; therefore, you must test those functions separately.

■   You might have to research the related RFCs to discover the detail of a particular transport or application layer protocol. Certain protocols/applications embed information such as addresses. Other applications might have special control, handshake, or authentication requirements.

**Table 11-2**   *General Commands for Isolating Application Layer Problems*

| Command | Description |
|---------|-------------|
| **traceroute** [*destination* ] | Identifies the path a packet takes through the network. The *destination* variable is the host name or IP address of the target system. This command is used with Cisco IOS, UNIX, and Mac OS X. |
| **cat /etc/resolv.conf** | Displays the identity of the name server from hosts that are running UNIX. |
| **ifconfig –a** | Displays IP information for UNIX and Mac OS X hosts. |
| **ipconfig /all** | Displays IP information for hosts that are running Windows NT/2000/XP. |
| **winipcfg /all** | Displays IP information for hosts that are running Windows 9x and Windows Me. |
| **tracert** [*destination* ] | Verifies connectivity to a destination device for Windows hosts. The *destination* variable is the IP alias or IP address of the target system. |
| **show running-config** | Displays the running configuration of the device (including the name server that a device uses). |
| **show hosts** | This Cisco IOS command displays the local device's host table. It also reveals the style of name lookup and the default IP domain name. |
| **ping** {*ip-address* I *domain name* } | Verifies connectivity and tests the functionality of address resolution services. |
| **nslookup** {*ip-address* I *domain name* } | Discovers the IP address of an IP host using its name, or discovers the host name for an IP address with the help of a name server. |

**Table 11-3**    *Commands Used to Isolate E-Mail Problems*

| Command | Description |
|---------|-------------|
| **telnet** {*ip-address* \| *host*} **25** | Tests SMTP protocol functionality |
| **telnet** {*ip-address* \| *host*} **110** | Tests POP protocol functionality |
| **telnet** {*ip-address* \| *host*} **143** | Tests IMAP protocol functionality |

**Table 11-4**    *Commands Used to Isolate Network Management Problems*

| Command | Description |
|---------|-------------|
| **debug snmp packets** | Displays packet activity related to the operation of SNMP |
| **debug ntp events** | Displays events related to the operation of NTP |
| **debug ntp packets** | Displays packet activity related to the operation of NTP |

**Table 11-5**    *Commands Used to Isolate File Management Problems*

| Command | Description |
|---------|-------------|
| **copy tftp** | You can test the functionality of the TFTP application by trying to copy a file from a TFTP server to the flash memory of the local router using the **copy tftp flash** command. |
| **telnet** {*ip-address* \| *host*} **21** | Tests FTP protocol functionality |
| **debug tftp** | Displays activity related to the operation of TFTP |

**Table 11-6**    *Commands Used to Isolate Telnet Problems*

| Command | Description |
|---------|-------------|
| **telnet** {*ip-address* \| *hostname*} | Tests functionality of the Telnet application |
| **debug telnet** | Displays events during the negotiation process of a Telnet connection |

**Table 11-7**    *Commands Used to Isolate DHCP Problems*

| Command | Description |
|---------|-------------|
| **show ip dhcp binding** | Displays address bindings on a DHCP server |
| **show dhcp lease** | Shows DHCP addresses leased from a server |
| **debug dhcp** [**detail**] | Displays DHCP client activities and monitors the status of DHCP packets |
| **debug ip dhcp server** [**events** \| **packets**] | Reports DHCP server events, such as address assignments and database updates, as well as packet activity |

# Q&A

As mentioned in the introduction, you have two choices for review questions. The questions that follow give you a bigger challenge than the exam does because they use an open-ended question format. By reviewing now with this more difficult question format, you can exercise your memory better and prove your conceptual and factual knowledge of this chapter. You can find the answers to these questions in Appendix A.

For more practice with exam-like question formats, including questions that use a router simulator and multiple choice format, use the exam engine on the CD.

1. List at least three possible symptoms of transport layer problems.

2. List at least three possible symptoms of application layer problems.

3. Provide at least one of the guidelines for isolating problems at the transport and application layers.

4. What do the commands **ipconfig** and **winipcfg** do? How are they different?

5. What are the well-known TCP ports for the SMTP and POP protocols?

6. Explain the purpose and result of the **copy flash tftp** command.

7. Provide the command that allows you to test Telnet functionality from a router using the address of a particular interface.

8. Which Cisco IOS debug command allows you to inspect real-time DHCP server events?

## This chapter covers the following subjects:

- Identifying commands and applications used to correct problems occurring at the transport layer

- Identifying commands and applications used to correct problems occurring at the application layer

- Identifying transport and application layer support resources

- Correcting problems occurring at the transport and application layers

# CHAPTER 12

# Correcting a Problem at the Transport or Application Layer

This chapter focuses on correcting the problems that you have already isolated using the commands and guidelines presented in Chapter 11, "Isolating a Problem at the Transport or Application Layer." The first section presents useful commands for correcting problems categorized as transport layer problems, and the second section provides the commands for correcting problems associated with the application layer. Next, this chapter lists the support resources available to network support personnel and provides some tips for making best use of Cisco's Technical Assistance Center. This chapter concludes by providing a set of guidelines for correcting transport and application layer problems.

## "Do I Know This Already?" Quiz

The purpose of the "Do I Know This Already?" quiz is to help you decide if you really need to read this entire chapter. If you already intend to read the entire chapter, you do not need to answer these questions now.

The 10-question quiz, derived from the major sections in the "Foundation Topics" portion of the chapter, helps you determine how to spend your limited study time.

Table 12-1 outlines the major topics discussed in this chapter and the "Do I Know This Already?" quiz questions that correspond to those topics.

**Table 12-1**  *"Do I Know This Already?" Foundation Topics Section-to-Question Mapping*

| Foundation Topics Section | Questions Covered in This Section |
|---|---|
| "Identifying Commands and Applications Used to Correct Problems Occurring at the Transport Layer" | 3 |
| "Identifying Commands and Applications Used to Correct Problems Occurring at the Application Layer" | 3 |
| "Identifying Transport and Application Layer Support Resources" | 2 |
| "Correcting Problems Occurring at the Transport and Application Layers" | 2 |

> **CAUTION** The goal of self-assessment is to gauge your mastery of the topics in this chapter. If you do not know the answer to a question or are only partially sure of the answer, you should mark this question wrong for purposes of the self-assessment. Giving yourself credit for an answer you correctly guess skews your self-assessment results and might provide you with a false sense of security.

1. Which statement of access list 100 would match and permit Telnet traffic?

   a. **access-list 100 permit udp any any**

   b. **access-list 100 permit tcp any any eq smtp**

   c. **access-list 100 permit tcp any any eq www**

   d. **access-list 100 permit tcp any any eq ftp**

   e. None of the above

2. Which definition is suitable for this statement:

   **access-list 200 permit tcp any 10.27.19.66 eq telnet**

   a. It defines an extended access list.

   b. It defines a Transmission Control Protocol (TCP) access group.

   c. It defines a standard access list.

   d. It defines an extended access group.

   e. It applies an extended access list to an interface.

3. Which definition is suitable for this command/statement?

   **ip access-group 200 in**

   a. It defines an extended access group.

   b. It applies an access list to an interface.

   c. It defines an access list.

   d. It defines a named or numbered access group.

   e. This command does not exist.

4. Simple Network Management Protocol (SNMP) traps can be generated and sent to an IP host (address) when a particular condition is created or a certain threshold is exceeded. Which of the following pairs of commands enables SNMP traps and configures a router with the address of the trap recipient device?

   a. **server-snmp enable informs** and **snmp community** {*access-list-number*}

   b. **snmp server enable** and **snmp-server host** *ip-address*

   c. **snmp-enable server traps** and **snmp-server host** *ip-address*

   d. **snmp-server enable traps** and **snmp-server host** *ip-address*

   e. **snmp-server enable informs** and **snmp-host** *ip-address*

5. Which of the following commands configures Network Time Protocol (NTP) to use the IP address of a particular interface?

   a. **ntp server** {*ip-address*}

   b. **ntp peer** {*ip-address*}

   c. **ntp source** {*interface-type number*}

   d. **ntp-server source** {*interface-type number*}

   e. None of the above

6. Which of the following commands configures a router to timestamp log or debug messages with the local date and time?

   a. **enable {log | debug} timestamps local datetime**

   b. **service timestamps {log | debug} datetime localtime**

   c. **service {log | debug} timestamps datetime localtime**

   d. **configure timestamp {log | debug} local date time**

   e. None of the above

7. Which of the following Web sites offers up-to-date technical documentation on open standards and developments with regards to Transmission Control Protocol/Internet Protocol (TCP/IP) protocols, such as SMTP and RTP?

   a. www.ietf.org

   b. www.itu.int

   c. www.sniffers.com

   d. www.latest-tech.docs

   e. www.atmforum.net

**8.** Which of the following is not necessary to have when contacting Cisco Technical Assistance Center?

    **a.** Network diagram.

    **b.** Gathered symptoms.

    **c.** Output of the **show tech-support** command for all devices.

    **d.** Telnet or dial-in access to your equipment.

    **e.** All of the above are necessary.

**9.** You are in the midst of correcting a problem. You have just made some changes to the configurations of a router. Following the procedure for correcting problems at the transport and application layers, what is the next step?

    **a.** Make more changes as required.

    **b.** Evaluate the results of the changes made.

    **c.** Undo the changes made.

    **d.** Complete the documentation.

    **e.** Seek help from outside sources.

**10.** You are in the process of correcting a problem. After making some changes, you notice that you have not solved the existing problems. Now there are new problems, and you have lost track of all the changes made. What is the best action to take next?

    **a.** Restore the configuration of the device to its initial settings.

    **b.** Erase the startup configuration and reload the router to start from scratch.

    **c.** Erase the flash and start from scratch.

    **d.** Copy a good IOS from a Trivial File Transfer Protocol (TFTP) server.

    **e.** None of the above.

You can find the answers to the "Do I Know This Already?" quiz in Appendix A, "Answers to the 'Do I Know This Already?' Quizzes and 'Q&A' Sections." The suggested choices for your next step are as follows:

- **8 or less overall score**—Read the entire chapter. This includes the "Foundation Topics" and "Foundation Summary" sections, as well as the "Q&A" section.

- **9 or 10 overall score**—If you want more review on these topics, skip to the "Foundation Summary" section and then go to the "Q&A" section. Otherwise, move to the next chapter.

# Foundation Topics

To correct internetworking problems, including those occurring at the transport and application layers, you must isolate and identify the problems first. You then need to know how to fix the problems. To fix the problems efficiently and effectively, you must follow a methodology, know the correct commands and tools, and have access to support resources. The following sections provide commands and applications, support resources, and procedures for correcting transport and application layer problems.

## Identifying Commands and Applications Used to Correct Problems Occurring at the Transport Layer

Network administrators and engineers occasionally use access lists, sometimes called *access control lists* (ACLs), to perform different types of tasks. One such task is controlling what packets can enter and which packets can exit particular router interfaces. You create an ACL in global configuration mode. If you apply the ACL to an interface from within interface configuration mode, it can control what packets can get in or out of that interface depending on whether it is applied in the in or out direction. Standard IP access lists qualify packets merely based on the source address of the packets. In contrast, extended IP access lists can discriminate packets based on source address, destination address, protocol number, source port, destination port, or any combination of these fields. Therefore, the content of an access list that is applied to an interface can dictate whether packets that carry a specific type of transport layer protocol data unit (PDU) sourced from or destined to a specific application's port number are allowed to enter or exit an interface.

If the isolated cause of a transport layer problem is an access list, then your familiarity with the syntax of the ACLs and how they are applied to router interfaces is crucial to the task of correcting the problem. You can create numbered or named access lists. Access lists 1 through 99 are considered standard IP access lists, and access lists 100 through 199 are considered extended IP access lists. Named access lists can be either standard or extended. Table 12-2 shows the syntax for creating IP access lists and applying them to router interfaces.

**Table 12-2**   *IP Access List Commands Useful for Correcting TCP and User Datagram Protocol (UDP) Problems*

| Command | Description |
|---------|-------------|
| **Access-list** {*access-list-number* } {**deny** \| **permit**} {**ip** \| **udp** \| **tcp** \| **...**} *source-address source-wildcard destination-address destination-wildcard* [*operator operand* ] [**log**] | Syntax for defining an extended access list. Allows you to specify more precise filtering conditions. You can check source and destination IP address (with wild-mask). Allows you to specify protocol and port number. |

*continues*

**Table 12-2** *IP Access List Commands Useful for Correcting TCP and User Datagram Protocol (UDP) Problems (Continued)*

| Command | Description |
|---|---|
| **ip access-list** {**standard** \| **extended**} {*access-list-name* } | Syntax for defining a standard or extended *named* access list. |
| **ip access-group** {*access-list-number* \| *access-list-name* } [**in** \| **out**] | This command, entered from within interface configuration mode, activates/applies an access list to the interface. When you activate an ACL on an interface by using this command, you can use the keyword **in** at the end to specify that the ACL is applied to the inbound traffic. If you do not type a keyword or if you specify the keyword **out**, the access list is applied to the outbound traffic. |

Isolating a problem and identifying the cause as a misconfigured or inappropriate access list applied to one or more interfaces requires that you be fully comfortable with its syntax and know whether to use it in the inbound or outbound direction. An access list applied to a router's interface only affects traffic that does not originate from the router.

Familiarize yourself with named access lists. Also, note that in the recent IOS releases, new ranges of access list numbers were added, just in case users needed more. Moreover, time-based access lists, which are active at certain times, and reflexive access lists, which allow traffic in one direction only if the traffic is responding to some traffic that has passed the interface in the other direction, are also exciting and worth studying, but they are not part of the CIT curriculum.

Finally, do not forget that access lists have numerous applications and are used at various places. For example, routing protocols might use access lists to control/filter the prefixes they advertise to or accept from peers. You can also apply access lists during redistribution of routes from one routing process to another to control which routes are sent from one process to another. Furthermore, you can use access lists to specify interesting traffic that triggers dial-on-demand routing. Other usages of access lists include policy routing, QoS commands and tools (such as queuing strategies), and so on.

## Access List Troubleshooting Example

You have isolated the cause of a Telnet problem. The problem is due to an access list that does not permit Telnet traffic to enter and transit through a router. (See the output in Example 12-1.)

**Example 12-1** *Contents of an Erroneous Access List*

```
Router#show access-lists
Extended IP access list 100
    permit icmp any any
    permit tcp any any eq smtp
    permit tcp any any eq www
```

**Example 12-1**  *Contents of an Erroneous Access List (Continued)*

```
     permit tcp any any eq ftp
     permit tcp any any eq ftp-data
Router#
```

To fix the problem, you must modify the access list so that Telnet traffic can transit through the identified router. You must add an extra line to the access list to permit TCP traffic with the destination port 23. See Example 12-2.

**Example 12-2**  *Adding a Line to Access List 100 to Permit Telnet Traffic*

```
Router#
Router#conf t
Enter configuration commands, one per line.  End with CNTL/Z.
Router(config)#access-list 100 permit tcp any any eq telnet
Router(config)#exit
03:29:18: %SYS-5-CONFIG_I: Configured from console by console
Router#show access-lists
Extended IP access list 100
    permit icmp any any
    permit tcp any any eq smtp
    permit tcp any any eq www
    permit tcp any any eq ftp
    permit tcp any any eq ftp-data
    permit tcp any any eq telnet
Router#
```

The transport layer problem that was isolated to an access list has been corrected; the Telnet traffic can now transit through the router.

# Identifying Commands and Applications Used to Correct Problems Occurring at the Application Layer

This section presents some commands that you can use to correct problems occurring at the application layer. The selected commands relate to SNMP, NTP, and Dynamic Host Configuration Protocol (DHCP). Of course, you can use other commands to configure and correct application layer problems. The Cisco Internetwork Troubleshooting (CIT) course intends to familiarize you with the troubleshooting process, rather than listing and explaining all Cisco IOS commands. This book also discusses those same commands so that you are well prepared for the CIT exam.

SNMP is an application layer member of the TCP/IP suite. Naturally, operation of this protocol depends on the transport, internet, and network interface layers. As the name implies, SNMP manages (configuration and troubleshooting) network entities. SNMP is based on open standards and can be utilized in multivendor environments. The output shown in Example 12-3 was captured on a Cisco router. Example 12-3 shows the **snmp-server** command options and a brief explanation for each of them. The **snmp-server enable**, **snmp-server community**, and **snmp-server host** commands are highlighted to emphasize their importance. The **snmp-server enable** command enables SNMP traps or informs on a Cisco router. The **snmp-server community** command sets the community string and access privileges (read-only, read, read-write, and view); it essentially configures a community string to act like a password to regulate read-write and read-only access to the agent (router). The **snmp-server host** command allows you to specify the IP address of the SNMP notification host (recipient).

**Example 12-3** *Cisco IOS* **snmp-server** *Commands and Options*

```
Router#conf t
Enter configuration commands, one per line.  End with CNTL/Z.
Router(config)#snmp-server ?
  chassis-id        String to uniquely identify this chassis
  community         Enable SNMP; set community string and access privs
  contact           Text for mib object sysContact
  enable            Enable SNMP Traps or Informs
  engineID          Configure a local or remote SNMPv3 engineID
  group             Define a User Security Model group
  host              Specify hosts to receive SNMP notifications
  ifindex           Enable ifindex persistence
  inform            Configure SNMP Informs options
  location          Text for mib object sysLocation
  manager           Modify SNMP manager parameters
  packetsize        Largest SNMP packet size
  queue-length      Message queue length for each TRAP host
  system-shutdown   Enable use of the SNMP reload command
  tftp-server-list  Limit TFTP servers used via SNMP
  trap              SNMP trap options
  trap-source       Assign an interface for the source address of all traps
  trap-timeout      Set timeout for TRAP message retransmissions
  user              Define a user who can access the SNMP engine
  view              Define an SNMPv2 MIB view

Router(config)#snmp-server enable ?
  informs  Enable SNMP Informs
  traps    Enable SNMP Traps

Router(config)#snmp-server community ?
  WORD  SNMP community string

Router(config)#snmp-server community somename ?
  <1-99>       Std IP accesslist allowing access with this community string
  <1300-1999>  Expanded IP accesslist allowing access with this community string
  ro           Read-only access with this community string
  rw           Read-write access with this community string
  view         Restrict this community to a named MIB view
  <cr>
```

**Example 12-3** *Cisco IOS* **snmp-server** *Commands and Options (Continued)*

```
Router(config)#snmp-server community somename ro ?
  <1-99>       Std IP accesslist allowing access with this community string
  <1300-1999>  Expanded IP accesslist allowing access with this community string
  <cr>

Router(config)#snmp-server community somename rw ?
  <1-99>       Std IP accesslist allowing access with this community string
  <1300-1999>  Expanded IP accesslist allowing access with this community string
  <cr>

Router(config)#snmp-server host ?
  Hostname or A.B.C.D  IP address of SNMP notification host
```

Time synchronization and accurate time and calendar on internetwork devices are of great importance in most environments. NTP serves that purpose; it is a UDP-based (port 123) standard protocol (RFC 1305 describes NTP version 3) that was designed to synchronize the time on a network of devices. Example 12-4 shows **ntp** commands and configuration options. **ntp server**, **ntp peer**, and **ntp source** commands are highlighted to emphasize their significance. The **ntp server** and **ntp peer** commands are straightforward. The first command allows you to specify the address of another device that plays a server role, and the latter allows you to specify another time server device as a peer. The **ntp source** command specifies which interface's IP address you should use during the NTP communications with other devices.

**Example 12-4** *Cisco IOS* **ntp** *Commands and Options*

```
Router(config)#ntp ?
  access-group        Control NTP access
  authenticate        Authenticate time sources
  authentication-key  Authentication key for trusted time sources
  broadcastdelay      Estimated round-trip delay
  clock-period        Length of hardware clock tick
  master              Act as NTP master clock
  max-associations    Set maximum number of associations
  peer                Configure NTP peer
  server              Configure NTP server
  source              Configure interface for source address
  trusted-key         Key numbers for trusted time sources

Router(config)#ntp peer ?
  Hostname or A.B.C.D  IP address of peer

Router(config)#ntp server ?
  Hostname or A.B.C.D  IP address of peer
```

*continues*

**Example 12-4**  *Cisco IOS* **ntp** *Commands and Options (Continued)*

```
Router(config)#ntp source ?
  Async                Async interface
  BVI                  Bridge-Group Virtual Interface
  CTunnel              CTunnel interface
  Dialer               Dialer interface
  Ethernet             IEEE 802.3
  Lex                  Lex interface
  Loopback             Loopback interface
  Multilink            Multilink-group interface
  Null                 Null interface
  Serial               Serial
  TokenRing            IEEE 802.5
  Tunnel               Tunnel interface
  Vif                  PGM Multicast Host interface
  Virtual-FrameRelay   Virtual Frame Relay interface
  Virtual-Template     Virtual Template interface
  Virtual-TokenRing    Virtual TokenRing
```

You can use the **service timestamps** command to configure how the system log messages and debug messages are time stamped: based on how long the device has been up for, or based on regular date/time. The information about system events and messages, including the time they occurred, is crucial. Example 12-5 displays the configuration options for the Cisco IOS **service timestamps** command.

**Example 12-5**  *Cisco IOS* **service timestamps** *Commands and Options*

```
Router(config)#service timestamps ?
  debug                Timestamp debug messages
  log                  Timestamp log messages
  <cr>

Router(config)#service timestamps log ?
  datetime             Timestamp with date and time
  uptime               Timestamp with system uptime
  <cr>

Router(config)#service timestamps log datetime ?
  localtime            Use local time zone for timestamps
  msec                 Include milliseconds in timestamp
  show-timezone        Add time zone information to timestamp
  <cr>

Router(config)#service timestamps debug uptime ?
  <cr>
```

**Example 12-5**  *Cisco IOS* **service timestamps** *Commands and Options (Continued)*

```
Router(config)#service timestamps debug datetime ?
  localtime      Use local time zone for timestamps
  msec           Include milliseconds in timestamp
  show-timezone  Add time zone information to timestamp
  <cr>
```

DHCP plays a significant role in today's TCP/IP networks. Traditionally, you would configure a special server (or two) as DHCP server(s) and many personal computers as DHCP clients requesting and receiving information such as IP address, subnet mask, default gateway, and so on from the server. You would configure the routers to forward these requests and responses (BOOTP Client and BOOTP Server messages), which are UDP-based broadcasts, by converting them to unicasts. The **ip helper-address** interface configuration command allows you to configure a router's interface to forward a client's bootp-request (in unicast form) to a DHCP server and insert the network address of the segment where the original requested was generated into the request's DHCP header. Some of today's network devices, such as Cisco routers, allow you to configure the router to be a DHCP server, rather than merely acting as a relay-agent, which has been routers' traditional role. The output captured and displayed in Example 12-6 shows the **ip helper-address** command and the **service dhcp** commands and descriptions.

**Example 12-6**  *Cisco IOS* **ip helper-address** *and* **service dhcp** *Commands and Options*

```
Router(config)#interface ethernet 0/0
Router(config-if)#ip helper-address ?
  A.B.C.D  IP destination address

Router(config-if)#exit
Router(config)#


Router(config)#service dhcp
Router(config)#ip dhcp ?
  conflict          DHCP address conflict parameters
  database          Configure DHCP database agents
  excluded-address  Prevent DHCP from assigning certain addresses
  ping              Specify ping parameters used by DHCP
  pool              Configure DHCP address pools
  relay             DHCP relay agent parameters
  smart-relay       Enable Smart Relay feature

Router(config)#
```

# Identifying Transport and Application Layer Support Resources

This section identifies some valuable support resources that are at your disposal. Cisco Connection Online (CCO), which is Cisco's official Web site, and Cisco's documentation pages offer a tremendous amount of useful information (see Figure 12-1). The Internet Engineering Task Force (IETF), International Telecommunications Union (ITU), Frame Relay Forum (FRF), and ATM Forum also provide valuable information on their Web pages.

**Figure 12-1** *Cisco Connection Online (CCO) and Documentation*

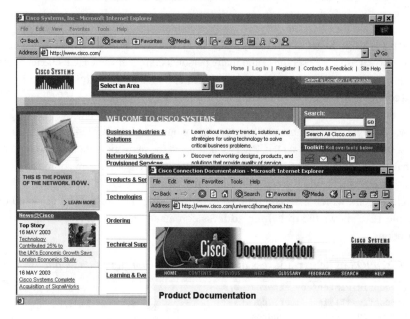

In case you decide to take advantage of the Cisco Systems Technical Assistance Center, this section identifies the information you need to gather and have ready to submit to Technical Assistance Center personnel so that they can assist you most effectively.

The following is a list of Web pages from Cisco and other standards organizations that offer valuable information:

- **Cisco Systems Technical Assistance Center**—www.cisco.com/tac/

- **CCO**—www.cisco.com

- **Cisco Systems Technologies Reference (Documentation)**—www.cisco.com/univercd/home/ home.htm

- **IETF**—www.ietf.org

- **ITU**—www.itu.int/home

- **FRF**—www.frforum.com

- **ATM Forum**—www.atmforum.com

So that you can take full advantage of Cisco's Technical Assistance Center, it is recommended that you gather and document the following information prior to contacting it:

■ An accurate network diagram of your network, or at least the part of your network that is experiencing problems. The diagram will be more helpful if it includes IP addresses and masks.

■ All the information you have gathered during the course of troubleshooting.

■ A capture of the **show tech-support** command output if fewer than four routers are suspected to be faulty.

■ Dial-in or Telnet access to the affected devices.

# Correcting Problems Occurring at the Transport and Application Layers

This section details a brief yet beneficial procedure to be followed when correcting problems occurring at the transport and application layers (or in general). Because the order of execution is important, the steps are presented as a numbered list:

1.  Be sure that you have a saved configuration for the device whose configuration you are about to change. During the course of troubleshooting, you should always be able to revert back to a known initial state. Casually speaking, you want to make sure that you do not make matters worse than they were originally.

2.  Start making changes that you have decided are necessary to correct the problem. However, make one atomic change at a time.

3.  Evaluate your change(s). If the results are not good or as expected, undo the changes.

4.  Verify that your changes did not introduce new problems. The goal is to return the network to its baseline, so no new or old symptoms must remain. If you cannot rectify the situation, undo your changes.

5.  Continue making changes until the problem is solved.

6.  You might need to seek assistance from outside resources, such as a co-worker, consultant, or Cisco Technical Assistance Center. In certain troubleshooting cases, a core dump might be necessary; therefore, take the necessary steps to familiarize yourself with the procedure for performing a core dump. Specialized Cisco Systems personnel analyze core dumps.

7.  Document your solution and all your changes.

# Foundation Summary

The "Foundation Summary" section of each chapter lists the most important facts from that chapter. Although this section does not list every fact from the chapter that will be on your CCNP exam, a well-prepared CCNP candidate should at a minimum know all the details in each "Foundation Summary" before taking the exam.

**Table 12-3**  *IP Access List Commands Useful for Correcting TCP and UDP Problems*

| Command | Description |
|---|---|
| **access-list** {*access-list-number* } {**deny** \| **permit**} {**ip** \| **udp** \| **tcp** \| ...} *source-address source-wildcard destination-address destination-wildcard* [*operator operand* ] [**log**] | Syntax for defining an extended access list. Allows you to specify more precise filtering conditions. You can check source and destination IP address (with wild-mask). Allows you to specify protocol and port number. |
| **ip access-list** {**standard** \| **extended**} {*access-list-name* } | Syntax for defining a standard or extended *named* access list. |
| **ip access-group** {*access-list-number* \| *access-list-name* } [**in** \| **out**] | Entered in interface configuration mode, this command applies an access list to the interface. Inbound traffic is affected if the trailing keyword **in** is used. If no keyword is entered or if the **out** keyword is used, the access list affects outbound traffic. |

**Table 12-4**  *Commands Used to Correct Application Layer Problems*

| Command | Description |
|---|---|
| **snmp-server enable** {**informs** \| **traps**} | Enables SNMP informs or traps. |
| **snmp-server community** *name* [**rw** \| **ro**] [*access-list-number* ] | Enables SNMP and sets community string. The standard or expanded access list that is referenced optionally specifies the address range of the IP hosts that are permitted to have read-write (**rw**) or read-only (**ro**) communication with this device. |
| **snmp-server host** {*name* \| *IP-address* } | Specifies the host name or IP address of the SNMP notification host that is receiving traps. |
| **ntp server** {*ip-address*} | Specifies the IP address of another device that will act in the capacity of an NTP server. |
| **ntp peer** {*ip-address*} | Specifies the IP address of another device that will have a peering relation with the local device. |

**Table 12-4**    *Commands Used to Correct Application Layer Problems (Continued)*

| Command | Description |
|---------|-------------|
| **ntp source** {*interface* } | Specifies which interface's IP address should be used during NTP communications with other devices. |
| **Service timestamps log datetime localtime** | Configures the router to timestamp log messages with the local date and time. |
| **service timestamps debug datetime localtime** | Configures the router to timestamp debug messages with the local date and time. |
| **ip helper-address** {*address*} | This is an interface configuration command, which means different interfaces can have different settings. The UDP broadcasts (with certain destination ports, such as 68, 67 for BootP) are converted to unicast and sent to the IP address specified. |
| **[no] service dhcp** | Enables/disables DHCP server and relay-agent functionality on the local router. When DHCP service is enabled, the related configuration parameters are then set with the **ip dhcp** global command. |

**Table 12-5**    *Support Resources for Correcting Transport and Application Layer Problems*

| Resource Name | Universal Resource Locator (URL) |
|---------------|----------------------------------|
| **Cisco Systems Technical Assistance Center** | www.cisco.com/tac/ |
| **CCO** | www.cisco.com |
| **Cisco Systems Technologies Reference** | www.cisco.com/univercd/home/home.htm |
| **IETF** | www.ietf.org |
| **IRU** | www.itu.int/home |
| **FRF** | www.frforum.com |
| **ATM Forum** | www.atmforum.com |

You should have the following information gathered before contacting Cisco Technical Assistance Center:

■ Complete network diagram, or at least the affected area. The IP address/mask of the IP devices should be shown if possible.

■ All the information and any facts gathered.

- The output of the **show tech-support** command if the number of affected routers is fewer than four.

- Dial-in or Telnet access to the devices under investigation.

**Table 12-6** *Guidelines for Correcting Problems Occurring at the Transport and Application Layers*

| Step | Description |
|------|-------------|
| 1 | For the device(s) whose configuration you intend to change, ensure that there is a saved valid configuration. |
| 2 | Make the intended changes. Make one change at a time. |
| 3 | Evaluate and document the results of the changes made. |
| 4 | Verify that the changes made did not introduce new problems/symptoms. |
| 5 | Continue making changes until problems are fixed. |
| 6 | Seek assistance from outside sources, such as other colleagues, consultants, and Cisco's Technical Assistance Center, if necessary. |
| 7 | Document the solution. |

# Q&A

As mentioned in the introduction, you have two choices for review questions. The questions that follow give you a bigger challenge than the exam does because they use an open-ended question format. By reviewing now with this more difficult question format, you can exercise your memory better and prove your conceptual and factual knowledge of this chapter. You can find the answers to these questions in Appendix A.

For more practice with exam-like question formats, including questions that use a router simulator and multiple choice format, use the exam engine on the CD.

1.  Which Cisco IOS command applies an access list to an interface?

2.  Which Cisco IOS command enables SNMP and sets community string?

3.  List the commands that configure the NTP server and the NTP peer.

4.  Which Cisco IOS command configures the router to timestamp log or debug messages with the local date and time?

5.  Which Cisco IOS command enables (or disables) DHCP server functionality on the local router?

6.  Which Cisco IOS interface configuration command converts the UDP broadcasts (with certain destination ports, such as 68, 67 for BootP) to unicast and sends them to the IP address specified?

7.  What are the URLs for the Web pages of the IETF, ITU, FRF, and ATM Forum?

8.  What are the URLs for Cisco Systems Technologies Reference, Cisco's Technical Assistance Center, and CCO?

9.  What information must you gather and have ready before contacting Cisco Technical Assistance Center?

10.  List the seven steps to correct problems occurring at the transport and application layers.

# Part VI: Scenarios

---

**Chapter 13    CIT Scenarios and Examples**

This chapter includes scenarios and examples that cover topics from throughout this book. These scenarios and examples will help solidify your mastery of the CIT topics. The following topics are covered in the scenarios and examples in this chapter:

- Network documentation

- Gathering symptoms

- Resolving problems at the physical or data link layer

- Resolving problems at the network layer

- Resolving problems at the transport and application layers

# CIT Scenarios and Examples

This chapter is composed of a few CIT scenarios and examples. The goal of this chapter is to show you how to put some of the techniques presented in the previous chapters to practical use. This will help you comprehend the material better and prepare you for the certification exam.

## Network Documentation

In Chapter 1, "Creating Network Configuration Documentation," you learned that to create effective network documentation, you must do the following:

- **Determine the scope of your work**—You must find out what part of the network you are responsible for and which devices you need to include in your work.

- **Know your objective**—Collect and document information about the elements within your scope. While making certain that you provide sufficient detail, you must also avoid collecting and documenting too much information because that usually has a negative effect and causes confusion.

- **Be consistent**—The terminology, abbreviations, and technical jargon you use in your documentation must be accurate and consistent. You must also use the presentation tools, such as tables, graphs, figures, and so on, consistently throughout the network documentation. Keeping a library of symbols and graphics icons that you can use and reuse in several documents is a handy practice.

- **Keep the documents accessible**—Although you must store at least one copy of your network documentation in a secure and safe place (hopefully at an off-site location), you must also have a copy of your network documentation readily available and accessible on the job.

- **Maintain your network documentation**—As your end systems, network devices, network topology, and other elements of your network change through time, you must reflect those changes in your network documentation to make sure it is up to date and accurate.

To obtain a more practical and tangible view of these points, consider the following scenario. You are about to start working as a network engineer in some firm. The person whose position you will be filling is retiring and more than willing to give you hints and tips. You have been granted access to the network documentation prior to your start date and have taken the time to study it before taking over the position. Imagine that you find the network documentation to be well written, organized, and easy to understand; therefore, you decide to interview the person who prepared the network documentation and is retiring. You want to learn all about good documentation skills and find out all the first-rate practices that went into the network documentation that impress you so much.

Here is the summary of what the retiring network engineer tells you and the actions you take:

- First, you find out exactly which part(s) of the network and devices you are responsible for and need to prepare the network documentation for. For example, you are told that the networks of the branch offices to which the central site connects are outside the scope of your work. Show those branches with cloud symbols. On the perimeter (edge) of the network topology diagram, show the type of connection to those branches and document the addresses and routing protocols/techniques used on those links.

- Next, find exactly what information and how much detail you need to gather and include in your network documentation. You receive numerous tips from other network personnel. Most people advise against too much extra and rather useless pieces of information.

- After some research, purchase some network documentation tools and a software package. Make sure that you use consistent tables, symbols, graphs, and so on. Also, make a conscious effort to use terms and acronyms consistently. Make a glossary of the terms used in the documentation and add it as an appendix. For this task, you might find Cisco's Internetworking Terms and Acronyms Dictionary located at http://www.cisco.com/univercd/cc/td/doc/cisintwk/ita/ useful.

- Make the network documentation available online on the intranet Web site. In addition, make the documentation hard copies available at the desktop publishing and mini-library office; someone can borrow the documentation there, but he must sign it out formally and return it as soon as he is done with it. This way, the documents are both accessible and secure.

- You make a policy in the organization that says changes to any piece of the network must be approved and then documented. If the changes affect other parts and pieces of the network, those parts of the network documentation must also be updated. For all changes, the reason for the change, the date of the change, and the department/group/people responsible for that change are recorded. This way, the network documentation always remains up to date. Also, if anyone needs explanation or clarification about any part of the network or any change, that person can contact the correct party.

# Gathering Symptoms

Chapter 5, "Gathering Symptoms," presents a flow diagram (see Figure 13-1) that depicts the process of gathering symptoms from a network.

**Figure 13-1**    *Gathering Network Symptoms*

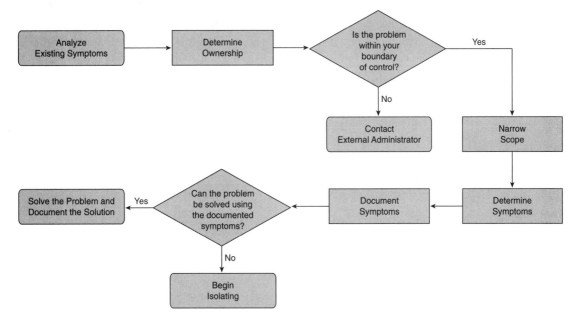

The process of gathering symptoms from a network is composed of the following steps:

1.  **Analyze Existing Symptoms**—After you gather symptoms from the users, end systems, or trouble ticket documents, you must analyze the symptoms and describe the problem.

2.  **Determine Ownership**—Based on the gathered symptoms, analysis of the symptoms, and resulting problem definition, you must decide whether the devices or the territories affected fall within your area of responsibility. If they do not, you must contact the administrator(s) or the personnel responsible; otherwise, go to the next step.

3.  **Narrow Scope**—Based on your knowledge, past experience, and symptoms observed, determine if the problem is at the access, distribution, or core layer. Then try to narrow the scope to one of a few devices or segments within the determined layer.

4.  **Determine Symptoms**—Using a layered troubleshooting approach, you must gather further data and symptoms from the suspected devices and decide whether the problem is hardware related or if it is a software configuration problem. Finally, you must determine what might be the most likely culprit.

5.  **Document Symptoms**—At this stage, you must document all your findings and the symptoms observed. If you can solve the problem(s), you must proceed to do so. Otherwise, you must start the Isolating stage of the general troubleshooting process.

The following scenario presents a realistic case that required a network support engineer to go through the stages of gathering network symptoms. The users within the Toronto branch office of a company have reported that they can no longer communicate with the users and servers who reside in other branches. Figure 13-2 depicts how the users are connected to the Toronto branch office's TorASW switch, and how the Toronto office is connected to the other company offices residing in Canada and the United States via a Frame Relay service.

**Figure 13-2**  *Diagram of the Toronto Branch Office*

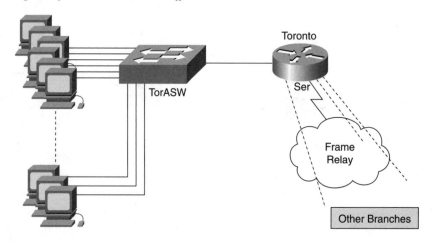

As per the guidelines for gathering symptoms from users, the network engineer asks the users the following questions and makes note of the answers:

- What works and what doesn't work?

  Users state that they can communicate among themselves, but they cannot communicate with the users or servers who reside outside their branch.

- Could you communicate with the users and servers residing in other branches before? When was the last time you did? And when did you first notice the problem?

  Users say that those functionalities were lost after their lunch break. They could communicate with the remote devices before noon.

- Did you change anything or are you aware of any changes that took place around noon?

  Most users do not report making changes or being aware of changes, but a couple of them said that they heard rumors in the cafeteria about some wide-area connection problems. (Whatever that means!)

Next, the network engineer decides to see the problem for herself and observes that as the local users stated, their computers can communicate, but they cannot connect to the devices in other branches.

The network engineer tests connectivity of user workstations to their default gateway (Toronto router) and notices that is also okay. Then the network engineer decides to Telnet to the Toronto router and test its Frame Relay (serial) connection to the other branches. She notices that the Toronto router has lost all its Frame Relay connections to the other branches. Evidently, what the users have heard in the cafeteria about the wide-area connection being down is valid. However, the wide-area connection and service is outside of this network engineer's ownership and responsibility, so she documents her findings and notifies the personnel in charge of the Toronto office's wide-area connection about the problem.

## Resolving Problems at the Physical or Data Link Layer

Chapter 7, "Isolating a Problem at the Physical or Data Link Layer," lists several common symptoms of problems occurring at the physical or data link layer. Table 13-1 provides a summary of those symptoms for your review.

**Table 13-1**  *Common Symptoms of Physical and Data Link Layer Problems*

| Common Symptoms of Problems Occurring at the Physical Layer | Common Symptoms of Problems Occurring at the Data Link Layer |
|---|---|
| No component above the physical layer works on the failing interface. | No component above the data link layer works on the failing interface. |
| Even though the network is functional, it is operating at a level below the baseline. | There is no connectivity on the link from the network layer's perspective. |
| Loss of connectivity occurs at the data link layer. | Encapsulation errors are present. |
| Framing, line coding, or synchronization errors are reported. | Address resolution errors occur. |
| Port LEDs are off, red, or at an alarming state. | CRC errors are excessive. |
| Interface errors are excessive. | Collisions are excessive. |
| Utilization occurs at a much higher level than the baseline. | Broadcasts are excessive. |
| Console, system log, management alarm, or trap messages appear. | Console, system log, management alarm, or trap messages appear. |

In Chapter 7, you were also given the following general guidelines for isolating problems at the physical and data link layers:

■ **Check the operational status and the error rates on the network device interface(s)**—Cisco IOS **show** commands, such as the **show interfaces** command, provide information on the physical and data link status of your device interfaces. The **show interfaces** command also provides statistics on drops, collisions, broadcasts, resets, restarts, overruns, and ignores.

- **Verify the correctness of interface configurations**—On routers, misconfiguration of parameters such as media type, duplex, and encapsulation type are common errors. In contrast, on LAN switch ports, incorrect speed, duplex, native VLAN, trunk, spanning tree, and channel settings are common errors.

- **Check for broken or loose cables or connections**—Cable conditions such as opens, kinks, crimps, sharp bends, and broken connectors or adapters, as well as loose screws, are common physical problems. You can discover some physical problems by visual inspection, whereas others require you to use tools, such as cable testers. Link LEDs are good indicators of link status. When in doubt, replace a suspicious cable with a known/good one for testing.

- **Check for correct cable pin-out**—Some Ethernet connections require a straight cable, and others require a crossover cable. Serial connections sometimes require a straight cable and other times require a rollover serial cable.

In the following scenario, a support engineer has been mandated to investigate and, if possible, correct the status, configuration, and error rates on two links. The first link is an Ethernet connection between a router named Router-O (ethernet0) and a router called Router-T (ethernet1). The second link is between Router-O's FastEthernet1 interface and the FastEthernet0/1 port of a switch named Switch-D. Figure 13-3 shows these connections.

**Figure 13-3**  *Ethernet Connection Between Router-O and Router-T, and the FastEthernet Connection Between Router-O and Switch-D*

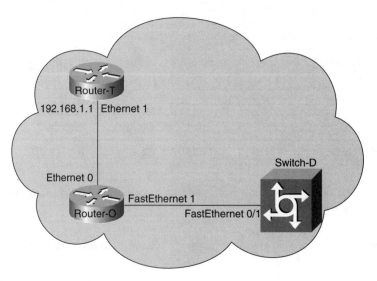

The support engineer decides to connect to the console of Router-O, ping Router-T's IP address on its Ethernet 1 interface, and see the results. He gets the results displayed in Example 13-1.

**Example 13-1** *Ping Results with Low Success*

```
Router-O#ping 192.168.1.1
Type escape sequence to abort.
Sending 5, 100-byte ICMP Echos to 192.168.1.1, timeout is 2 seconds:
!.!..
Success rate is 40 percent (2/5), round-trip min/avg/max = 1/3/5 ms
```

The 40 percent success rate of ping with a directly connected device is a sign of a problem on the interface or link. To investigate further, the engineer decides to clear counters (by using the Cisco IOS **clear counters** command) to reset all the data and error counters, redo the ping test, and inspect the Ethernet 0 interface on Router-O. He gets the results shown in Example 13-2.

**Example 13-2** *Results of* **show** *Command for Ethernet0 Interface of Orlando Router*

```
Router-O#show interfaces ethernet 0
Ethernet0 is up, line protocol is up
  Hardware is Lance, address is 0000.0c12.3456 (bia 0000.0c12.3456)
  Internet address is 192.168.1.2/24
  MTU 1500 bytes, BW 10000 Kbit, DLY 1000 usec, rely 255/255, load 1/255
  Encapsulation ARPA, loopback not set, keepalive set (10 sec)
  ARP type: ARPA, ARP Timeout 04:00:00
  Last input 00:00:00, output 00:00:00, output hang never
  Last clearing of "show interface" counters never
  Input queue: 0/75/0/0 (size/max/drops/flushes); Total output drops: 0
  Queueing strategy: fifo
  Output queue 0/40 (size/max)
  5 minute input rate 0 bits/sec, 0 packets/sec
  5 minute output rate 0 bits/sec, 0 packets/sec
     2220 packets input, 3146442 bytes, 0 no buffer
     Received 6 broadcasts, 0 runts, 0 giants, 0 throttles
     0 input errors, 0 CRC, 0 frame, 0 overrun, 0 ignored, 0 abort
     0 input packets with dribble condition detected
     2801 packets output, 3222650 bytes, 0 underruns
     16 output errors, 0 collisions, 10 interface resets
     0 babbles, 0 late collision, 0 deferred
     16 lost carrier, 0 no carrier
     0 output buffer failures, 0 output buffers swapped out
```

Based on the guidelines for isolating problems at the physical and data link layers, the engineer becomes curious about the reason for the errors, resets, and lost carriers.

Based on his training and past experience, and again, based on the guidelines, the engineer decides to inspect the cable and physical connection to Router-O's Ethernet 0 interface. There, he notices that the cable is not properly seated in the connector. He disconnects the cable, properly reconnects/reseats it, and clears the counters on Router-O. Once again, he tests the connection by issuing a ping from

Router-O to Router-T's adjacent IP address (192.168.1.1) and reinspecting the error rates in the interface. The ping results are shown in Example 13-3. The output of **show interfaces Ethernet 0** shows no more input errors, interface resets, or lost carriers.

**Example 13-3**  *Ping Results with Perfect Success*

```
Router-O#ping 192.168.1.1
Type escape sequence to abort.
Sending 5, 100-byte ICMP Echos to 192.168.1.1, timeout is 2 seconds:
!!!!!
Success rate is 100 percent (5/5), round-trip min/avg/max = 1/1/2 ms
```

Next, the network engineer goes after the problem on the FastEthernet connection between Router-O and Switch-D. Users have complained about the performance of their applications that travel across that link. The engineer decides to look at the status and error rates on the FastEthernet1 interface of the Router-O router, again using the **show interfaces** command. Example 13-4 shows the results.

**Example 13-4**  *Results of* **show** *Command for FastEthernet1 Interface of Router-O Router*

```
Router-O#show interfaces fastethernet 1
FastEthernet1 is up, line protocol is up
  Hardware is Fast Ethernet, address is 0000.0c66.7788 (bia 0000.0c66.7788)
MTU 1500 bytes, BW 100000 Kbit, DLY 100 usec,
     reliability 255/255, txload 1/255, rxload 1/255
  Encapsulation ARPA, loopback not set
  Keepalive set (10 sec)
  Half-duplex, 100Mb/s
  input flow-control is off, output flow-control is off
  ARP type: ARPA, ARP Timeout 04:00:00
  Last input 00:00:00, output 00:00:00, output hang never
  Last clearing of "show interface" counters never
  Input queue: 0/75/0/0 (size/max/drops/flushes); Total output drops: 0
  Queueing strategy: fifo
  Output queue :0/40 (size/max)
  5 minute input rate 0 bits/sec, 0 packets/sec
  5 minute output rate 0 bits/sec, 0 packets/sec
     26 packets input, 3233 bytes, 0 no buffer
     Received 25 broadcasts, 0 runts, 0 giants, 0 throttles
     0 input errors, 0 CRC, 0 frame, 0 overrun, 0 ignored
     0 watchdog, 25 multicast, 0 pause input
     0 input packets with dribble condition detected
     135237 packets output, 15687924 bytes, 0 underruns
     0 output errors, 0 collisions, 1 interface resets
     0 babbles, 255 late collision, 0 deferred
     0 lost carrier, 0 no carrier, 0 PAUSE output
     0 output buffer failures, 0 output buffers swapped out
```

The network engineer notices that the FastEthernet1 interface of Router-O router is up, and there are no drops or output errors. That is good news. Despite the good news, a surprising number (255) of late collisions is reported on the FastEthernet1 interface. Based on his past experience and the guidelines for isolating problems at the physical and data link layers, the engineer suspects that either the total length of the cable connecting Router-O's FastEthernet1 interface is longer than the recommended maximum, or Router-O's FastEthernet1 interface's half duplex setting does not match the setting on FastEthernet0/1 port of Switch-D at the other end. Therefore, the engineer decides to check the FastEthernet0/1 interface of Switch-D. The results are shown in Example 13-5.

**Example 13-5**  *Results of* **show** *Command for FastEthernet0/1 Interface of Switch-D*

```
Switch-D#show interfaces fastethernet 0/1
FastEthernet0/1 is up, line protocol is up
  Hardware is Fast Ethernet, address is 0000.0c02.2222 (bia 0000.0c02.2222)
  MTU 1500 bytes, BW 100000 Kbit, DLY 1000 usec,
     reliability 255/255, txload 1/255, rxload 1/255
  Encapsulation ARPA, loopback not set
  Keepalive set (10 sec)
  Full-duplex, 100Mb/s
  input flow-control is off, output flow-control is off
  ARP type: ARPA, ARP Timeout 04:00:00
  Last input never, output 00:00:00, output hang never
  Last clearing of "show interface" counters never
  Input queue: 0/75/0/0 (size/max/drops/flushes); Total output drops: 0
  Queueing strategy: fifo
  Output queue :0/40 (size/max)
  5 minute input rate 0 bits/sec, 0 packets/sec
  5 minute output rate 0 bits/sec, 0 packets/sec
     15835 packets input, 2215305 bytes, 0 no buffer
     Received 1358 broadcasts, 0 runts, 0 giants, 0 throttles
     10 input errors, 10 CRC, 0 frame, 0 overrun, 0 ignored
     0 watchdog, 0 multicast, 0 pause input
     0 input packets with dribble condition detected
     174455 packets output, 38446758 bytes, 0 underruns
     0 output errors, 0 collisions, 2 interface resets
     0 babbles, 0 late collision, 0 deferred
     0 lost carrier, 0 no carrier, 0 PAUSE output
     0 output buffer failures, 0 output buffers swapped out
```

After inspecting the results of the **show interfaces FastEthernet 0/1** command, the network engineer quickly notices that the interface is set up for full duplex. Therefore, it seems that the mismatch of Duplex setting on the two ends of the fast Ethernet connection between Router-O's FastEthernet1 and Switch-D's FastEthernet0/1 is the root of the problem on this link. The engineer changes the duplex setting on Router O's FastEthernet1, clears the counters, and observes the statistics on that interface. The results are positive. Example 13-6 displays the work done and the output of the **show interfaces** command after the corrections are made and the counters are cleared.

**Example 13-6**  *Change of Duplex Setting of FastEthernet 1 on Router-O and the Results*

```
Router-O(config)#interface fastethernet 1
Router-O(config-if)#duplex full
Router-O(config-if)#^Z
Router-O#
August 03 01:06:06: %SYS-5-CONFIG_I: Configured from console by console

Router-O#clear counters
Clear "show interface" counters on all interfaces [confirm]
Router-O#

Router-O#show interfaces fastethernet 1
FastEthernet1 is up, line protocol is up
  Hardware is Fast Ethernet, address is 0000.0c66.7788 (bia 0000.0c66.7788)
MTU 1500 bytes, BW 100000 Kbit, DLY 100 usec,
     reliability 255/255, txload 1/255, rxload 1/255
  Encapsulation ARPA, loopback not set
  Keepalive set (10 sec)
  Full-duplex, 100Mb/s
  input flow-control is off, output flow-control is off
  ARP type: ARPA, ARP Timeout 04:00:00
  Last input 00:00:00, output 00:00:00, output hang never
  Last clearing of "show interface" counters never
  Input queue: 0/75/0/0 (size/max/drops/flushes); Total output drops: 0
  Queueing strategy: fifo
  Output queue :0/40 (size/max)
  5 minute input rate 0 bits/sec, 0 packets/sec
  5 minute output rate 0 bits/sec, 0 packets/sec
     26 packets input, 3233 bytes, 0 no buffer
     Received 25 broadcasts, 0 runts, 0 giants, 0 throttles
     0 input errors, 0 CRC, 0 frame, 0 overrun, 0 ignored
     0 watchdog, 25 multicast, 0 pause input
     0 input packets with dribble condition detected
     138001 packets output, 16799924 bytes, 0 underruns
     0 output errors, 0 collisions, 2 interface resets
     0 babbles, 0 late collision, 0 deferred
     0 lost carrier, 0 no carrier, 0 PAUSE output
     0 output buffer failures, 0 output buffers swapped out
```

The engineer's next responsibility is to document his efforts and the work done.

# Resolving Problems at the Network Layer

You learned in Chapter 9, "Isolating a Problem at the Network Layer," that common and possible symptoms of network layer problems include the following:

■ On the failing link, no component appears to be functional above the network layer.

- The network is operating, but it is operating either consistently or intermittently below the baseline level.

- The transport layer cannot transfer data or achieve connectivity.

- Routing tables are empty, inconsistent, or incomplete.

- Routing behavior is unexpected.

- Packets are not delivered/forwarded to correct destinations; pings are either fully or partially unsuccessful.

- Console, system log, or management system alarms indicate failures/problems.

Chapter 9 lists some valuable Cisco IOS commands that you can use to isolate network layer problems, such as routing issues. A few examples of such commands follow.

The following command displays a summary of router interfaces, along with their IP address and status:

```
show ip interface [brief]
```

The following command displays the current content of the IP routing table:

```
show ip route
```

The following command displays useful information about the active IP routing protocols:

```
show ip protocols
```

The following command displays the content of the BGP table:

```
show ip bgp
```

The following command lists the neighbors of the local router's BGP process, along with some information about each one of those neighbors, such as the status of their neighbor relationship with the local BGP router:

```
show ip bgp summary
```

The following command builds and displays the current configuration of the local router in text format:

```
show running-config
```

To practice using the guidelines and commands for isolating problems at the network layer, consider that you have been given a troubleshooting assignment. The assignment is based on the network diagram depicted in Figure 13-4.

**Figure 13-4**   *Network Diagram of eBGP Relations Among Autonomous Systems 111, 222,*
*77, and 21*

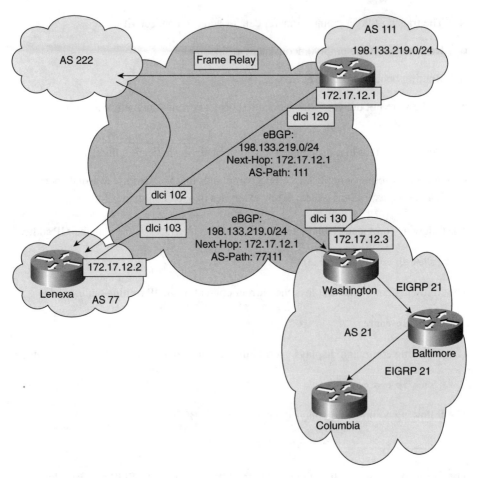

Users in autonomous system 21 have reported that they can no longer access resources in network 198.133.219.0. Using the Cisco IOS **show ip route** command, examine the content of Columbia, Baltimore, and Washington routers' routing table and notice that neither of those routers has the prefix 198.133.219.0 in its routing table. Knowing that Washington is supposed to learn the route from its external BGP neighbor (Lenexa) in autonomous system 77, examine the content of Washington router's BGP table and see if the prefix is present. You can display the IP routing table by using the command **show ip route**, and you can display the BGP table by using the **show ip bgp** command. The results are displayed in Example 13-7.

**Example 13-7**  *Content of Washington Router's BGP Table*

```
Washington#show ip route
Codes: C - connected, S - static, I - IGRP, R - RIP, M - mobile, B - BGP
       D - EIGRP, EX - EIGRP external, O - OSPF, IA - OSPF inter area
       N1 - OSPF NSSA external type 1, N2 - OSPF NSSA external type 2
       E1 - OSPF external type 1, E2 - OSPF external type 2, E - EGP
       i - IS-IS, L1 - IS-IS level-1, L2 - IS-IS level-2, ia - IS-IS inter area
       * - candidate default, U - per-user static route, o - ODR
       P - periodic downloaded static route

Gateway of last resort is not set
...
     172.17.0.0 255.255.255.255 is subnetted, 2 subnets
C       172.17.12.3 is directly connected, Loopback0
S       172.17.12.2 is directly connected, Serial0/0.1
B     77.0.0.0 255.0.0.0 [20/0] via 172.17.12.2, 00:00:42
...
Washington#show ip bgp
BGP table version is 3, local router ID is 172.17.12.3
Status codes: s suppressed, d damped, h history, * valid, > best, i - internal
Origin codes: i - IGP, e - EGP, ? - incomplete

   Network          Next Hop         Metric LocPrf Weight Path
*> 21.0.0.0         0.0.0.0               0         32768 ?
*> 77.0.0.0         172.17.12.2           0             0 77 ?
*  198.133.219.0    172.17.12.1                         0 77 111 ?
...
Washington#
```

When you examine Washington router's BGP table, you notice that the prefix 198.133.219.0 is present in the BGP table. However, when you examined Washington's IP routing table, the entry was not present. In the BGP table, you notice that the entry for 198.133.219.0 does not have a > sign behind it; in other words, the entry is not chosen as a best route. Now you understand why the route was not offered to the IP routing table and hence, it was not installed in Washington's IP routing table.

You are curious to find out why BGP still doesn't mark 198.133.219.0 as the best route even though it has only one path to it. You think of BGP's path selection process and recall that the first step in BGP's path selection states that the next-hop value of a prefix must be reachable. The next-hop value of 172.17.12.1 on the 198.133.219.0 entry is not reachable from Washington, and that explains why this entry is not selected as a best route by BGP and is not offered to IP. Example 13-8 shows the result of issuing a **ping**. As you can see, Washington can **ping** Lenexa's address (172.17.12.2), but it cannot **ping** 172.17.12.1, which is the next-hop value on the route (198.133.219.0) received from Lenexa via eBGP.

**Example 13-8** *Results of Testing Reachability of BGP Next-Hop Values from Washington*

```
Washington#ping 172.17.12.2
Type escape sequence to abort.
Sending 5, 100-byte ICMP Echos to 172.17.12.2, timeout is 2 seconds:
!!!!!
Success rate is 100 percent (5/5), round-trip min/avg/max = 60/71/100 ms

Washington#ping 172.17.12.1
Type escape sequence to abort.
Sending 5, 100-byte ICMP Echos to 172.17.12.1, timeout is 2 seconds:
.....
Success rate is 0 percent (0/5)
Washington#
```

Finally, you ask yourself why the Washington router's eBGP neighbor (Lenexa) in autonomous system 77 is not attaching its own address on the next-hop attribute of the 198.133.219.0 prefix when it sends the update toward Washington. When you notice that the router learned the route from another eBGP neighbor over Frame Relay, you remember that not altering the next-hop in this case (over multiaccess network) is the normal behavior. To change this behavior and effectively rectify the problem at hand, the administrator of Washington router's eBGP neighbor (Lenexa in autonomous system 77) must manually force the next-hop value to be replaced by its own IP address (using the BGP configuration command **neighbor** *address* **next-hop-self**). The alternative solution is to enter a static route for 172.17.12.1 in the Washington router (via its Frame Relay serial interface) and effectively make that address reachable on Washington. The network layer problem is isolated. You must now document and report the isolated network layer problem and the possible rectification options.

# Resolving Problems at the Transport and Application Layers

Chapter 11, "Isolating a Problem at the Transport or Application Layer," presented a set of common symptoms for each of the transport and application layer-related problems. Table 13-2 provides a summary of those symptoms for your review.

**Table 13-2** *Common Symptoms of Transport and Application Layer Problems*

| Common Symptoms of Problems Occurring at the Transport Layer | Common Symptoms of Problems Occurring at the Application Layer |
| --- | --- |
| There is a lack of connectivity, or resources are unreachable, while the physical, data link, and network layers are functioning properly. | Resources are not available or are unreachable, while the physical, data link, network, and transport layers are functioning properly. |

**Table 13-2**   *Common Symptoms of Transport and Application Layer Problems (Continued)*

| Common Symptoms of Problems Occurring at the Transport Layer | Common Symptoms of Problems Occurring at the Application Layer |
|---|---|
| Even though the network is functional, it is either intermittently or consistently performing at a level below the baseline. | A network service or application is not meeting the normal expectations of one or more users. (That is, it is performing at a substandard level.) |
| The application layer reports a lack of connectivity, or the application cannot connect to the intended resource. | Several users complain about a slow or sluggish network, while performance tests at the transport or network layers give good results. |
| Error messages are generated by the application or the application layer protocol. | One or more applications do not function.<br><br>A certain afflicted application reports errors. |
| Users complain or report of a lack of connectivity, functionality, or a slow network. | Console or system log messages indicate problems. |
| Console or system log messages indicate problems. | Management alarm or trap messages indicate problems. |
| Management alarm or trap messages indicate problems. | |

Now look at a scenario that demonstrates how and why an application layer protocol or program will not function, even though network and lower layer protocols might be in mint operating shape. A while ago I was contacted by one of my colleagues. He was worried because the IOS of one of the office routers had been corrupted or erased, and he could not restore it. The router had reloaded and was in ROMMON (ROM Monitor) mode. He was informed of the problem because the office had lost its connectivity to the rest of the corporation and the Internet. He quickly discovered the problem, but he said that everyone in the office was upset and complaining and that made his panic worse. Although this problem seems like a network layer problem, you will soon realize that if my colleague did not have problem(s) at upper layer(s), he could have restored the missing/corrupted operating system and in a short time, the network and its applications would resume their operation as usual.

I asked my colleague to calm down and tell me why he simply did not download the IOS from our TFTP server. We have a TFTP server in our office that stores the IOS and the up-to-date configuration of all our routers and switches. My colleague responded that that was exactly what he was trying to do, but he was not having any luck with it. However, he suspected that his lack of success might have to do with his state of mind, and that was the reason he sought my assistance. I told my colleague to connect his laptop to the console port of the failed router while we were on the phone, and while in ROMMON mode, type **?** for help. When he did that, the router listed the commands available to him in that mode, similar to the output shown in Example 13-9.

**Example 13-9**   *A Sample of Commands That Might Be Available in ROMMON Mode*
            *(Model Dependent)*

```
rommon 18 > ?
alias              set and display aliases command
boot               boot up an external process
break              set/show/clear the breakpoint
confreg            configuration register utility
cont               continue executing a downloaded image
context            display the context of a loaded image
cookie             display contents of cookie PROM in hex
dev                list the device table
dir                list files in file system
dis                display instruction stream
dnld               serial download a program module
frame              print out a selected stack frame
help               monitor builtin command help
history            monitor command history
meminfo            main memory information
repeat             repeat a monitor command
reset              system reset
set                display the monitor variables
stack              produce a stack trace
sync               write monitor environment to NVRAM
sysret             print out info from last system return
tftpdnld           tftp image download
unalias            unset an alias
unset              unset a monitor variable
xmodem             x/ymodem image download
rommon 19 >
```

I then asked him to look for and type the command for TFTP. He told me that there was a **tftpdnld** command available. I told him to enter it. My colleague, who was feeling better already, entered the command, and the router displayed information similar to that shown in Example 13-10.

**Example 13-10**   *Sample Output Result of Typing **tftpdnld** in ROMMON Mode*

```
rommon 20 > tftpdnld

Missing or illegal ip address for variable IP_ADDRESS
Illegal IP address.

usage: tftpdnld [-r]
  Use this command for disaster recovery only to recover an image via TFTP.
```

**Example 13-10**  *Sample Output Result of Typing* **tftpdnld** *in ROMMON Mode (Continued)*

```
    Monitor variables are used to set up parameters for the transfer.
    (Syntax: "VARIABLE_NAME=value" and use "set" to show current variables.)
    "ctrl-c" or "break" stops the transfer before flash erase begins.
    The following variables are REQUIRED to be set for tftpdnld:
            IP_ADDRESS: The IP address for this unit
        IP_SUBNET_MASK: The subnet mask for this unit
       DEFAULT_GATEWAY: The default gateway for this unit
           TFTP_SERVER: The IP address of the server to fetch from
             TFTP_FILE: The filename to fetch
    The following variables are OPTIONAL:
          TFTP_VERBOSE: Print setting. 0=quiet, 1=progress(default), 2=verbose
      TFTP_RETRY_COUNT: Retry count for ARP and TFTP (default=7)
          TFTP_TIMEOUT: Overall timeout of operation in seconds (default=7200)
         TFTP_CHECKSUM: Perform checksum test on image, 0=no, 1=yes (default=1)

  Command line options:
    -r: do not write flash, load to DRAM only and launch image
rommon 21 >
```

After reading the information displayed by the router, my colleague realized that several pieces of information needed to be entered before the router could attempt to download an IOS image from the TFTP server. The needed pieces of information were as follows:

- An IP address for the local router

- A subnet mask for the local router

- A default gateway for the local router

- The IP address of the TFTP server

- The name of the file (IOS image stored for the local router) on the TFTP server

I helped my colleague enter all that information by using the "VARIABLE_NAME=value" syntax as per the instructions given in Example 13-9. He typed all the required information, as shown in the upper part of Example 13-10. The router was then ready for downloading the IOS from the TFTP server. Therefore, he re-entered the command **tftpdnld**. This time the attempt was successful, as shown in the middle part of Example 13-10. At last, the router was ready to be reloaded with the appropriate IOS image recovered and restored in the flash memory. I told my colleague to enter the **boot** command; the router booted and loaded the just-restored IOS from the flash memory, as shown in the bottom section of Example 13-11. The network went into normal operation shortly thereafter.

**Example 13-11** *Entering Information Required by* **tftpdnld** *in ROMMOM to Recover an IOS Image*

```
rommon 22 > IP_ADDRESS=10.66.10.27
rommon 23 > IP_SUBNET_MASK=255.255.255.0
rommon 24 > DEFAULT_GATEWAY=10.66.10.1
rommon 25 > TFTP_SERVER=10.66.8.3
rommon 26 > TFTP_FILE=c3640-js-mz.122-2.T.bin
rommon 27 > tftpdnld
           IP_ADDRESS: 10.66.10.27
       IP_SUBNET_MASK: 255.255.255.0
      DEFAULT_GATEWAY: 10.66.10.1
          TFTP_SERVER: 10.66.8.3
            TFTP_FILE: flash:/c3640-js-mz.122-2.T.bin
Invoke this command for disaster recovery only.
WARNING: all existing data in all partitions on flash will be lost!
Do you wish to continue? y/n:  [n]:  y
Receiving c3640-js-mz.122-2.T.bin from 10.66.8.3 !!!!!!!!!!!!!!!!!!!!!!!!!!!!!!!!!!
!!!!!!!!!!!!!!!!!!!!!!!!!!!!!!!!!!!!!!!!!!!!!!!!!!!!!!!!!!!!!!!!!!!!!!!!!!!!!!!!!!!!!
!!!!!!!!!!!!!!!!!!!!!!!!!!!!!!!!!!!!!!!!!!!!!!!!!!!!!
File reception completed.
Copying file c3640-js-mz.122-2.T to flash.
Erasing flash at 0x73cf0000
Programming location 84230000
rommon 28 > boot
program load complete, entry point: 0x9000B000, size: 0xCD7C00
Self decompressing the image : #############################################
################################################################################
############################################## [OK]
...
Cisco Internetwork Operating System Software
IOS (tm) C3640 Software (C3640-JSMZ-M), Version 12.2(8)YL,
    EARLY DEPLOYMENT RELEASE SOFTWARE (fc1)
Synched to technology version 12.2(10.3)T1
TAC Support: http://www.cisco.com/tac
Copyright (c) 1986-2002 by cisco Systems, Inc.
Compiled Wed 17-Jul-02 14:04 by ealyon
Image text-base: 0x80008124, data-base: 0x8122D408
...
Press RETURN to get started!
```

Before closing, I would like to briefly analyze this scenario to clarify the initial claim that the scenario just presented was indeed related to the application layer. In the scenario just presented, the IOS image of a router was erased or was corrupted; that caused the router to reload. Upon reload, because the router could not find a good IOS image to load, it went into the ROMMON (ROM Monitor) mode. During reload or while in the ROMMON mode, the router could not and did not perform its normal and routine tasks. Many network components felt the results of this router's crash, and eventually, the users experienced connectivity and application problems. So far, all the problems sprang from the failure of a network layer device (the router). However, when I was contacted for assistance, the problem at hand and presented to me was not to isolate and correct the network problems experienced. I was asked to help because my colleague could not set up a TFTP client (the router in ROMMON mode) to copy a file from a TFTP server. I helped my colleague enter the required and appropriate commands to set up the broken router in the ROMMON mode as TFTP client and specify the location (IP address of the TFTP server) and name of the file (IOS). Therefore, we can conclude that the problem I helped troubleshoot was an application layer problem.

# Part VII: Appendix

# Answers to the "Do I Know This Already?" Quizzes and "Q&A" Sections

## Chapter 1

### "Do I Know This Already?"

1. c
2. a, d
3. c
4. d
5. c
6. d
7. b
8. a, b, d
9. b
10. c
11. d
12. a
13. b
14. a
15. c

### "Q&A"

1. What are the two components of network baseline documentation?

   Following are the two components of network baseline documentation:

   - Network configuration documentation
   - End system (network) configuration documentation

**2.** Name at least three pieces of information that a network configuration table must document.

A network configuration table must document the following information:

- Device name
- Data link layer addresses and implemented features
- Network layer addresses and implemented features
- Important information about the physical aspects of the device
- Other information that someone who is familiar with the network or who has experience troubleshooting it considers important to document

**3.** The network topology diagram is a graphical representation of the network that must illustrate all the devices and how they are connected. Name at least three pieces of information that reveal physical, data link, or network layer information about a device.

The following reveal physical, data link, or network layer information about a device:

- Device name
- Media type
- MAC address
- IP address
- Subnet mask
- Interface name
- Routing protocol(s)

**4.** List at least three commands that are useful for discovering network configurations on routers and multilayer switches.

The following commands are useful for discovering network configurations on routers and multilayer switches:

- **show version**
- **show interfaces**
- **show interfaces** *interface-type number*
- **show ip interfaces**
- **show ip interfaces brief**
- **show ip protocols**
- **show spanning-tree summary**

- **show spanning-tree vlan** *vlan-number*
- **show cdp neighbors [detail]**
- **show cdp entry** *device-id*
- **show ip ospf neighbors**
- **show ip eigrp neighbors**

**5.** List at least three commands that are useful for discovering network configurations on standard switches.

The following commands are useful for discovering network configurations on standard switches:

- **show version**
- **show interfaces description**
- **show interfaces status**
- **show etherchannel summary**
- **show interfaces trunk**
- **show spanning-tree**
- **show spantree**
- **show cdp neighbors**
- **show cdp entry** *device-id*

**6.** List the five stages of the process of creating network documentation.

Following are the five stages in the process of creating network documentation:

- Stage 1: Login
- Stage 2: Interface Discovery
- Stage 3: Document
- Stage 4: Diagram
- Stage 5: Device Discovery

**7.** What are the rules/guidelines for creating network documentation?

The following are the rules/guidelines for creating network documentation:

- Determine the scope.

- Know your objective.

- Be consistent.

- Keep the documents accessible.

- Maintain the documentation.

# Chapter 2

## "Do I Know This Already?"

1. d
2. d
3. b
4. d
5. c
6. b
7. c
8. c
9. c
10. c

## "Q&A"

1. Name the two main components of end system network documentation.

   The two main components of end system network documentation are an end system network configuration table and an end system network topology diagram.

2. Identify at least three pieces of information recorded in the end system network configuration table that relate to the TCP/IP physical layer.

   Following is the information recorded in the end system network configuration table that relates to the TCP/IP physical layer:

   - Physical location

   - Manufacturer/model

   - CPU type/speed

   - RAM

Chapter 2 **263**

- Storage

- Device name

- Device purpose

3. List at least three types of information recorded in the end system network configuration table that relate to the TCP/IP Internet/network layer.

   Following is the information recorded in the end system network configuration table that relates to the TCP/IP Internet/network layer:

   - IP address

   - Subnet mask

   - Default gateway

   - DNS address

   - WINS address

4. Name at least two types of information recorded in the end system network configuration table that relate to the TCP/IP application layer.

   Following is the information recorded in the end system network configuration table that relates to the TCP/IP application layer:

   - Operating system/version

   - Network applications

   - High-bandwidth applications

   - Delay-sensitive applications

5. What is the end system network topology diagram, and what should it depict?

   The end system network topology diagram graphically represents how the end device(s) logically and physically fit into the network. The diagram should illustrate every device along with its name and how it connects to the network.

6. Identify the end system network configuration information-gathering command(s) that list the set of active routes on an end system running Windows and on an end system running a UNIX/MAC operating system.

   The command **route print** lists the set of active routes on an end system that is running a Windows operating system.

   The command **route -n** lists the set of active routes on an end system that is running a UNIX/MAC operating system.

7. Name the general end system network configuration information-gathering command that displays the content of the local end system's ARP cache table.

   The command **arp -a** displays the content of the local end system's ARP cache table.

8. Provide the command that displays IP information for hosts that are running Windows NT/Windows 2000/Windows XP and its counterpart command for Windows 9x/Windows Me.

   The **ipconfig** and **winipcfg** commands display IP information for hosts that are running Windows NT/Windows 2000/Windows XP and Windows 9x/Windows Me, respectively.

9. Identify the command that displays IP information for UNIX and MAC OS X hosts.

   The command **ifconfig -a** displays IP information for UNIX and MAC OS X hosts.

10. Name at least three guidelines for creating end system network configuration documentation.

    The following are the guidelines for creating end system network configuration documentation:

    - Determine the scope.
    - Know the objective.
    - Be consistent.
    - Keep the documents accessible.
    - Maintain the documentation.

# Chapter 3

## "Do I Know This Already?"

1. c
2. d
3. b
4. b
5. a
6. d
7. c
8. a
9. e
10. b

## "Q&A"

**1.** At which stage of the encapsulated data flow process is a header that includes network address information added to each segment?

Stage 1: Encapsulation

**2.** Explain Stage 2 of the encapsulated data flow process.

Stage 2 of the encapsulated data flow process is about passing the data over the physical medium as bits.

**3.** Explain Stage 3 of the encapsulated data flow process.

Stage 3 is about how the intermediate network devices (routers, switches, and so on) change or alter and forward, flood, or block the data. Standard switches and hubs read physical addressing information and forward frames to an interface. Routers, firewalls, and multilayer switches read network addressing information and forward packets to an interface.

**4.** Explain Stage 4 of the encapsulated data flow process.

The interface of the receiving end system receives the data from the physical medium, removes the data control information, and converts the data as needed for use with the target application.

**5.** List the layers of the OSI model that TCP/IP's network interface layer maps to.

TCP/IP's network interface layer maps to the OSI model's physical and data link layers.

**6.** Name the layer or layers of the OSI model that TCP/IP's Internet layer maps to.

TCP/IP's Internet layer maps to the OSI model's network layer.

**7.** Identify the layer or layers of the OSI model that TCP/IP's application layer maps to.

TCP/IP's application layer maps to the OSI model's session, presentation, and application layers.

**8.** List the layer or layers of the OSI model that TCP/IP's transport layer maps to.

TCP/IP's transport layer maps to the OSI model's transport layer.

**9.** Which logical layers does a router map to?

A router maps to the physical, data link, network, and transport layers.

**10.** Name the logical layers that a firewall maps to.

A firewall maps to the physical, data link, network, and transport layers.

11.    List the logical layers that a multilayer switch maps to.

A multilayer switch maps to the physical, data link, network, and transport layers.

12.    What are the logical layers that a standard Layer 2 switch maps to?

A standard switch maps to the physical and data link layers.

13.    Identify the logical layer that a hub maps to.

A hub maps to the physical layer.

14.    Name the logical layers that an end system maps to.

An end system maps to the physical, data link, network, transport, and application layers.

# Chapter 4

## "Do I Know This Already?"

1.    b

2.    a, c, d

3.    a

4.    d

5.    b

6.    c

7.    a

8.    b

9.    c

10.    a

## "Q&A"

1.    What are the stages of the general troubleshooting process?

The stages of the general troubleshooting process are as follows:

- Gather Symptoms

- Isolate the Problem

- Correct the Problem

2. What do you do in the first stage of the troubleshooting process?

   At the Gather Symptoms stage, you gather and document symptoms from the network, end systems, or users. You must determine what network components have been affected and how the functionality of the network has changed compared to the baseline.

3. What do you do in the second stage of the troubleshooting process?

   At the Isolate the Problem stage, you identify the characteristics of problems at the logical layers of the network so that you can select the most likely cause.

4. What do you do in the third stage of the troubleshooting process?

   At the Correct the Problem stage, you correct an identified problem by implementing, testing, and documenting a solution.

5. True or false: You should establish a policy for each stage of the troubleshooting process.

   True. The way that symptoms and facts are gathered; changes are authorized, implemented, and documented; and testing and final documentation are accomplished must be based on policies. This ensures reliability and standardization of the troubleshooting process.

6. True or false: You have not truly isolated the problem until you have identified a single problem or a set of related problems.

   True. Many people confuse a well-gathered set of symptoms with an isolated problem. An isolated problem is clearly recognized, and if corrected, should eliminate the observed symptoms.

# Chapter 5

## "Do I Know This Already?"
1. d
2. a
3. e
4. c
5. b

**6.** c

**7.** a, c, d

**8.** a, c, e

**9.** e

**10.** b

# "Q&A"

**1.** What is the first stage in the general troubleshooting process, and why is it important and useful?

Gathering Symptoms is the first stage of the general troubleshooting process. Gathering a comprehensive collection of symptoms allows you to understand and recognize the problem, be able to describe and document it, and focus on the problem at hand.

**2.** What three categories can the Gathering Symptoms process be broken into?

The three categories that Gathering Symptoms can be broken into are Gathering Network Symptoms, Gathering User Symptoms, and Gathering End System Symptoms.

**3.** What are the five stages of the Gathering Network Symptoms process?

The five stages of the Gathering Network Symptoms process are Analyze Existing Symptoms, Determine Ownership, Narrow Scope, Determine Symptoms, and Document Symptoms.

**4.** Provide three Cisco IOS **show** commands for gathering network symptoms.

**show ip interface brief**

**show ip route**

**show running-config**

**5.** Provide three Cisco IOS diagnostic and troubleshooting commands for gathering network symptoms (No **show** or **debug** commands).

**ping** {*host* | *ip-address*}

**traceroute** {*host* | *ip-address*}

**telnet** {*host* | *ip-address*}

**6.** Provide at least four guidelines for gathering symptoms for a user's hardware or software.

Guidelines for gathering symptoms for a user's hardware or software are as follows:

- Ask questions that are pertinent to the problem.
- Use each question as a means to either eliminate or discover possible problems.
- Speak at a technical level that a user can understand.
- Ask the user when he first noticed the problem.
- If possible, ask the user to re-create the problem.
- Determine the sequence of events that took place before the problem occurred.
- Match the symptoms that the user describes with common problem causes.

**7.** List at least four general questions you can ask a user during the process of gathering user symptoms.

General questions you can ask a user during the process of gathering user symptoms are as follows:

- What does not work? What does work?
- Are the things that do and do not work related?
- Has the thing that does not work ever worked before?
- When did you first notice/experience the problem?
- What has changed since the last time it worked?
- When exactly does the problem occur?
- Can you reproduce the problem? If yes, how do you reproduce it?

**8.** What are the four stages in the process of gathering symptoms from an end system?

The four stages in the process of gathering symptoms from an end system are Interview User, Analyze Symptoms, Determine Symptoms, and Document Symptoms.

**9.** What Windows command identifies the path a packet takes through the network? What is the Mac/UNIX counterpart for this command?

Windows: **tracert** {*host* | *ip-address*}

Mac/UNIX: **traceroute** {*host* | *ip-address*}

**10.** What Windows command displays information relating to the IP configuration of the end system?

**ipconfig /all**

# Chapter 6

## "Do I Know This Already?"

 1. b

 2. a

 3. c

 4. c

 5. a

 6. b

 7. d

 8. d

 9. c, d

 10. a

## "Q&A"

 1. What is the benefit of following a method for troubleshooting?

   With a method to follow, you can solve the problem more quickly and cost effectively.

 2. What are the main troubleshooting approaches?

   The main troubleshooting approaches are bottom-up, top-down, and divide-and-conquer.

 3. Which approach is best for complex cases?

   The bottom-up approach is best for complex cases.

 4. Which approach is usually adapted for user-initiated and simple cases?

   The top-down approach is usually adapted for user-initiated and simple cases.

 5. What are the drawbacks of the bottom-up approach?

   The downside to selecting the bottom-up approach is that it requires you to check every device, interface, and so on in the network until you find the possible cause of the problem along with documenting each conclusion and possibility.

6.  What are the drawbacks of the top-down approach?

    You usually take the top-down approach for simpler cases. The disadvantage to selecting this approach is that if the problem turns out to be more complex or happens to spring from lower layer culprits (physical, data link, or network), you will have wasted time and effort on examining the user applications or upper OSI layer components. Furthermore, if you have internetwork expertise, you might not necessarily have the expertise to diagnose or correct application layer issues.

7.  What are the guidelines for selecting the most effective troubleshooting approach?

    The guidelines for selecting the most effective troubleshooting approach are determining the scope of the problem, applying experience, and analyzing the symptoms.

8.  What does it mean to determine the scope of the problem?

    Determining the scope of the problem means selecting the troubleshooting approach based on the perceived complexity of the problem.

9.  What does it mean to apply experience?

    Applying experience means that if you have troubleshot a particular problem previously, you might know of a way to shorten the troubleshooting process.

10. What is the main benefit of analyzing the symptoms?

    Analyzing the symptoms allows you to have a better chance of solving a problem if you know more about it. You might find that you can immediately correct a problem simply by analyzing the symptoms.

11. At which layer of the OSI model does the bottom-up approach to troubleshooting begin?

    The bottom-up approach to troubleshooting begins at the physical layer.

12. You have isolated a problem to be an encapsulation type mismatch between point-to-point serial interfaces (data link layer). Given this problem, which troubleshooting approach would be the least effective to select?

    The top-down troubleshooting approach would be the least effective to select in this case. Based on the given information, testing the application and the upper layers is wasteful.

13. A user has reported that a certain application does not run from his end system. You know that no filters are applied that would prevent the application from working. Running a **traceroute** command verifies that a connection exists between the end system of the user and the application server. Applying a layered approach to troubleshooting, which layer should you troubleshoot next?

    You should troubleshoot the application layer because the network layer seems to be in good working order. With the lack of filters (or ACLs), the problem is most likely application related.

**14.**    If you know that a user can access some resources but not others, which layer is the least likely culprit?

The physical layer is the least likely culprit. If there were physical layer problems, *no* resources would be accessible.

**15.**    When you learn that the users cannot browse the World Wide Web, you decide to first check the network layer and, based on your findings, decide what to troubleshoot next. Which approach have you adapted?

This is the divide-and-conquer approach.

# Chapter 7

## "Do I Know This Already?"

**1.**    b

**2.**    d

**3.**    b

**4.**    b

**5.**    b

**6.**    b

**7.**    d

**8.**    b, d

**9.**    a

**10.**    b

## "Q&A"

**1.**    List at least four common symptoms of physical layer problems.

The following are common symptoms of physical layer problems:

- No component on the failing interface appears to be functional above the physical layer.

- The network is functional, but it is operating either consistently or intermittently less than the baseline level.

- No connectivity on the interfaces is seen from the data link layer.

- Framing errors are present.

- Line coding errors occur.

- Synchronization errors appear.

- LEDs are off, flashing, or in a state other than the expected state during normal operation.

- Utilization is excessive.

- Interface errors have increased.

- Console messages (reporting error) emerge.

- System log file messages (reporting error) occur.

- Management system alarms indicate problems.

**2.**   List at least four common symptoms of data link layer problems.

The following are common symptoms of data link layer problems:

- No component on the failing link appears to be functional above the data link layer.

- The link is functional, but it is operating either consistently or intermittently less than the baseline level.

- No connectivity on the link is seen from the network layer.

- Framing errors appear.

- Encapsulation errors occur.

- Address resolution errors exist.

- Excessive CRC errors are present.

- Frame check sequence errors pop up.

- Broadcast traffic increases.

- MAC address cycling between ports occurs.

- Console messages (reporting error) appear.

- System log file messages (reporting error) emerge.

- Management system alarms indicate problems.

**3.**   Name an end system command for isolating physical and data link layer problems.

**ping**, **arp –a**, and **netstat [–rn]** are end system commands that help isolate physical and data link layer problems.

**4.** What does the end system command **netstat –rn** do?

The end system command **netstat –rn** displays the status of all connected devices and links without querying a DNS server.

**5.** Name a Microsoft Windows command that is useful for isolating physical and data link layer problems.

**Ipconfig /all**, **tracert**, and **winipcfg** are Microsoft Windows commands that help isolate physical and data link layer problems.

**6.** Name a UNIX/Mac OS X command that is useful for isolating physical and data link layer problems.

**Ifconfig –a** and **traceroute** are UNIX/Mac OS X commands that help isolate physical and data link layer problems.

**7.** List at least two Cisco IOS commands for isolating physical and data link layer problems.

The following Cisco IOS commands help isolate physical and data link layer problems:

- **show version**
- **show ip interface brief**
- **show interfaces**
- **show cdp neighbor [detail]**
- **show controllers**
- **debug**

**8.** Which Cisco IOS command would be useful for troubleshooting data link address resolution?

The following Cisco IOS commands would be useful for troubleshooting data link address resolution:

- **show arp**
- **debug {arp | lapb | stun}**

**9.** List at least two valid guidelines for isolating problems at the physical and data link layers.

The following are guidelines for isolating problems at the physical and data link layers:

- Check operational status and data error rates.
- Verify proper interface configurations.
- Check cable configuration.

- Check for bad cables or connections.

- Check for incorrect cables.

# Chapter 8

## "Do I Know This Already?"

   **1.** d

   **2.** d

   **3.** c

   **4.** c

   **5.** b

   **6.** a

   **7.** d

   **8.** a

   **9.** c

   **10.** a

## "Q&A"

   **1.** Which Cisco IOS commands allow you to deactivate and activate a Cisco router's interface? In which configuration mode can you do that?

   The **shutdown** and **no shutdown** Cisco IOS commands are entered in interface configuration mode to deactivate and activate a Cisco router's interface.

   **2.** Which Cisco IOS command displays the status of all router interfaces along with their IP addresses (if the interface has one) in a brief table format?

   **show ip interface brief**

   **3.** Specify the Cisco IOS commands (in sequence) that you need to enter to 1) go from privileged mode to global configuration mode; 2) get into interface configuration mode for serial1/0; 3) set the clock rate to 64000 on serial 1/0.

   1. **configure terminal**

   2. **interface serial1/0**

   3. **clock rate 64000**

4.  Which Cisco IOS command allows you to test connectivity to an IP host or device?

    **ping** {*destination*}

5.  Name the Cisco IOS command that allows you to set the encapsulation type on a router interface. Specify the mode in which the command must be entered.

    The command that allows you to set the encapsulation type on a router interface is **encapsulation**, and you must enter it from within interface configuration mode.

6.  Which command allows you to change the Frame Relay LMI type on an interface?

    The command that allows you to change the Frame Relay LMI type on an interface is **frame-relay lmi-type**, and you enter it from interface configuration mode.

7.  When troubleshooting physical and data link layers, what support resources are available to you?

    Many resources are available to troubleshooters. Colleagues, certified Cisco consultants, and Cisco Technical Assistance Center personnel are valuable resources. CCO has information on various legacy and new technologies, configuration and troubleshooting of Cisco devices, design and migration solutions, and so on. Web sites of the IETF, ITU-T, Frame Relay Forum, and ATM Forum are also valuable sources of information and troubleshooting resources.

8.  Before you modify the configuration of a Cisco device, what is the first thing you must ensure?

    Ensure that you have a valid saved configuration for any device on which you intend to modify the configuration. This provides for eventual recovery to a known initial state.

9.  Name at least two guidelines that are important to follow when you have isolated a problem and are ready to correct it.

    Following are the guidelines that are important to follow when you have isolated a problem and are ready to correct it:

    1.  Ensure that you have a valid saved configuration for any device on which you intend to modify the configuration. This provides for eventual recovery to a known initial state.

    2.  Make initial changes to the configuration.

    3.  Evaluate and document the results of each change that you make.

    4.  Verify that the changes you make actually fix the problem without introducing new problems.

5. Continue making changes until the original problem appears to be solved.

6. Get input from outside resources.

7. Document the solution.

**10.** What is CCO's Web (HTTP) address?

www.cisco.com

# Chapter 9

## "Do I Know This Already?"

**1.** d

**2.** c

**3.** b

**4.** c

**5.** c

**6.** c

**7.** e

**8.** d

**9.** a

**10.** b

## "Q&A"

**1.** Is it possible to have network layer problems while the addresses are correct and routing is operational and functional?

Yes. The network might be functional, but it might be operating either consistently or intermittently at a lower capacity (speed, response, or throughput) than the baseline level.

**2.** Is it possible to have a network layer problem—such as a router's address being duplicated by another router or device—but see no log messages on the console? Explain.

Yes. If console message logging is turned off manually by using the **no logging console** command, system log messages are no longer displayed on the console. You can review these messages from the logging buffer by typing the **show logging** command.

3. Is it possible that only a percentage of ping messages sent to an IP address succeed? Explain.

   Yes. Only a percentage of pings might succeed if the echo request messages sent to the IP address or the echo replies sent from the IP address take alternate and different paths and, based on the path taken, some of those messages become lost or time out.

4. What does the command **route print** do? Is it an end system or a Cisco IOS command?

   The **route print** command is an end system command that displays the content of the end system's routing table.

5. Provide three commands—one for Windows NT/2000/XP, one for Windows 9x/Me, and one for UNIX/MAC OS X—that display information about that device's IP settings (address and other information).

   Windows NT/2000/XP: **ipconfig**

   Windows 9x/Me: **winipcfg**

   UNIX/MAC OS X: **ifconfig -a**

6. Which two Cisco IOS commands display and clear the content of the ARP cache table?

   **show ip arp** (or **show arp**)

   **clear arp-cache**

7. Which Cisco IOS command displays the list of local router interfaces, their IP addresses, and their physical and logical status?

   **show ip interface [brief]**

8. List two Cisco IOS commands that display all BGP neighbors (peers) and the status of their peering with the local router. (One provides more detail than the other.)

   **show ip bgp summary**

   **show ip bgp neighbors**

9. Which Cisco IOS command displays the content of the BGP table?

   **show ip bgp**

10. It is important to use an effective and systematic technique to successfully isolate a problem at the network layer. Provide at least two of the recommended guidelines for isolating network layer problems.

    Following are the recommended guidelines for isolating network layer problems:

    • Identify a single pair of problematic source and destination devices.

- Ping a device across the connection.
- Test connectivity at each hop of a connection.
- Troubleshoot in both directions along an IP path.
- Use a network diagram.

# Chapter 10

## "Do I Know This Already?"

1. b
2. c
3. d
4. d
5. e
6. b
7. a
8. b
9. c
10. e

## "Q&A"

1. Explain the effect of the command **ip address 192.168.1.20 255.255.255.0 secondary**.

   The command **ip address 192.168.1.20 255.255.255.0 secondary** sets the IP address 192.168.1.20 255.255.255.0 as a secondary address for an interface.

2. What will the command **interface Ethernet 0** do?

   The command **interface Ethernet 0** switches the command prompt from global configuration mode (in fact, from any configuration mode) to interface configuration mode for the Ethernet 0 interface.

3. Explain the purpose of *distance* in the command **ip route** *prefix mask address* [*distance*].

   *distance* allows you to specify an administrative distance other than the default administrative distance that is assigned to static routes.

4. What end system command allows you to configure IP information on hosts that are running UNIX?

   **ifconfig**

5. Which Cisco IOS command enables or disables console logging?

   **[no] logging console**

6. Which Cisco IOS command can you use to display the configured access lists on a router?

   **show access-lists**

7. What is the URL for Cisco Systems' Technical Assistance Center?

   www.cisco.com/tac/

8. What is the last task that you should perform after correcting a problem?

   Document the solution.

9. List the seven recommended steps for correcting problems at the network layer.

   1. Verify that you have a valid saved configuration for the device whose configuration you intend to modify.

   2. Make initial configuration changes.

   3. Evaluate and document the results of each change that you make.

   4. Verify that the changes you make actually fix the problem without introducing new problems.

   5. Continue making changes until the original problem appears to be solved.

   6. If necessary, get input from outside resources.

   7. After you have resolved the problem, document the solution.

# Chapter 11

## "Do I Know This Already?"

1. c

2. e

**3.**  a

**4.**  b, c, d

**5.**  b

**6.**  e

**7.**  d

**8.**  a, e

**9.**  e

**10.**  b

## "Q&A"

**1.**  List at least three possible symptoms of transport layer problems.

The following are possible symptoms of transport layer problems:

- Unreachable resources and connectivity problems are an issue, while the physical, data link, and network layers are functional.

- The network is operating either consistently or intermittently less than the baseline level.

- Users perceive link connectivity issues at the application layer, or network applications generate error messages.

- Users complain that the network is slow.

- Console messages report abnormal events; unexpected events are observed in system logs messages.

- Management system alarms indicate problems.

- Partial or intermittent connectivity or erratic performance results from TCP windowing problems, long round-trip times, excess retransmissions, and so on.

**2.**  List at least three possible symptoms of application layer problems.

The following are possible symptoms of application layer problems:

- Resources are unreachable or unusable, while the physical, data link, network, and transport layers are functional.

- Operation of a network service or application does not meet the normal expectations of a user.

- Applications generate error messages or report lack of functionality.

- Users complain that the network is slow or that their network applications are not functioning, are unavailable, or are too slow.

- Console messages indicate abnormal events; system log file messages report errors.

- Management system alarms deliver unexpected news.

3.  Provide at least one of the guidelines for isolating problems at the transport and application layers.

The guidelines for isolating problems at the transport and application layers are as follows:

- Establish that the problem is not at the network or lower layers by testing and proving IP connectivity between two points of interest.

- If you are troubleshooting e-mail–related problems, beware of the fact that sending and receiving e-mail utilize and depend on different protocols and might involve multiple components; therefore, you must test those functions separately.

- You might have to research the related RFCs to discover the detail of a particular transport or application layer protocol. Certain protocols/applications embed information such as addresses. Other applications might have special control, handshake, or authentication requirements.

4.  What do the commands **ipconfig** and **winipcfg** do? How are they different?

**ipconfig** and **winipcfg** both display IP information (IP address, subnet mask, and default gateway) about the host. **ipconfig** is supported on Windows NT/2000/XP, whereas **winipcfg** is supported on Windows 9x and Windows Me operating systems.

5.  What are the well-known TCP ports for the SMTP and POP protocols?

Ports 25 and 110, respectively, are the well-known TCP ports for the SMTP and POP protocols.

6.  Explain the purpose and result of the **copy flash tftp** command.

You can test the functionality of the TFTP application by trying to copy/back up the IOS file from the flash memory of the local router to a TFTP server that is present in the network using the **copy flash tftp** command.

7.  Provide the command that allows you to test Telnet functionality from a router using the address of a particular interface.

**telnet** {*ip-address* | *host*} **/source-interface** *interface*

8. Which Cisco IOS debug command allows you to inspect real-time DHCP server events?

**debug ip dhcp server [events | packets]**

# Chapter 12

## "Do I Know This Already?"

1. e

2. a

3. b

4. d

5. c

6. b

7. a

8. c

9. b

10. a

## "Q&A"

1. Which Cisco IOS command applies an access list to an interface?

**ip access-group** {*access-list-number* | *access-list-name*} [**in** | **out**]

2. Which Cisco IOS command enables SNMP and sets community string?

**snmp-server community** *name* [**rw** | **ro**] [*access-list-number*]

3. List the commands that configure the NTP server and the NTP peer.

**ntp server** {*ip-address*}

**ntp peer** {*ip-address*}

4. Which Cisco IOS command configures the router to timestamp log or debug messages with the local date and time?

**service timestamps** {**log** | **debug**} **datetime localtime**

5. Which Cisco IOS command enables (or disables) DHCP server functionality on the local router?

   **service dhcp**

6. Which Cisco IOS interface configuration command converts the UDP broadcasts (with certain destination ports, such as 68, 67 for BootP) to unicast and sends them to the IP address specified?

   **ip helper-address** {*ip-address*}

7. What are the URLs for the Web pages of the IETF, ITU, FRF, and ATM Forum?

   **Internet Engineering Task Force**—www.ietf.org

   **International Telecommunications Union**—www.itu.int/home

   **Frame Relay Forum**—www.frforum.com

   **ATM Forum**—www.atmforum.com

8. What are the URLs for Cisco Systems Technologies Reference, Cisco's Technical Assistance Center, and CCO?

   **Cisco Systems Technologies Reference**—www.cisco.com/univercd/home/home.htm

   **Cisco's Technical Assistance Center**—www.cisco.com/tac/

   **CCO**—www.cisco.com

9. What information must you gather and have ready before contacting Cisco Technical Assistance Center?

   You should have the following information prepared before contacting Technical Assistance Center:

   - A complete network diagram, or at least the affected area. The IP address/mask of the IP devices should be shown if possible.

   - All the information and any facts gathered.

   - The output of the **show tech-support** command if the number of affected routers is fewer than four.

   - Dial-in or Telnet access to the devices under investigation.

**10.** List the seven steps to correct problems occurring at the transport and application layers.

Following are the seven steps to correct problems occurring at the transport and application layers:

1. For the device(s) whose configuration you intend to change, ensure that there is a saved valid configuration.

2. Make the intended changes. Make one change at a time.

3. Evaluate and document the results of your changes.

4. Verify that your changes did not introduce new problems/symptoms.

5. Continue making changes until problems are fixed.

6. Seek assistance from outside sources, such as other colleagues, consultants, and Cisco's Technical Assistance Center, if necessary.

7. Document the solution.

# GLOSSARY

**access list**  A list kept by routers and switches to control access to or from the router or switch for a number of services (such as to prevent packets with a certain IP address from leaving a particular interface on the router or switch).

**administratively down**  A state that an interface might be in. An interface with the **shutdown** command stays in this state until the **no shutdown** command is entered.

**ANSI**  American National Standards Institute. A voluntary organization composed of corporate, government, and other members that coordinates standards-related activities, approves U.S. standards, and develops positions for the United States in international standards organizations. ANSI helps develop international and U.S. standards relating to, among other things, communications and networking. ANSI is a member of the IEC and the ISO.

**application layer**  Layer 7 of the OSI reference model. This layer provides services to application processes (such as e-mail, file transfer, and terminal emulation) that are outside the OSI model. The application layer identifies and establishes the availability of intended communication partners and the resources required to connect with them. It also synchronizes cooperating applications and establishes an agreement on the procedures for error recovery and the control of data integrity.

**ARP**  Address Resolution Protocol. An Internet protocol that is used to map an IP address to a MAC address. Defined in RFC 826.

**ATM**  Asynchronous Transfer Mode. The international standard for cell relay in which multiple service types (such as voice, video, or data) are conveyed in fixed-length (53-byte) cells. Fixed-length cells allow cell processing to occur in hardware, thereby reducing transit delays. ATM is designed to take advantage of high-speed transmission media, such as E3, SONET, and T3.

**ATM Forum**  An international organization jointly founded in 1991 by Cisco Systems, NET/ADAPTIVE, Northern Telecom, and Sprint. This organization develops and promotes standards-based implementation agreements for ATM technology. The ATM Forum expands on official standards developed by ANSI and ITU-T and develops implementation agreements in advance of official standards.

**autonomous system**    A collection of networks under a common administration sharing a common routing strategy. An autonomous system must be assigned a unique 16-bit number.

**availability**    The amount of time that a telephone system or other device is operational—that is, how long it processes telephone calls or other transactions. Availability is represented as the ratio of the total time a device is operational during a given time interval to the length of that interval.

**bandwidth**    The difference between the highest and lowest frequencies available for network signals. Also, the rated throughput capacity of a given network medium or protocol. The frequency range necessary to convey a signal is measured in hertz (Hz); for example, voice signals typically require approximately 7 kHz of bandwidth, and data traffic typically requires approximately 50 kHz of bandwidth.

**baseline**    All information about a network that is in normal operating condition; includes diagrams, address specifications and lists, list of protocols in use, performance information, and so on.

**BGP**    Border Gateway Protocol. The interdomain routing protocol that replaces EGP. BGP exchanges reachability information with other BGP systems. It is defined in RFC 1163.

**bottom-up troubleshooting approach**    An approach to troubleshooting that starts with the physical components of the network and works its way up the layers of the OSI model until the problem's cause is identified.

**broadcast**    A data packet that is sent to all nodes within a single logical network. Broadcasts are identified by a broadcast address.

**cache**    A piece of (fast) memory that is used to hold information that frequently needs to be accessed. Different types of cache are available, and they hold different types of information. ARP cache, Fast Switching cache, and Multilayer Switching cache are examples of different types of cache.

**CDP**    Cisco Discovery Protocol. A media- and protocol-independent device-discovery protocol that runs on all Cisco-manufactured equipment, including routers, access servers, bridges, and switches. Using CDP, a device can advertise its existence to other devices and receive information about other devices on the same LAN or on the remote side of a WAN. CDP runs on all media that support SNA systems, including LANs, Frame Relay, and ATM media.

**CDP neighbors**    Neighbors that are discovered (adjacent) through receiving of their CDP multicast frames.

**Cisco IOS Software**    Cisco operating system software that provides common functionality, scalability, and security for all Cisco products. Cisco IOS Software allows centralized, integrated, and automated installation and management of internetworks while ensuring support for a wide variety of protocols, media, services, and platforms.

**Cisco Technical Assistance Center**    The focal point of all Cisco software and hardware maintenance and support services. Contact the Cisco Technical Assistance Center for help with installation and testing, performance, training, documentation, equipment repair, Return Material Authorization (RMA) service, and equipment specifications.

**clock rate**    This command is used to set the clocking rate on a serial interface that has the DCE end of the serial cable plugged into it.

**collision**    In Ethernet, the result of two nodes transmitting simultaneously. The frames from each device impact and are damaged when they meet on the physical medium.

**congestion**    A condition caused by traffic in excess of network capacity.

**Correct the Problem stage**    The stage of troubleshooting at which the isolated cause of the problem is corrected.

**CPU**    Central Processing Unit. A complex microcomputer chip that controls most of the important tasks performed by other components of the computing device.

**CRC**    Cyclic redundancy check. An error-checking technique in which the frame recipient calculates a remainder by dividing frame contents by a prime binary divisor and compares the calculated remainder to a value stored in the frame by the sending node.

**data flow**    A grouping of traffic, identified by a combination of source address/mask, destination address/mask, IP next protocol field, and source and destination ports, where the protocol and port fields can have the values of any. In effect, all traffic that matches a specific combination of these values is grouped logically in a data flow. A data flow can represent a single TCP connection between two hosts, or it can represent all the traffic between two subnets. IPSec protection is applied to data flows.

**data flow control layer**    Layer 5 of the architectural model. This layer determines and manages interactions between session partners, particularly data flow. Corresponds to the session layer of the OSI reference model.

**datagram**   A logical grouping of information sent as a network layer unit over a transmission medium without prior establishment of a virtual circuit. IP datagrams are the primary information units in the Internet. The terms *cell, frame, message, packet,* and *segment* are also used to describe logical information groupings at various layers of the OSI reference model and in various technology circles.

**DCE**   1. data communications equipment (EIA expansion). Provides clocking to the data terminal equipment (DTE). 2. data circuit-terminating equipment (ITU-T expansion). Devices and connections of a communications network that compose the network end of the user-to-network interface. The DCE provides a physical connection to the network, forwards traffic, and provides a clocking signal that synchronizes data transmission between DCE and DTE devices. Modems and interface cards are examples of DCE.

**debugging**   A term that is used for tools and commands that help remove culprits from computing software or configuration files.

**default gateway**   An address to which an IP host forwards the data whose destination is outside the IP host's local subnet.

**default route**   A routing table entry that directs packets for which a next hop is not explicitly listed in the routing table.

**default VLAN**   The VLAN to which all switch interfaces are associated, unless specified otherwise. Naturally, the default VLAN for Ethernet, Token Ring, and the rest is different. The Ethernet default VLAN is usually VLAN 1.

**DHCP**   Dynamic Host Configuration Protocol. A protocol that provides a mechanism for allocating IP addresses dynamically so that addresses can be reused when hosts no longer need them.

**divide-and-conquer troubleshooting approach**   This approach to troubleshooting selects a layer and performs tests in both directions from the starting layer. The troubleshooter chooses the starting layer based on his past experience and any information at hand about the problem. When a layer is identified as working, the layer above it is suspected and examined. If a layer is detected as faulty, the layer below it is examined.

**DNS**   Domain Name System. A system used on the Internet to translate names of network nodes into addresses.

**DNS server**   Domain Name System server.

**DRAM**    dynamic random-access memory. RAM that stores information in capacitors that must be refreshed periodically. Delays can occur because DRAM is inaccessible to the processor when refreshing its contents. However, DRAM is less complex and has greater capacity than SRAM.

**DTE**    data terminal equipment. A device at the user end of a user-network interface that serves as a data source, destination, or both. DTE connects to a data network through a DCE device (such as a modem) and typically uses clocking signals that the DCE generates. DTE includes devices such as computers, protocol translators, and multiplexers.

**duplex**    Specifies whether a device's interface sends and receives data on the same circuit (not at the same time), or whether the send and receive circuits are distinct and the interface can send data at the same time it receives data.

**EIGRP**    Enhanced Interior Gateway Routing Protocol. An advanced version of IGRP that Cisco developed. Provides superior convergence properties and operating efficiency and combines the advantages of link-state protocols with those of distance vector protocols.

**EMI**    electromagnetic interference. Interference by electromagnetic signals that can cause reduced data integrity and increased error rates on transmission channels.

**encapsulation**    The wrapping of data in a particular protocol header. For example, Ethernet data is wrapped in a specific Ethernet header before network transit. Also, when you are bridging dissimilar networks, the entire frame from one network is placed in the header used by the other network's data link layer protocol.

**end system**    Servers, workstations, personal computers, and laptop computers are examples of end systems.

**end system network configuration table**    This table is baseline documentation that shows accurate records of the hardware and software used in end systems.

**EtherChannel technology**    Developed and copyrighted by Cisco Systems, this is a logical aggregation of multiple Ethernet interfaces used to form a single higher-bandwidth routing or bridging endpoint.

**Fast Ethernet**    Any of a number of 100-Mbps Ethernet specifications. Fast Ethernet offers a speed increase 10 times that of the 10BASE-T Ethernet specification while preserving such qualities as frame format, MAC mechanisms, and MTU. Such similarities allow the use of existing 10BASE-T applications and network management tools on Fast Ethernet networks. Based on an extension to the IEEE 802.3 specification.

**Faststart**   A feature that can be used on switch ports (of certain switches such as 19xx) to which end systems or nonbridging devices connect. Allows the port to go into the spanning tree forwarding state in a few seconds. (The similar command on other switches, such as 5xxx, is PortFast.)

**FCS**   frame check sequence. Extra characters added to a frame for error-control purposes. Used in high-level data link control (HDLC), Frame Relay, and other data link layer protocols.

**firewall**   A router or access server, or several routers or access servers, designated as a buffer between any connected public networks and a private network. A firewall router uses access lists and other methods to ensure the private network's security.

**flapping**   A routing problem in which an advertised route between two nodes alternates (flaps) between two paths because of a network problem that causes intermittent interface failures.

**flash memory**   A special type of electrically erasable programmable read-only memory (EEPROM) that can be erased and reprogrammed in blocks instead of one byte at a time. Many modern PCs have their BIOS stored on a flash memory chip so that it can be updated easily if necessary. Such a BIOS is sometimes called a *Flash BIOS*. Flash memory is also popular in modems because it lets the modem manufacturer support new protocols as they become standardized.

**frame**   A logical grouping of information sent as a data link layer unit over a transmission medium. Often refers to the header and trailer, used for synchronization and error control, that surround the user data contained in the unit. The terms *cell, datagram, message, packet,* and *segment* also are used to describe logical information groupings at various layers of the OSI reference model and in various technology circles.

**frame error**   One of many error statistics reported on the output of the Cisco IOS **show interface** command. This counter reports on the frames read (input frames) that had noninteger number of bytes. (The lengths of those frames were not integer numbers.)

**Frame Relay**   An industry-standard switched data link layer protocol that handles multiple virtual circuits using HDLC encapsulation between connected devices. Frame Relay is more efficient than X.25, the protocol for which it generally is considered a replacement.

**FTP**   File Transfer Protocol. An application protocol, part of the TCP/IP protocol stack, that transfers files between network nodes. FTP is defined in RFC 959.

**gateway of last resource**   A routing table entry that all packets not matching against any other routing table entry will match to and be sent to their next hop address.

**Gather Symptoms stage**   The stage of the troubleshooting process in which symptoms of the problem(s) are collected.

**general troubleshooting process** A three-stage troubleshooting model composed of the following: 1. Gather the Symptoms stage; 2. Isolate the Problem stage; 3. Correct the Problem stage.

**helper address** An address configured on an interface to which broadcasts received on that interface are sent. Helper addresses are typically used when clients are configured as DHCP clients, and the DHCP server is connected to a different logical network than the clients.

**high-bandwidth application** An application that, because of its nature, requires high bandwidth. Multimedia network applications are examples of such applications.

**HTTP** Hypertext Transfer Protocol. The protocol used by Web browsers and Web servers to transfer files, such as text and graphics.

**hub** 1. Generally, a term used to describe a device that serves as the center of a star-topology network. 2. A hardware or software device that contains multiple independent but connected modules of network and internetwork equipment. Hubs can be active (they repeat signals sent through them) or passive (they do not repeat, but merely split, signals sent through them). 3. In Ethernet and IEEE 802.3, an Ethernet multiport repeater, sometimes called a *concentrator*.

**IANA** Internet Assigned Numbers Authority. An organization that is operated under the auspices of the ISOC as part of the IAB. The IANA delegates authority for IP address space allocation and domain-name assignment to the InterNIC and other organizations. IANA also maintains a database of assigned protocol identifiers used in the TCP/IP stack, including autonomous system numbers.

**ICMP** Internet Control Message Protocol. A network-layer Internet protocol that reports errors and provides other information that is relevant to IP packet processing. Documented in RFC 792.

**IETF** Internet Engineering Task Force. A task force consisting of more than 80 working groups that is responsible for developing Internet standards. The IETF operates under the auspices of ISOC.

**IGP** Interior Gateway Protocol. An Internet protocol used to exchange routing information within an autonomous system. Examples of common Internet IGPs include IGRP, OSPF, and RIP.

**interface** 1. A connection between two systems or devices. 2. In routing terminology, a network connection. 3. In telephony, a shared boundary defined by common physical interconnection characteristics, signal characteristics, and meanings of interchanged signals. 4. A boundary between adjacent layers of the OSI model.

**interface reset** This is one of many counters/statistics reported on the output of the Cisco IOS **show interface** command. This counter increments every time the interface is cleared (using the **clear interface** *interface* command), when the **shutdown** command is issued for that interface, when the **no shutdown** command is issued for that interface, and when the state of the interface changes from up to down or from down to up. When an interface is reset for any of these reasons, its hardware buffers are cleared.

**IP**    Internet Protocol. The network layer protocol in the TCP/IP stack that offers a connectionless internetwork service. IP provides features for addressing, type of service (ToS) specification, fragmentation and reassembly, and security. Defined in RFC 791.

**IP address**    A 32-bit address that is assigned to hosts using TCP/IP. An IP address belongs to one of five classes—A, B, C, D, or E—and is written as four octets separated by periods (dotted-decimal format). Each address consists of a network number, an optional subnetwork number, and a host number. The network and subnetwork numbers together are used for routing, and the host number is used to address an individual host within the network or subnetwork. Also called an *Internet address*.

**IPTV**    A multimedia, multicast-based software application.

**IS-IS Protocol**    Intermediate System-to-Intermediate System Protocol. An OSI link-state hierarchical routing protocol based on DECnet Phase V routing whereby ISs (routers) exchange routing information based on a single metric to determine network topology.

**ISOC**    Internet Society. An international nonprofit organization, founded in 1992, that coordinates the evolution and use of the Internet. In addition, ISOC delegates authority to other groups related to the Internet, such as the Internet Architecture Board (IAB). ISOC is headquartered in Reston, Virginia.

**Isolate the Problem stage**    The stage of troubleshooting at which the cause of the problem is isolated (determined).

**ITU**    International Telecommunication Union. An organization established by the United Nations to set international telecommunications standards and to allocate frequencies for specific uses.

**jabber**    1. An error condition characterized by a network device continually transmitting random, meaningless data onto the network. 2. In IEEE 802.3, a data packet whose length exceeds that prescribed in the standard.

**jitter**    1. Interpacket delay variance; that is, the difference between interpacket arrival and departure. Jitter is an important quality of service (QoS) metric for voice and video applications. 2. Analog communication line distortion caused by the variation of a signal from its reference timing positions. Jitter can cause data loss, particularly at high speeds.

**keepalive interval**    A period of time between each keepalive message sent by a network device.

**keepalive message**   A message sent by one network device to inform another network device that the virtual circuit between the two is still active.

**latency**   1. The delay between the time that a device requests access to a network and the time that it is granted permission to transmit. 2. The delay between the time that a device receives a frame and the time that the frame is forwarded out the destination port.

**latency-sensitive application**   An application that cannot perform well or completely fails in the presence of network delays (latency).

**LED**   light emitting diode. A semiconductor device that emits light produced by converting electrical energy. Status lights on hardware devices typically are LEDs.

**line coding error**   An error related to the line coding setting/mismatch on T1/E1 or Primary Rate Interfaces (PRIs).

**line protocol**   Line protocol is often interpreted as the layer immediately above the physical layer (Media Access Control in Ethernet terminology). This layer is responsible for submitting Layer 2 frames (or protocol data units in general) and receiving Layer 2 frames to and from the physical layer. The ability to send and receive frames requires more than just the physical layer's health. For example, an Ethernet interface that is not connected to the cable media will go into "line protocol down" state because the keepalives fail and the device concludes that it cannot send and receive frames to and from the cable media.

**LMI**   Local Management Interface. A set of enhancements to the basic Frame Relay specification. LMI includes support for a keepalive mechanism that verifies that data is flowing; a multicast mechanism that provides the network server with its local DLCI and the multicast DLCI; global addressing, which gives DLCIs global rather than local significance in Frame Relay networks; and a status mechanism, which provides an ongoing status report on the DLCIs known to the switch.

**loopback interface**   A logical interface (or sometimes called software interface) that is often created on routers with an IP address assigned to it. This interface is stable; if present, its IP address is used as the router ID for routing protocols such as BGP and OSPF.

**MAC address**   A standardized data link layer address that is required for every port or device that connects to a LAN. Other devices in the network use these addresses to locate specific ports in the network and to create and update routing tables and data structures. MAC addresses are 6 bytes long and are controlled by the IEEE. Also known as a *hardware address, MAC layer address,* and *physical address*.

**Mac OS**   Apple Macintosh operating system.

**management alarm system**   Implemented in the form of beeping, sending e-mail, generating log messages, and so on, the management alarm system monitors such things as devices, CPUs, memories, and links. It notifies the support personnel of an event such as an error, crash, threshold exceeded, and so on.

**management IP address**   A device's address that is used for managing the device. On routers, the loopback 0 address (and on Catalyst 5xxx switches, the SC0 [system console] address) is often used as the management IP address. This address is used when you ping the device, Telnet into it, or communicate with it using SNMP.

**management VLAN**   The VLAN that administrators are urged to reserve for network management, management traffic, and protocols such as VTP, CDP, HSRP, and so on.

**media type**   A Cisco IOS interface configuration command that allows the administrator to configure the interface for connectivity through its RJ45, AUI, or any other type of connector (such as MII) that it might have.

**multicast**   A stream of single packets copied by the network and sent to a specific subset of network addresses. These addresses are specified in the destination address field.

**multicast application**   A network application that generates multicast traffic on the server and expects the traffic to be directed to the segments at which the clients that have joined the multicast group reside. IPTV is an example of a multicast application.

**multilayer switch**   A switch that filters and forwards packets on the basis of Media Access Control (MAC) addresses and network addresses.

**multiplexing**   A scheme that allows multiple logical signals to be transmitted simultaneously across a single physical channel.

**native VLAN**   The VLAN that a switch port is associated to and that receives all the broadcasts released in that VLAN.

**network layer**   Layer 3 of the OSI reference model. This layer provides connectivity and path selection between two end systems. The network layer is the layer at which routing occurs.

**network topology diagram**   A graphical representation of a network. It illustrates how each device in the network is connected and reveals the logical architecture of the network.

**NMS**   network management system. A system that is responsible for managing at least part of a network. An NMS is generally a reasonably powerful and well-equipped computer, such as an engineering workstation. NMSs communicate with agents to help keep track of network statistics and resources.

**noise**   A set of undesirable communications channel signals.

**NTP**   Network Time Protocol. A protocol built on top of TCP that ensures accurate local timekeeping with reference to radio and atomic clocks located on the Internet. This protocol can synchronize distributed clocks within milliseconds over long time periods.

**NTP peer**   This Cisco IOS command allows you to specify the address of another time server device as a peer.

**NTP server**   This Cisco IOS command allows you to specify the address of another device that plays the NTP server role.

**NTP source**   This Cisco IOS command allows you to specify, on an NTP server, the IP address of which of its interfaces should be used when the device communicates with other NTP devices.

**OSI reference model**   Open System Interconnection reference model. A network architectural model that ISO and ITU-T developed. The model consists of seven layers, each of which specifies particular network functions, such as addressing, flow control, error control, encapsulation, and reliable message transfer. The lowest layer (the physical layer) is closest to the media technology. The highest layer (the application layer) is closest to the user. From Layer 1 to Layer 7, the layers are as follows: physical, data link, network, transport, session, presentation, and application. The OSI reference model is used universally as a method of teaching and understanding network functionality.

**OSPF**   Open Shortest Path First. A link-state, hierarchical Interior Gateway Protocol (IGP) routing algorithm proposed as a successor to the Routing Information Protocol (RIP) in the Internet community. OSPF features include least-cost routing, multipath routing, and load balancing. OSPF was derived from an early version of the Intermediate System-to-Intermediate System (IS-IS) protocol.

**packet**   A logical grouping of information that includes a header containing control information and (usually) user data. Packets most often refer to network layer units of data.

**passive-interface**   A router configuration command used for RIP and (E)IGRP that prevents the routing process from sending routing updates out of the interface referenced by this command.

**PDU**   protocol data unit. An OSI term for *packet*.

**peak rate**   The maximum rate, in kilobits per second, at which a virtual circuit can transmit.

**physical layer**    Layer 1 of the OSI reference model. The physical layer defines the electrical, mechanical, procedural, and functional specifications for activating, maintaining, and deactivating the physical link between end systems.

**ping**    packet Internet groper. An Internet Control Message Protocol (ICMP) echo message and its reply. ping is often used in IP networks to test a network device's reachability.

**policy map**    This command/structure associates class maps to QoS policies. A policy map is applied to router interfaces using the service policy command.

**POP**    1. point of presence. A physical location where an interexchange carrier has equipment installed to interconnect with a *local exchange carrier (LEC)*. 2. Post Office Protocol. A protocol that client e-mail applications use to retrieve mail from a mail server.

**port security**    This feature allows the administrator to restrict usage of a switch port to a particular or a specific set of MAC addresses.

**PortFast**    This feature can be used on switch ports to which end systems or nonbridging devices connect. Allows the port to go into the spanning tree forwarding state in a few seconds.

**PPP**    Point-to-Point Protocol. A successor to Serial Line Internet Protocol (SLIP) that provides router-to-router and host-to-network connections over synchronous and asynchronous circuits. PPP was designed to work with several network layer protocols, such as IP, IPX, and AppleTalk Remote Access (ARA). PPP also has built-in security mechanisms, such as Challenge Handshake Authentication Protocol (CHAP) and Password Authentication Protocol (PAP). PPP relies on two protocols: Link Control Protocol (LCP) and Network Control Protocol (NCP).

**presentation layer**    Layer 6 of the OSI reference model. This layer ensures that information sent by one system's application layer can be read by another system's application layer. The presentation layer also is concerned with the data structures that programs use; therefore, it negotiates data transfer syntax for the application layer.

**PVC**    permanent virtual circuit. A virtual circuit that is permanently established. PVCs save bandwidth associated with circuit establishment and teardown in situations in which certain virtual circuits must exist all the time.

**queue**    1. An ordered list of elements waiting to be processed. 2. A backlog of packets waiting to be forwarded over a router interface.

**redundancy**    1. In internetworking, the duplication of devices, services, or connections so that, in the event of a failure, the redundant devices, services, or connections can perform the work of those that failed. 2. The portion of the total information contained in a message that can be eliminated without losing essential information or meaning.

**reliability**   1. A determination of a network's or system's capability to continue operating if a single component fails. 2. A ratio of expected to received keepalives from a link. If the ratio is high, the line is reliable. Used as a routing metric.

**RFC**   Request For Comments. A series of documents used as the primary means of communicating information about the Internet. The Internet Architecture Board (IAB) designates some RFCs as Internet standards. Most RFCs document protocol specifications, such as Telnet and File Transfer Protocol (FTP), but some are humorous or historical. RFCs are available online from numerous sources.

**RMON**   Remote Monitoring. A Management Information Base (MIB) agent specification described in RFC 1271 that defines functions for the remote monitoring of networked devices. The RMON specification provides numerous monitoring, problem detection, and reporting capabilities.

**router**   A network layer device that uses one or more metrics to determine the optimal path along which network traffic should be forwarded. Routers forward packets from one network to another based on network layer information.

**router ID (RID)**   A protocol such as OSPF or BGP selects one of the router's IP addresses as its RID. The highest loopback interface's IP is preferred; otherwise, with no loopback addresses present, merely the highest IP address is chosen as the RID.

**RTP**   1. Routing Table Protocol. A Virtual Integrated Network Service (VINES) routing protocol based on Routing Information Protocol (RIP). Distributes network topology information and helps VINES servers find neighboring clients, servers, and routers. Uses delay as a routing metric. 2. Rapid Transport Protocol. A protocol that provides pacing and error recovery for Advanced Peer-to-Peer Networking (APPN) data as it crosses the APPN network. With RTP, error recovery and flow control are performed end-to-end rather than at every node. RTP prevents congestion rather than reacting to it. 3. Real-Time Transport Protocol. A protocol commonly used with IP networks. RTP is designed to provide end-to-end network transport functions for applications that transmit real-time data—such as audio, video, or simulation data—over multicast or unicast network services. RTP provides such services as payload type identification, sequence numbering, time-stamping, and delivery monitoring to real-time applications.

**secondary IP address**   Cisco routers allow you to assign multiple IP addresses to an interface using the command **ip address secondary**. The addresses other than the primary IP address are thereby called the secondary IP addresses for that interface.

**segment**   1. A section of a network that is bound by bridges, routers, or switches. 2. In a LAN that uses a bus topology, a continuous electrical circuit that often is connected to other such segments with repeaters. 3. A term used in the TCP specification to describe a single transport layer unit of information.

**server**   A node or software program that provides services to clients.

**service timestamps**   A service that you can enable for logging or debugging on Cisco routers. It puts a timestamp beside every line of the log or debug output.

**session layer**   Layer 5 of the OSI reference model. This layer establishes, manages, and terminates sessions between applications and manages the data exchange between presentation layer entities.

**SMTP**   Simple Mail Transfer Protocol. An Internet protocol that provides e-mail services.

**SNMP**   Simple Network Management Protocol. A network management protocol that is used almost exclusively in TCP/IP networks. SNMP provides a means to monitor and control network devices and to manage configurations, statistics collection, performance, and security.

**SNMP communities**   An authentication scheme that allows an intelligent network device to validate SNMP requests.

**SNMP server**   This is the server that sets or clears SNMP parameters or accepts SNMP traps from SNMP agents.

**SNMPv2**   SNMP version 2. SNMP2 supports centralized as well as distributed network management strategies and includes improvements in the Structure of Management Information (SMI), protocol operations, management architecture, and security.

**spanning tree**   A loop-free subset of a network topology.

**spanning-tree algorithm**   The algorithm used by the Spanning-Tree Protocol to create a spanning tree. Sometimes abbreviated as STA.

**speed**   Speed of an interface or port might be configurable (such as 10/100 Mbps). This command allows you to set the speed to the appropriate value.

**split-horizon updates**   A routing technique in which information about routes is prevented from exiting the router interface through which that information was received. Split-horizon updates are useful in preventing routing loops.

**SRAM**   static random-access memory. A type of RAM that retains its contents for as long as power is supplied. SRAM does not require constant refreshing, like dynamic RAM (DRAM) does.

**STP**   1. Spanning-Tree Protocol. A bridge protocol that uses the spanning-tree algorithm, allowing a learning bridge to dynamically work around loops in a network topology by creating a spanning tree. Bridges exchange bridge protocol data unit (BPDU) messages with other bridges to detect loops; then they remove the loops by shutting down selected bridge interfaces. Refers to both the

IEEE 802.1 Spanning-Tree Protocol standard and the earlier Digital Equipment Corporation Spanning-Tree Protocol upon which it is based. The IEEE version supports bridge domains and allows the bridge to construct a loop-free topology across an extended LAN. The IEEE version generally is preferred over the Digital version. 2. signal transfer point. An element of a Signaling System 7 (SS7)-based intelligent network that performs routing of the SS7 signaling.

**STP designated bridge**   When spanning tree runs, a designated device is chosen on each segment based on the best BPDU it advertises.

**STP root bridge**   When spanning tree runs, one device is chosen as the root for the entire spanning tree.

**STP state**   Based on the classic Spanning-Tree Protocol, a port can be in the Disabled, Listening, Learning Forwarding, or Blocking states.

**subnet mask**   A 32-bit address mask used in IP to indicate the bits of an IP address that are used for the subnet address. Sometimes simply called a *mask*.

**switch**   1. A network device that filters, forwards, and floods frames based on each frame's destination address. The switch operates at the data link layer of the OSI reference model. 2. A general term applied to an electronic or mechanical device that allows a connection to be established as necessary and terminated when there is no longer a session to support. 3. In telephony, a general term for any device, such as a private branch exchange (PBX), that connects individual phones to phone lines.

**T1**   A digital WAN carrier facility. T1 carries DS1-formatted data at 1.544 Mbps through the telephone-switching network by using AMI or B8ZS coding.

**TCP/IP**   Transmission Control Protocol/Internet Protocol. A common name for the suite of protocols developed by the U.S. Department of Defense in the 1970s to support the construction of worldwide internetworks. TCP and IP are the two best-known protocols in the suite.

**TDM**   time-division multiplexing. A technique in which information from multiple channels can be allocated bandwidth on a single wire based on preassigned time slots. Bandwidth is allocated to each channel regardless of whether the station associated with the channel has data to transmit.

**Telnet**   The standard terminal emulation protocol in the TCP/IP protocol stack. Telnet is used for remote terminal connections, allowing users to log in to remote systems and use resources as if they were connected to those systems. Telnet is defined in RFC 854.

**TFTP**   Trivial File Transfer Protocol. A simplified version of File Transfer Protocol (FTP) that allows files to be transferred from one computer to another over a network, usually without the use of client authentication (such as username and password).

**throughput**    The rate at which information arrives at, and possibly passes through, a particular point in a network system.

**top-down troubleshooting approach**    An approach to troubleshooting that starts with the end user application and works its way down from the upper layers of the OSI model until the problem's cause is identified.

**topology**    A physical arrangement of network nodes and media within an enterprise networking structure.

**traceroute**    A program available on many systems that traces the path a packet takes to a destination. It is used mostly to debug routing problems between hosts. A traceroute protocol is also defined in RFC 1393.

**transport layer**    Layer 4 of the OSI reference model. This layer is responsible for reliable network communication between end nodes. The transport layer provides mechanisms for the establishment, maintenance, and termination of virtual circuits, transport fault detection and recovery, and information flow control. Corresponds to the transmission control layer of the Systems Network Architecture (SNA) model.

**trunk**    1. A physical and logical connection between two switches across which network traffic travels. A backbone is composed of a number of trunks. 2. A phone line between two central offices (COs) or between a CO and a private branch exchange (PBX).

**tunnel interface**    A logical interface that is created and used to build tunnels, such as IP GRE tunnels.

**UDP**    User Datagram Protocol. A connectionless transport layer protocol in the TCP/IP protocol stack. UDP is a simple protocol that exchanges datagrams without acknowledgments or guaranteed delivery, requiring that other protocols handle error processing and retransmission. UDP is defined in RFC 768.

**unicast**    A message sent to a single network destination.

**UNIX**    An operating system developed in 1969 at Bell Laboratories. UNIX has gone through several iterations since its inception, including UNIX 4.3 BSD (Berkeley Standard Distribution), developed at the University of California at Berkeley, and UNIX System V, Release 4.0, developed by AT&T.

**VLAN**    virtual LAN. Devices on one or more LANs that are configured (using management software) so that they can communicate as if they were attached to the same wire, when, in fact, they are located on a number of different LAN segments. Because VLANs are based on logical instead of physical connections, they are extremely flexible.

**WAN**   wide-area network. A data communications network that serves users across a broad geographic area and often uses transmission devices that common carriers provide. Frame Relay, SMDS, and ATM are examples of WANs.

**WAN circuit**   A circuit such as a PVC or SVC connecting two remote sites over the WAN.

**WINS server**   A Microsoft service that facilitates NetBIOS name to IP resolution. Machines register with the WINS server dynamically. Any machine that needs the IP address of another machine (that is, its NetBIOS name) can send a request to the WINS server for that name.

# Index

## A

**access lists**

    correcting misconfiguration of, 181–182

    correcting transport layer problems, 221–223

**analyzing command output, 156–158, 160–161**

**application layer (OSI model), 55**

    correcting problems, 229, 250–255

    *with commands, 223–225*

    isolating problems, 209–210

    support resources, 227

    symptoms of problems, 201

**application layer (TCP/IP model), 55**

**applications, isolating physical/data link layer problems, 109–116**

**arp –a command, 154**

**arp –d command, 127**

**autonomous systems, reachability, 248–250**

## B

**BGP (Border Gateway Protocol), reachability, 248–250**

**bottom-up troubleshooting method, 91–92**

## C

**CCO (Cisco Connection Online), 227**

**CDP (Cisco Discovery Protocol), 140**

**change control, 20**

**collecting**

    end system data, 35–36

    network configuration information, 16–18

**commands**

    application layer problems, isolating, 209–210

    arp-a, 154

    arp-d, 127

    controller, 128

    copy flash tftp, 210

    data link layer problems, isolating, 109–116

    debug arp, 157

    debug ip bgp, 157

    debug ip icmp, 157

    debug ip packet, 157

    debug ip routing, 157

    debug snmp requests, 210

    encapsulation, 127

    framing, 129

    helper address, 177

    ifconfig -a, 208

    interface, 127

    ip helper-address, 227

    ipconfig -a, 156

    linecode, 129

    netstat, 155, 201

    no shutdown, 127

    nslookup, 209

    ntp source, 225

    output, analyzing, 156–161

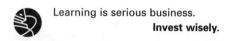

# learn

NOW
I HAVE THE POWER TO MAKE
YOU MORE PRODUCTIVE ON THE JOB.
I CAN PREPARE YOU TO MEET
NEW CHALLENGES.

I AM A CISCO CAREER CERTIFICATION.
ADD ME TO YOUR TOOLBOX WITH
AUTHORIZED TRAINING FROM
CISCO LEARNING PARTNERS...
PAY EASILY WITH CISCO
LEARNING CREDITS.

It is the power to acquire new skillsets, and expand your capabilities. Only Cisco Learning Partners can put you ahead of
the curve. Visit **www.cisco.com/go/learningpartners.**

THIS IS THE POWER OF THE NETWORK. now.

# Cisco Press

Learning is serious business.

**Invest wisely.**

# CCIE Security

### CCNP BCRAN Exam Certification Guide, Second Edition
1-58720-084-8 • Available Now

Prepare for the new CCNP 642-821 BCRAN Exam with the official exam preparation guide. Comprehensive coverage of all exam topics ensures readers will arrive at a complete understanding of what they need to master to succeed on the exam. This book follows a logical organization of the BCRAN exam objectives, and is written in a modular, small-chapter format that breaks elements into easy-to-absorb parts. It also contains the other valuable learning elements of an Exam Certification Guide from Cisco Press that ensure concept comprehension and retention. These include pre- and post-chapter quizzes, foundational review sections, scenario-based exercises and a CD-ROM testing engine with more than 200 questions, including simulation-based questions like on the actual exam.

### CCNP Certification Library, Third Edition
1-58720-104-6 • Available December 2003

Prepare for all four of the CCNP exams introduced in 2003 with the No. 1 selling Exam Certification Guides from Cisco Press. Includes four CD-ROMs with PC test engines and complete text in electronic format. The *CCNP Certification Library*, Third Edition, is a comprehensive self-study preparation library for any CCNP candidate. Combining all four of the CCNP Exam Certification Guides from Cisco Press at a discounted price, this library incorporates the most current versions of the CCNP self-study titles. Written to the new CCNP exams introduced in 2003, the books were created by the same authors who wrote the previous editions of the same titles.

The four books, *CCNP BSCI Exam Certification Guide, CCNP BCMSN Exam Certification Guide, CCNP BCRAN Exam Certification Guide*, and *CCNP CIT Exam Certification Guide*, apply to the following four exams, respectively: BSCI 642-801, BCMSN 642-811, BCRAN 642-821, and CIT 642-831. These books all include the standard features of Exam Certification Guides like the CD-ROM testing engine, foundation summaries, and pre- and post-chapter quizzes. These books are also created in the new modular format that breaks learning into small blocks of information that are both easy to absorb and retain.

### CCNP BSCI Exam Certification Guide, Third Edition
1-58720-085-6 • Available December 2003

Prepare for the CCNP 642-801 BSCI exam with the only Cisco Systems authorized self-study preparation book. With updated technology and testing content, *CCNP BSCI Exam Certification Guide* provides exceptional tutorial learning and exam preparation on advanced routing techniques and practices. It matches all the objectives of the new 642-801 BSCI exam launched in April 2003. Written in smaller, easier to absorb chapters than previous Exam Certification Guides, this book breaks down larger concepts into manageable blocks of learning. This, combined with other new learning elements and a complete rewriting of the material, make it even easier to comprehend and retain the large amount of learning required for this exam.